江苏师范大学“十三五”本科教育教学教材
2018 年江苏省高等学校重点教材

世界历史文献选读

SELECTED READINGS OF WORLD HISTORICAL DOCUMENTS

主　编　蒋　保
副主编　宋严萍　赵辉兵

合肥工業大學出版社

图书在版编目(CIP)数据

世界历史文献选读/蒋保主编. —合肥:合肥工业大学出版社,2019.8
ISBN 978-7-5650-4529-5

Ⅰ.①世… Ⅱ.①蒋… Ⅲ.①世界史—高等学校—教材—汉、英 Ⅳ.①K1

中国版本图书馆 CIP 数据核字(2019)第 137767 号

世界历史文献选读

蒋 保 主编

责任编辑 章 建 张 燕
出版发行 合肥工业大学出版社
地 址 (230009)合肥市屯溪路 193 号
网 址 www.hfutpress.com.cn
电 话 总 编 室:0551-62903038
市场营销部:0551-62903198
开 本 710 毫米×1000 毫米 1/16
印 张 19
字 数 361 千字
版 次 2019 年 8 月第 1 版
印 次 2019 年 8 月第 1 次印刷
印 刷 安徽昶颉包装印务有限责任公司
书 号 ISBN 978-7-5650-4529-5
定 价 54.00 元

前　言

《世界历史文献选读》是江苏师范大学“十三五”本科教育教学教材和 2018 年江苏省高等学校重点教材，由江苏师范大学历史文化与旅游学院世界史教学团队集体编写完成。教材内容涉及世界古代史、世界近代史、世界现当代史三部分文献，共计 25 篇。在选取文献的过程中，我们一是注意文献材料分布的区域性，尽量兼顾到更多的国家或地区的文献；二是在选取一手材料的同时，适当关注有影响的现代学者的研究成果；三是限于篇幅，所选文献有的是全文，有的是节选，但在内容上做到相对完整，独立成篇。每篇文献按照“正文”“导读”“注释”“问题探讨”和“参考文献”五部分内容进行编写。其中，“正文”是所选文献的部分或全部；“导读”是对所选文献的内容、作者以及节选部分内容的评介；“注释”是对正文中专有名词以及术语的解释；“问题探讨”是围绕所选文献内容设计相关思考题，帮助学生理解、运用文献；“参考文献”是关于所选文献的相关研究成果，为读者提供进一步阅读和研究信息。

编写《世界历史文献选读》教材，旨在培养历史学专业学生英语语言学习能力和英文历史文献解读能力，从而为历史研究打下良好的基础，同时帮助学生巩固、反思“世界通史”课程内容的学习。因此，在汲取以往教材编写经验的基础之上，本教材编写试图打破以往教材编写常规，创新编写思路，拓宽选材内容，将实用性、知识性、学术性和创新性结合起来。教材编写力求突出以下几点特色：第一，教材定位上，注重英语语言学习与历史文献解读并重，有利于学生学习语言、探究问题；第二，内容选取上，注重与“世界通史”教材内容的衔接，尽量兼顾到不同国家或地区的历史文献；第三，内容编写上，除了正文之外，力求在导读、注释、问题探讨和参考文献等方面体现出知识性、学术性、前沿性和创新性。

《世界历史文献选读》主要是面对普通高校历史学专业、世界史专业和外国语言与外国历史专业本科学生而编写的教材，适用于“世界历史文献选读”和“专业英语”等课程。《世界历史文献选读》教材讲授原则上不低于108学时，并且“世界历史文献选读”和“专业英语”等相关课程应与“世界通史”课程同步开设，这样更有利于学生学习，以提高学生学习的兴趣和学习的效率。

从某种意义上说，历史的学习不仅是专业的学习，也是语言的学习。我们这样说只是想强调语言学习是历史专业学习的基础和前提，强调语言在历史专业学习和研究过程中的重要性。显然，只有在较好地掌握一门甚至更多门语言的前提下，才能获取、掌握更多的直接的一手资料，才能更好地进行深入的历史学习和研究。另外，对于历史学研究与教学的从业者来说，多掌握一门语言就等于多打开历史学习和研究的一扇窗户，多一条学习和研究历史的路径。因此，我们希望通过编写这本《世界历史文献选读》教材，强化学生的语言学习意识，为历史专业尤其是世界史专业学生学习和阅读英文文献提供方便，也为历史学尤其是世界史专业人才培养贡献一点绵薄之力。

编　者

2019年4月于江苏师范大学

目　录

CONTENT

UNIT 1

THE CODE OF HAMMURABI[1]

Hammurabi

[Selections]

1. If a man accuses another man and charges him with homicide but cannot bring proof against him, his accuser shall be killed.

2. If a man charges another man with practicing witchcraft but cannot bring proof against him, he who is charged with witchcraft shall go to the divine River Ordeal[2], he shall indeed submit to the divine River Ordeal; if the divine River Ordeal should overwhelm him, his accuser shall take full legal possession of his estate; if the divine River Ordeal should clear that man and should he survive, he who made the charge of witchcraft against him shall be killed; he who submitted to the divine River Ordeal shall take full legal possession of his accuser's estate.

3. If a man comes forward to give false testimony in a case but cannot bring evidence for his accusation, if that case involves a capital offense, that man shall be killed.

4. If he comes forward to give (false) testimony for (a case whose penalty is) grain or silver, he shall be assessed the penalty for that case.

5. If a judge renders a judgment, gives a verdict, or deposits a sealed opinion, after which he reverses his judgment, they shall charge and convict that judge of having reversed the judgment which he rendered and he shall give twelvefold the claim of that judgment; moreover, they shall unseat him from his judgeship in the assembly, and he shall never again sit in judgment with the judges.

6. If a man steals valuables belonging to the god or to the palace, that man shall be killed, and also he who received the stolen goods from him shall be killed.

7. If a man should purchase silver, gold, a slave, a slave woman, an ox, a sheep, a donkey, or anything else whatsoever, from a son of a man or from a

slave of a man without witnesses or a contract — or if he accepts the goods for safekeeping — that man is a thief, he shall be killed.

8. If a man steals an ox, a sheep, a donkey, a pig, or a boat — if it belongs either to the god or to the palace, he shall give thirtyfold; if it belongs to a commoner, he shall replace it tenfold; if the thief does not have anything to give, he shall be killed.

14. If a man should kidnap the young child of another man, he shall be killed.

15. If a man should enable a palace slave, a palace slave woman, a commoner's slave, or a commoner's slave woman to leave through the main city-gate, he shall be killed.

16. If a man should harbor a fugitive slave or slave woman of either the palace or of a commoner in his house and not bring him out at the herald's public proclamation, that householder shall be killed.

17. If a man seizes a fugitive slave or slave woman in the open country and leads him back to his owner, the slave owner shall give him 2 shekels[3] of silver.

18. If that slave should refuse to identify his owner, he shall lead him off to the palace, his circumstances shall be investigated, and they shall return him to his owner.

19. If he should detain that slave in his own house and afterward the slave is discovered in his possession, that man shall be killed.

20. If the slave should escape the custody of the one who seized him, that man shall swear an oath by the god to the owner of the slave, and he shall be released.

21. If a man breaks into a house, they shall kill him and hang him in front of that very breach.

22. If a man commits a robbery and is then seized, that man shall be killed.

23. If the robber should not be seized, the man who has been robbed shall establish the extent of his lost property before the god; and the city and the governor in whose territory and district the robbery was committed shall replace his lost property to him.

24. If a life (is lost during the robbery), the city and the governor shall weigh and deliver to his kinsmen 60 shekels of silver.

25. If a fire breaks out in a man's house, and a man who came to help put it out covets the household furnishings belonging to the householder, and takes household furnishings belonging to the householder, that man shall be cast into

that very fire.

26. If either a soldier or a fisherman who is ordered to go on a royal campaign does not go, or hires and sends a hireling as his substitute, that soldier or fisherman shall be killed; the one who informs against him shall take full legal possession of his estate.

27. If there is either a soldier or a fisherman who is taken captive while serving in a royal fortress, and they give his field and his orchard to another to succeed to his holdings, and he then performs his service obligation — if he (the soldier or fisherman) should return and get back to his city, they shall return to him his field and orchard and he himself shall perform his service obligation.

28. If there is either a soldier or a fisherman who is taken captive while serving in a royal fortress, and his son is able to perform the service obligation, the field and orchard shall be given to him and he shall perform his father's service obligation.

29. If his son is too young and is unable to perform his father's service obligation, one third of the field and orchard shall be given to his mother, and his mother shall raise him.

30. If either a soldier or a fisherman abandons his field, orchard, or house because of the service obligation and then absents himself, another person takes possession of his field, orchard, or house to succeed to his holdings and performs the service obligation for three years — if he then returns and claims his field, orchard, or house, it will not be given to him; he who has taken possession of it and has performed his service obligation shall be the one to continue to perform the obligation.

31 If he should absent himself for only one year and then return, his field, orchard, and house shall be given to him, and he himself shall perform his service obligation.

32. If there is either a soldier or a fisherman who is taken captive while on a royal campaign, a merchant redeems him and helps him to get back to his city — if there are sufficient means in his own estate for the redeeming, he himself shall redeem himself; if there are not sufficient means in his estate to redeem him, he shall be redeemed by his city's temple; if there are not sufficient means in his city's temple to redeem him, the palace shall redeem him; but his field, orchard, or house will not be given for his redemption.

41. If a man accepts a field, orchard, or house of a soldier, fisherman, or state tenant in an exchange and gives him a compensatory payment (for the difference in value), the soldier, fisherman, or state tenant shall reclaim his field, orchard, or house and shall also keep full legal possession of the compensatory payment which was given to him.

42. If a man rents a field in tenancy but does not plant any grain, they shall charge and convict him of not performing the required work in the field, and he shall give to the owner of the field grain in accordance with his neighbor's yield.

43. If he does not cultivate the field at all but leaves it fallow, he shall give to the owner of the field grain in accordance with his neighbor's yield, and he shall plow and harrow the field which he left fallow and return it to the owner of the field.

44. If a man rents a previously uncultivated field for a three-year term with the intention of opening it for cultivation but he is negligent and does not open the field, in the fourth year he shall plow, hoe, and harrow the field and return it to the owner of the field; and in addition he shall measure and deliver 3,000 silas[4] of grain per 18 ikus[5] (of field).

45. If a man leases his field to a cultivator and receives the rent for his field, and afterwards the stormgod Adad[6] devastates the field or a flood sweeps away the crops, the loss is the cultivator's alone.

46. If he (the owner) should not receive the rent for his field (before the catastrophe destroys the field) or he leases out the field on terms of a half share or a third share (of the yield), the cultivator and the owner of the field shall divide whatever grain there is remaining in the agreed proportions.

47 If the cultivator should declare his intention to cultivate the field (in the next year) because in the previous year he did not recover his expenses, the owner of the field will not object; his same cultivator shall cultivate his field and he shall take (his share of) the grain at the harvest in accordance with his contract.

48. If a man has a debt lodged against him, and the stormgod Adad devastates his field or a flood sweeps away the crops, or there is no grain grown in the field due to insufficient water — in that year he will not repay grain to his creditor; he shall suspend performance of his contract and he will not give interest payments for that year.

49. If a man borrows silver from a merchant and gives the merchant a field prepared for planting with either grain or sesame (as a pledge for the loan) and declares to him. "You cultivate the field and collect and take away as much grain or sesame as will be grown" — if the cultivator should produce either grain or sesame in the field, at the harvest it is only the owner of the field who shall take the grain or sesame that is grown in the field, and he shall give to the merchant the grain equivalent to his silver which he borrowed from the merchant and the interest on it and also the expenses of the cultivation.

52. If the cultivator should not produce grain or sesame in the field, he will not alter his agreement.

53. If a man neglects to reinforce the embankment of (the irrigation canal of) his field and does not reinforce its embankment, and then a breach opens in its embankment and allows the water to carry away the common irrigated area, the man in whose embankment the breach opened shall replace the grain whose loss he caused.

54. If he cannot replace the grain, they shall sell him and his property, and the residents of the common irrigated area whose grain crops the water carried away shall divide (the proceeds).

55. If a man opens his branch of the canal for irrigation and negligently allows the water to carry away his neighbor's field, he shall measure and deliver grain in accordance with his neighbor's yield.

60. If a man gives a field to a gardener to plant as a date orchard and the gardener plants the orchard, he shall cultivate the orchard for four years; in the fifth year, the owner of the orchard and the gardener shall divide the yield in equal shares; the owner of the orchard shall select and take his share first.

61. If the gardener does not complete the planting of (the date orchard in) the field, but leaves an uncultivated area, they shall include the uncultivated area in his share.

62. If he does not plant as a date orchard the field which was given to him — if it is arable land, the gardener shall measure and deliver to the owner of the field the estimated yield of the field for the years it is left fallow in accordance with his neighbor's yield; furthermore he shall perform the required work on the field and return it to the owner of the field.

102. If a merchant should give silver to a trading agent for an investment

venture, and he incurs a loss on his journeys, he shall return silver to the merchant in the amount of the capital sum.

103. If enemy forces should make him abandon whatever goods he is transporting while on his business trip, the trading agent shall swear an oath by the god and shall be released.

104. If a merchant gives a trading agent grain, wool, oil, or any other commodity for local transactions, the trading agent shall return to the merchant the silver for each transaction; the trading agent shall collect a sealed receipt for (each payment in) silver that he gives to the merchant.

105. If the trading agent should be negligent and not take a sealed receipt for (each payment in) silver that he gives to the merchant, any silver that is not documented in a sealed receipt will not be included in the final accounting.

106. If the trading agent takes silver from the merchant but then denies the claim of his merchant, that merchant shall bring charges and proof before the god and witnesses against the trading agent concerning the silver taken, and the trading agent shall give to the merchant threefold the amount of silver that he took.

107. If a merchant entrusts silver to a trading agent and the trading agent then returns to his merchant everything that the merchant had given him but the merchant denies (having received) everything that the trading agent had given him, that trading agent shall bring charges and proof before the god and witnesses against the merchant, and because he denied the account of his trading agent, the merchant shall give to the trading agent sixfold the amount that he took.

108. If a woman innkeeper should refuse to accept grain for the price of beer but accepts (only) silver measured by the large weight, thereby reducing the value of beer in relation to the value of grain, they shall charge and convict that woman innkeeper and they shall cast her into the water.

109. If there should be a woman innkeeper in whose house criminals congregate, and she does not seize those criminals and lead them off to the palace authorities, that woman innkeeper shall be killed.

110. If a *naditu* or an *ugbabtu*[7] who does not reside within the cloister should open (the door to?) a tavern or enter a tavern for some beer, they shall burn that woman.

111. If a woman innkeeper gives one vat[8] of beer as a loan(?), she shall take 50 silas of grain at the harvest.

112. If a man is engaged in a trading expedition and gives silver, gold, precious stones, or any other goods to another under consignment for transportation, and the latter man does not deliver that which was consigned to him where it was to be consigned but appropriates it, the owner of the consigned property shall charge and convict that man of whatever consignment he failed to deliver, and that man shall give to the owner of the consigned property fivefold the property that had been given to him.

113. If a man has a claim of grain or silver against another man and takes grain from the granary or from the threshing floor without obtaining permission from the owner of the grain, they shall charge and convict that man of taking grain from the granary or from the threshing floor without the permission of the owner of the grain, and he shall return as much grain as he took; moreover, he shall forfeit whatever he originally gave as the loan.

117. If an obligation is outstanding against a man and he sells or gives into debt service his wife, his son, or his daughter, they shall perform service in the house of their buyer or of the one who holds them in debt service for three years; their release shall be secured in the fourth year.

118. If he should give a male or female slave into debt service, the merchant may extend the term (beyond the three years), he may sell him; there are no grounds for a claim.

119. If an obligation is outstanding against a man and he therefore sells his slave woman who has borne him children, the owner of the slave woman shall weigh and deliver the silver which the merchant weighed and delivered (as the loan) and he shall thereby redeem his slave woman.

120. If a man stores his grain in another man's house, and a loss occurs in the storage bin or the householder opens the granary and takes the grain or he completely denies receiving the grain that was stored in his house — the owner of the grain shall establish his grain before the god, and the householder shall give to the owner of the grain twofold the grain that he took (in storage).

122. If a man intends to give silver, gold, or anything else to another man for safekeeping, he shall exhibit before witnesses anything which he intends to give, he shall draw up a written contract, and (in this manner) he shall give goods for

safekeeping.

123. If he gives goods for safekeeping without witnesses or a written contract, and they deny that he gave anything, that case has no basis for a claim.

124. If a man gives silver, gold, or anything else before witnesses to another man for safekeeping and he denies it, they shall charge and convict that man, and he shall give twofold that which he denied.

125. If a man gives his property for safekeeping and his property together with the householder's property is lost either by (theft achieved through) a breach or by scaling over a wall, the householder who was careless shall make restitution and shall restore to the owner of the property that which was given to him for safekeeping and which he allowed to be lost; the householder shall continue to search for his own lost property, and he shall take it from the one who stole it from him.

128. If a man marries a wife but does not draw up a formal contract for her, that woman is not a wife.

129. If a man's wife should be seized lying with another male, they shall bind them and cast them into the water; if the wife's master allows his wife to live, then the king shall allow his subject (i. e., the other male) to live.

130. If a man pins down another man's virgin wife who still residing in her father's house, and they seize him lying with her, that man shall be killed; that woman shall be released.

131. If her husband accuses his own wife (of adultery), although she has not been seized lying with another male, she shall swear (to her innocence by) an oath by the god, and return to her house.

132. If a man's wife should have a finger pointed against her in accusation involving another male, although she has not been seized lying with another male, she shall submit to the divine River Ordeal for her husband.

134. If a man should be captured and there are not sufficient provisions in his house, his wife may enter another's house; that woman will not be subject to any penalty.

135. If a man should be captured and there are not sufficient provisions in his house, before his return his wile enters another's house and bears children, and afterwards her husband returns and gets back to his city, that woman shall return to her first husband; the children shall inherit from their father.

136. If a man deserts his city and flees, and after his departure his wife enters another's house — if that man then should return and seize his wife, because he repudiated his city and fled, the wife of the deserter will not return to her husband.

138. If a man intends to divorce his first-ranking wife who did not bear him children, he shall give her silver as much as was her bridewealth and restore to her the dowry that she brought from her father's house, and he shall divorce her.

139. If there is no bridewealth, he shall give her 60 shekels of silver as a divorce settlement.

140. If he is a commoner, he shall give her 20 shekels of silver.

141. If the wife of a man who is residing in the man's house should decide to leave, and she appropriates goods, squanders her household possessions, or disparages her husband, they shall charge and convict her; and if her husband should declare his intention to divorce her, then he shall divorce her: neither her travel expenses, nor her divorce settlement, nor anything else shall be given to her. If her husband should declare his intention to not divorce her, then her husband may marry another woman and that (first) woman shall reside in her husband's house as a slave woman.

150. If a man awards to his wife a field, orchard, house, or movable property, and makes out a sealed document for her, after her husband's death her children will not bring a claim against her; the mother shall give her estate to whichever of her children she loves, but she will not give it to an outsider.

151. If a woman who is residing in a man's house should have her husband agree by binding contract that no creditor of her husband shall seize her (for his debts) — if that man has a debt incurred before marrying that woman, his creditors will not seize his wife; and if that woman has a debt incurred before entering the man's house, her creditors will not seize her husband.

152. If a debt should be incurred by them after that woman enters the man's house, both of them shall satisfy the merchant.

153. If a man's wife has her husband killed on account of (her relationship with) another male, they shall impale that woman.

157. If a man, after his father's death, should lie with his mother, they shall burn them both.

158. If a man, after his father's death, should be discovered in the lap of his

(the father's) principal wife who had borne children, that man shall be disinherited from the paternal estate.

159. If a man who has the ceremonial marriage prestation brought to the house of his father-in-law, and who gives the bridewealth, should have his attention diverted to another woman and declare to his father-in-law, "I will not marry your daughter," the father of the daughter shall take full legal possession of whatever had been brought to him.

160. If a man has the ceremonial marriage prestation brought to the house of his father-in-law and gives the bridewealth, and the father of the daughter then declares. "I will not give my daughter to you." he shall return twofold everything that had been brought to him.

161. If a man has the ceremonial marriage prestation brought to the house of his father-in-law and gives the bridewealth, and then his comrade slanders him (with the result that) his father-in-law declares to the one entitled to the wife, "You will not marry my daughter," he shall return twofold everything that had been brought to him; moreover, his comrade will not marry his (intended) wife.

162. If a man marries a wife, she bears him children, and that woman then goes to her fate, her father shall have no claim to her dowry; her dowry belongs only to her children.

163. If a man marries a wife but she does not provide him with children, and that woman goes to her fate — if his father-in-law then returns to him the bridewealth that that man brought to his father-in-law's house, her husband will have no claim to that woman's dowry; her dowry belongs only to her father's house.

164. If his father-in-law should not return to him the bridewealth, he shall deduct the value of her bridewealth from her dowry and restore (the balance of) her dowry to her father's house.

165. If a man awards by sealed contract a field, orchard, or house to his favorite heir, when the brothers divide the estate after the father goes to his fate, he (the favorite son) shall take the gift which the father gave to him and apart from that gift they shall equally divide the property of the paternal estate.

166. If a man provides wives for his eligible sons but does not provide a wife for his youngest son, when the brothers divide the estate after the father goes to his fate, they shall establish the silver value of the bridewealth for their young

unmarried brother from the property of the paternal estate, in addition to his inheritance share, and thereby enable him to obtain a wife.

167. If a man marries a wife and she bears him children, and later that woman goes to her fate, and after her death he marries another woman and she bears children, after which the father then goes to his fate, the children will not divide the estate according to the mothers; they shall take the dowries of their respective mothers and then equally divide the property of the paternal estate.

168. If a man should decide to disinherit his son and declares to the judges, "I will disinherit my son," the judges shall investigate his case and if the son is not guilty of a grave offense deserving the penalty of disinheritance, the father may not disinherit his son.

169. If he should be guilty of a grave offense deserving the penalty of disinheritance by his father, they shall pardon him for his first one; if he should commit a grave offense a second time, the father may disinherit his son.

170. If a man's first-ranking wife bears him children and his slave woman bears him children, and the father during his lifetime then declares to (or: concerning) the children whom the slave woman bore to him, "My children," and he reckons them with the children of the first-ranking wife — after the father goes to his fate, the children of the first-ranking wife and the children of the slave woman shall equally divide the property of the paternal estate; the preferred heir is a son of the first-ranking wife, he shall select and take a share first.

171. But if the father during his lifetime should not declare to (or: concerning) the children whom the slave woman bore to him, "My children," after the father goes to his fate, the children of the slave woman will not divide the property of the paternal estate with the children of the first-ranking wife. The release of the slave woman and of her children shall be secured; the children of the first-ranking wife will not make claims of slavery against the children of the slave woman. The first-ranking wife shall take her dowry and the marriage settlement which her husband awarded to her in writing, and she shall continue to reside in her husband's dwelling; as long as she is alive she shall enjoy the use of it, but she may not sell it; her own estate shall belong (as inheritance) only to her own children.

172. If her husband does not make a marriage settlement in her favor, they shall restore to her in full her dowry, and she shall take a share of the property of

her husband's estate comparable in value to that of one heir. If her children pressure her in order to coerce her to depart from the house, the judges shall investigate her case and shall impose a penalty on the children; that woman will not depart from her husband's house. If that woman should decide on her own to depart, she shall leave for her children the marriage settlement which her husband gave to her; she shall take the dowry brought from her father's house and a husband of her choice shall marry her.

173. If that woman should bear children to her latter husband into whose house she entered, after that woman dies, her former and latter children shall equally divide her dowry.

174. If she does not bear children to her latter husband, only the children of her first husband shall take her dowry.

177. If a widow whose children are still young should decide to enter another's house, she will not enter without (the prior approval of) the judges. When she enters another's house, the judges shall investigate the estate of her former husband, and they shall entrust the estate of her former husband to her later husband and to that woman, and they shall have them record a tablet (inventorying the estate). They shall safeguard the estate and they shall raise the young children; they will not sell the household goods. Any buyer who buys the household goods of the children of a widow shall forfeit his silver; the property shall revert to its owner.

185. If a man takes in adoption a young child at birth and then rears him, that rearing will not be reclaimed.

186. If a man takes in adoption a young child, and when he takes him, he (the child?) is seeking his father and mother, that rearing shall return to his father's house.

188. If a craftsman takes a young child to rear and then teaches him his craft, he will not be reclaimed.

189. If he should not teach him his craft, that rearing shall return to his father's house.

190. If a man should not reckon the young child whom he took and raised in adoption as equal with his children, that rearing shall return to his father's house.

一、导读

《汉谟拉比法典》（以下简称《法典》）是古巴比伦王国的第六任国王汉谟拉比（Hammurabi）颁布的法律汇编，是迄今为止世界上保存较为完整的最早的一部成文法典。《法典》全文刻于一座黑色玄武岩的石碑上，高约 2.25 米。1901—1902 年，法国考古队在苏萨发掘出这块石碑，并将其运回法国。石碑现藏于巴黎卢浮宫博物馆。

《法典》石碑的顶部是一幅浮雕，刻画的是太阳神沙马什把绳环和木杖授予汉谟拉比的场景。绳和木杖是古代两河流域传统的丈量工具，象征司法与正义。浮雕中，沙马什端坐于宝座，汉谟拉比站立在沙马什面前，左手水平弯曲 90 度，右臂曲起，肘部置于左手前臂上，右手手掌到达嘴部高度。这一姿势是两河流域艺术作品中常用的祈祷的姿势。

《法典》用楔形文字刻于石碑上。全文分为三部分：序、法典条款和跋。一般认为，《法典》保存下来的条款有 282 条。序言陈述了汉谟拉比的丰功伟绩，说明了立法的目的是为人民提供立身行事的正确引导，以确保他们的正直作为。结尾部分勉励子孙后代遵守法律，呼吁众神诅咒并惩处违法的人。《法典》条款涵盖的内容包括司法程序、刑事犯罪、婚姻家庭和经济活动等方面，是了解、学习古巴比伦王国社会、政治、经济、法律以及婚姻家庭生活的重要史料。

在内容和形式上，《法典》对古代近东其他文明的成文法典产生了深刻的影响。《旧约·出埃及记》第 21～23 章记录的相关法律条文与《法典》无论在形式还是内容上都有很大的相似性，比如法律条文采用的“如果……那么……”的句式，关于对人身伤害、财产侵犯等问题的处罚等。这也是古代近东文明相互交融的一个重要体现。

学者研究指出，两河流域流传下来的包括《法典》在内的一系列成文法典，更多地代表了公平和正义，而非具体指导司法实践的规则，其实是地方议会和长老会从公元前 3000 年左右一直到波斯时期（前 559—前 330 年）在发挥着仲裁和决策的作用。本书节选的《法典》相关条文，主要反映古巴比伦王国社会经济生活等状况。

二、注释

1. Selected from Martha T. Roth(ed.), *Law Collections from Mesopotamia and Asia Minor*, Society of Biblical Literature, 1997.

2. Ordeal，即神明裁判，或称神判法、神断法、神明审判，指的是借助神的力量，为定夺诉讼纷争之输赢或确定罪犯，而对当事人或嫌疑者施行考验的原始审判方法。神明裁判曾存在于世界许多民族中，当时人们相信神力可以对人世间的是非做出判定，并帮助人们给罪犯量刑。其方式多种多样，常用的有吞食某种有毒的东西、手下油锅取物、决斗、将嫌疑者投入河中，等等。

3. shekel，音译“舍客勒”，古代两河流域的重量单位，1“舍客勒”约合8.33克，后来为希伯来人借鉴使用。

4. sila，音译“希拉”，古代两河流域的容积单位，1“希拉”约合1升。

5. iku，音译“依库”，古代两河流域的土地面积单位，1“依库”约合3600平方米。

6. Adad，音译“阿达”，古代两河流域雷电神、暴风雨神等，《法典》中指暴风雨神。

7. naditu，音译“纳迪图”，ugbabtu，音译“乌格巴博图”，她们是古巴比伦王国女祭司，神的配偶，终身居住在女观院，献身于神。

8. vat，音译“瓦特”，古代两河流域的一种器皿。

三、问题探讨

1. 结合《汉谟拉比法典》节选的条文内容，评述古巴比伦王国的妇女地位。
2. 结合《汉谟拉比法典》节选的条文内容，评述古巴比伦王国的经济状况。

四、参考文献

1. 欧阳晓莉：《〈汉谟拉比法典〉真是用来判刑的吗?》，《澎湃新闻》2015年3月21日。

2. J. Dyneley Prince, “Review: The Code of Hammurabi”, *The American Journal of Theology*, Vol.8, No.3 (Jul. , 1904), pp.601 – 609.

3. Martha T. Roth, *Law Collections from Mesopotamia and Asia Minor*, Society of Biblical Literature, 1997.

4. Phillip C. Boardman, *Enduring Legacies*, Simon & Schuster Custom Publishing, 1996.

5. *The Code of Hammurabi*, translated by Robert Francis Harper, the University of Chicago Press, 1904.

UNIT 2

EGYPTIAN CUSTOMS[1]

Herodotus

About Egypt I shall have a great deal more to relate because of the number of remarkable things which the country contains, and because of the fact that more monuments which beggar description are to be found there than anywhere else in the world. That is reason enough for my dwelling on it at greater length. Not only is the Egyptian climate peculiar to that country, and the Nile different in its behaviour from other rivers elsewhere, but the Egyptians themselves in their manners and customs seem to have reversed the ordinary practices of mankind. For instance, women attend market and are employed in trade, while men stay at home and do the weaving. In weaving the normal way is to work the threads of the weft upwards, but the Egyptians work them downwards. Men in Egypt carry loads on their heads, women on their shoulders; women pass water standing up, men sitting down. To ease themselves they go indoors, but eat outside in the streets, on the theory that what is unseemly but necessary should be done in private, and what is not unseemly should be done openly. No woman holds priestly office, either in the service of goddess or god; only men are priests in both cases. Sons are under no compulsion to support their parents if they do not wish to do so, but daughters must, whether they wish it or not. Elsewhere priests grow their hair long; in Egypt they shave their heads. In other nations the relatives of the deceased in time of mourning cut their hair, but the Egyptians, who shave at all other times, mark a death by letting the hair grow both on head and chin. They live with their animals — unlike the rest of the world, who live apart from them. Other men live on wheat and barley, but any Egyptian who does so is blamed for it, their bread being made from spelt, or *Zea* as some call it. Dough they knead with their feet, but clay with their hands — and even handle dung. They practise circumcision, while men of other nations — except those who have learnt from Egypt — leave their private parts as nature made them. Men in Egypt have two garments each, women only one. The ordinary practice at sea is to make sheets fast to ring-bolts fitted outboard; the Egyptians fit them inboard. In writing or calculating, instead of going, like the Greeks, from left to right, the Egyptians go from right to left — and obstinately maintain that theirs is the dexterous method, ours being left-handed and awkward. They have two sorts of writing, the sacred and the common. They are religious to excess, beyond any other nation in the world, and here are some of the customs which illustrate the fact; they drink from brazen cups which they scour every day — everyone, without exception. They wear linen clothes which they make a special point of continually washing. They circumcise themselves for cleanliness' sake, preferring to be clean rather than comely. The priests shave their bodies all over every other day to guard against the presence of lice, or anything else equally unpleasant, while they are about their religious duties; the priests, too, wear linen only, and shoes made from the papyrus plant — these materials, for dress and shoes, being the only ones allowed them. They bath in cold water twice a day and twice every night — and observe innumerable other ceremonies besides. Their life, however, is not by any means all hardship, for they enjoy advantages too: for instance, they are free from all personal expense, having bread made for them out of the sacred grain, and a plentiful daily supply of goose — meat and beef, with wine in addition. Fish they are forbidden to touch; and as for beans, they cannot even bear to look at them, because they imagine they are unclean (in point of fact the Egyptians never sow beans, and even if any happen to grow wild, they will not eat them, either raw or boiled). They do not have a single priest for each god, but a number, of which one is chief-priest, and when a chief-priest dies his son is appointed to succeed him. Bulls are considered the property of the god Epaphus — or Apis[2] — and are therefore tested in the following way: a priest appointed for the purpose examines the animal, and if he finds even a single black hair upon him, pronounces him unclean; he goes over him with the greatest care, first making him stand up, then lie on his back, after which he pulls out his tongue to see if that, too, is "clean" according to the recognized marks — what those are I will explain later[3]. He also inspects the tail to make sure the hair on it grows properly; then, if the animal passes all these tests successfully, the priest marks him by twisting round his horns a band of papyrus, which he seals with wax and stamps with his signet ring. The bull is finally taken away, and the penalty is death for anybody who sacrifices an animal which has not been marked in this manner. The method of sacrifice is as follows: they take the beast (one of those marked with the seal) to the appropriate altar and light a fire; then, after pouring a libation of wine and invoking the god by name, they slaughter it, cut off its head, and flay the carcase. The head is loaded with curses and taken away — if there happen to be Greek traders in the market, it is sold to them; if not, it is thrown into the river. The curses they pronounce take the form of a prayer that any disaster which threatens either themselves or their country may be diverted and fall upon the severed head of the beast. Both the libation and the practice of cutting off the heads of sacrificial beasts are common to all Egyptians in all their sacrifices, and the latter explains why it is that no Egyptian will use the head of any sort of animal for food. The methods of disembowelling and burning are various, and I will describe the one which is followed in the worship of the goddess whom they consider the greatest and honour with the most important festival. In this case, when they have flayed the bull, they first pray and then take its paunch out whole, leaving the intestines and fat inside the body; next they cut off the legs, shoulders, neck, and rump, and stuff the carcase with loaves of bread, honey, raisins, figs, frankincense, myrrh, and other aromatic substances; finally they pour a quantity of oil over the carcase and burn it. They always fast before a sacrifice, and while the fire is consuming it they beat their breasts. That part of the ceremony done, they serve a meal out of the portions left over.

...

I was told that this Heracles was one of the twelve gods. Of the other Heracles, with whom the Greeks are familiar, I could get no information anywhere in Egypt. Nevertheless it was not the Egyptians who took the name Heracles from the Greeks. The opposite is true: it was the Greeks who took it from the Egyptians — those Greeks, I mean, who gave the name to the son of Amphitryon. There is plenty of evidence to prove the truth of this, in particular the fact that both the parents of Heracles — Amphitryon and Alcmene[4] — were of Egyptian origin. Again, the Egyptians say they do not know the names of Poseidon or the Dioscuri, or receive them as gods amongst the rest. But surely, if they had taken the name of any gods from the Greeks, it is precisely these they would have been most likely to notice — unless I am greatly mistaken in my belief that the Egyptians were already at that time a sea-faring nation, and that some of the Greeks, too, used the sea. Being sailors, the Egyptians would have learnt the name of Poseidon and the Dioscuri even before that of Heracles.

Nevertheless the Egyptians have had a god named Heracles from time immemorial. They say that seventeen thousand years before the reign of Amasis[5] the twelve gods were produced from the eight; and of the twelve they hold Heracles to be one. To satisfy my wish to get the best information I possibly could on this subject, I made a voyage to Tyre in Phoenicia, because I had heard that there was a temple there, of great sanctity, dedicated to Heracles. I visited the temple, and found that the offerings which adorned it were numerous and valuable, not the least remarkable being two pillars, one of pure gold, the other of emerald which gleamed in the dark with a strange radiance. In the course of conversation with the priests I asked how long ago the temple had been built, and found by their answer that they, too, did not share the Greek view; for they said that the temple was as ancient as Tyre itself, and that Tyre had already stood for two thousand three hundred years. I also saw another temple there, dedicated to the Thasian Heracles; and I have also been to Thasos, where I found a temple of Heracles built by the Phoenicians who settled there after they had sailed in search of Europa. Even this was five generations before Heracles the son of Amphitryon made his appearance in Greece. The result of these researches is a plain proof that the worship of Heracles is very ancient; and I think that the wisest course is taken by those Greeks who maintain a double cult of this deity, with two temples, in one of which they worship him as Olympian and divine, and in the other pay him such honour as is due to a demi-god, or hero. The Greeks have many stories with no basis of fact. One of the silliest is the story of how Heracles came to Egypt and was taken away by the Egyptians to be sacrificed to Zeus, with all due pomp and the sacrificial wreath upon his head; and how he quietly submitted until the moment came for the beginning of the actual ceremony at the altar, when he exerted his strength and killed them all. For me at least such a tale is proof enough that the Greeks know nothing whatever about Egyptian character and custom. The Egyptians are forbidden by their religion even to kill animals for sacrifice, except sheep and such bulls and bull-calves as have passed the test for "cleanness" — and geese: is it likely, then, that they would sacrifice human beings? Besides, if Heracles was a mere man (as they say he was) and single-handed, how is it conceivable that he should have killed tens of thousands of people? And now I hope that both gods and heroes will forgive me for saying what I have said on these matters!

...

About the oracles — that of Dodona[6] in Greece and of Ammon in Libya — the Egyptians have the following legend: according to the priests of the Theban Zeus, two women connected with the service of the temple were carried off by the Phoenicians and sold, one in Libya and the other in Greece, and it was these women who founded the oracles in the two countries. I asked the priests at Thebes what grounds they had for being so sure about this, and they told me that careful search had been made for the women at the time, and that though it was unsuccessful, they had afterwards learned that the facts were just as they had reported them. At Dodona, however, the priestesses who deliver the oracles have a different version of the story: two black doves, they say flew away from Thebes in Egypt, and one of them alighted at Dodona, the other in Libya. The former, perched on an oak, and speaking with a human voice, told them that there, on that very spot, there should be an oracle of Zeus. Those who heard her understood the words to be a command from heaven, and at once obeyed. Similarly the dove which flew to Libya told the Libyans to found the oracle of Ammon — which is also an oracle of Zeus. The people who gave me this information were the three priestesses at Dodona — Promeneia the eldest, Timarete the next, and Nicandra the youngest — and their account is confirmed by the other Dodonaeans connected with the temple. Personally, however, I would suggest that if the Phoenicians really carried off the women from the temple and sold them respectively in Libya and Greece, the one who was brought to Greece (or Pelasgia as it was then called) must have been sold to the Thesprotians; and later, while she was working as a slave in that part of the country, she built, under an oak that happened to be growing there, a shrine to Zeus; for she would naturally remember in her exile the god whom she had served in her native Thebes. Subsequently, when she had learned to speak Greek, she established an oracle there, and mentioned, in addition, that the same Phoenicians who had sold her, also sold her sister in Libya. The story which the people of Dodona tell about the doves came, I should say, from the fact that the women were foreigners, whose language sounded to them like the twittering of birds; later on the dove spoke with a human voice, because by that time the woman had stopped twittering and learned to talk intelligibly. That, at least, is how I should explain the obvious impossibility of a dove using the language of men. As to the bird being black, they merely signify by this that the woman was an Egyptian. It is certainly true that the oracles at Thebes and Dodona are similar in character. Another form of divination — by the inspection of sacrificial victims — also came from Egypt.

It was the Egyptians too who originated, and taught the Greeks to use, ceremonial meetings, processions, and liturgies: a fact which can be inferred from the obvious antiquity of such ceremonies in Egypt, compared with Greece, where they have been only recently introduced. The Egyptians meet in solemn assembly not once a year only, but on a number of occasions, the most important and best attended being the festival of Artemis at Bubastis: second in importance is the assembly at Busiris — a city in the middle of the Delta, containing a vast temple dedicated to Isis, the Egyptian equivalent of Demeter, in whose honour the meeting is held. Then there are the assemblies in honour of Athene at Sais, of the Sun at Heliopolis, of Leto at Buto, and of Ares[7] at Papremis. The procedure at Bubastis is this: they come in barges, men and women together, a great number in each boat; on the way, some of the women keep up a continual clatter with castanets and some of the men play flutes, while the rest, both men and women, sing and clap their hands. Whenever they pass a town on the river-bank, they bring the barge close in-shore, some of the women continuing to act as I have said, while others shout abuse at the women of the place, or start dancing, or stand up and hitch up their skirts. When they reach Bubastis they celebrate the festival with elaborate sacrifices, and more wine is consumed than during all the rest of the year. The numbers that meet there, are, according to native report, as many as seven hundred thousand men and women — excluding children. I have already mentioned the festival of Isis at Busiris: it is here that everybody — tens of thousands of men and women — when the sacrifice is over, beat their breasts: in whose honour, however, I do not feel it is proper for me to say. Any Carians who happen to live in Egypt go even further and cut their foreheads with knives, thus proving that they are foreigners and not Egyptians. At Sais, on the night of the sacrifices, everybody burns a great number of lights in the open air round the houses; the lamps they use are flat dishes filled with oil and salt, with a floating wick which keeps burning throughout the night. The festival is called the Festival of Lamps, and even the Egyptians who cannot attend it mark the night of the sacrifice by lighting lamps, so that on that night lamps are burning not in Sais only but throughout the country. There is a sacred tradition which accounts both for the date and for the manner of these observances.

...

It was the Egyptians who first made it an offence against piety to have intercourse with women in temples, or to enter temples after intercourse without having previously washed. Hardly any nation except the Egyptians and Greeks has any such scruple, but nearly all consider men and women to be, in this respect, no different from animals, which, whether they are beasts or birds, they constantly see coupling in temples and sacred places-and if the god concerned had any objection to this, he would not allow it to occur. Such is the theory, but, in spite of it, I must continue to disapprove the practice. The Egyptians are meticulous in their observance of this point, as indeed they are in everything else which concerns their religion.

There are not a great many wild animals in Egypt, in spite of the fact that it borders on Libya. Such as there are — both wild and tame — are without exception held to be sacred[8]. To explain the reason for this, I should have to enter into a discussion of religious principles which is a subject I particularly wish to avoid-any slight mention I have already made of such matters having been forced upon me by the needs of my story. But, reasons apart, how they actually behave towards animals I will proceed to describe. The various sorts have guardians appointed for them, sometimes men, sometimes women, who are responsible for feeding them; and the office of guardian is handed down from father to son. Their manner, in the various cities, of performing vows is as follows: praying to the god to whom the particular creature, whichever it may be, is sacred, they shave the heads of their children — sometimes completely, sometimes only a half or a third part — and after weighing the hair in a pair of scales, give an equal weight of silver to the animals' keeper, who then cuts up fish (the animals' usual food) to an equivalent value and gives it to them to eat. Anyone who deliberately kills one of these animals, is punished with death;

should one be killed accidentally, the penalty is whatever the priests choose to impose; but for killing an ibis or a hawk, whether deliberately or not, the penalty is inevitably death.

...

The Egyptians who live in the cultivated parts of the country, by their practice of keeping records of the past, have made themselves much the most learned of any nation of which I have had experience. I will describe some of their habits: every month for three successive days they purge themselves, for their health's sake, with emetics and clysters, in the belief that all diseases come from the food a man eats; and it is a fact — even apart from this precaution — that next to the Libyans they are the healthiest people in the world. I should put this down myself to the absence of changes in the climate; for change, and especially change of weather, is the prime cause of disease. They eat loaves made from spelt — *cyllestes* is their word for them — and drink a wine made from barley, as they have no vines in the country. Some kinds of fish they eat raw, either dried in the sun, or salted; quails, too, they eat raw, and ducks and various small birds, after pickling them in brine; other sorts of birds and fish, apart from those which they consider sacred, they either roast or boil. When the rich give a party and the meal is finished, a man carries round amongst the guests a wooden image of a corpse in a coffin, carved and painted to look as much like the real thing as possible, and anything from eighteen inches to three foot long; he shows it to each guest in turn, and says: "Look upon this body as you drink and enjoy yourself; for you will be just like it when you are dead."

The Egyptians keep to their native customs and never adopt any from abroad. Many of these customs are interesting, especially, perhaps, the "Linus" song. This person, under different names, is celebrated in song not only in Egypt but in Phoenicia, Cyprus, and other places, and appears to be the person whom the Greeks celebrate as Linus; if this is so, it is yet one more of the many surprises that Egypt has to offer: for where did the Egyptians get this song from? It is clearly very ancient, the Egyptian name for Linus is Maneros, and their story is that their first king had an only son, who died young, and that this dirge — their first and, at the time, their only melody — was invented to be sung in his honour.

There is another point in which the Egyptians resemble one section of the

Greek people — the Lacedaemonians[9]: I mean the custom of young men stepping aside to make room for their seniors when they meet them in the street, and of getting up from their seats when older men come in. But they are unlike any of the Greeks in that they do not greet one another by name in the streets, but make a low bow and drop one hand to the knee. The clothes they wear consist of a linen tunic with a fringe hanging round the legs (called in their language *calasiris*), and a white woollen garment on top of it. It is, however, contrary to religious usage to be buried in a woollen garment, or to wear wool in a temple. This custom agrees with the rites known as Orphic[10] and Bacchic[11] (actually Egyptian and Pythagorean); for anyone initiated into these rites is similarly debarred from burial in a garment of wool. They have a myth which explains the reason for this.

The Egyptians were also the first to assign each month and each day to a particular deity, and to foretell by the date of a man's birth his character, his fortunes, and the day of his death — a discovery which Greek poets have turned to account. The Egyptians, too, have made more use of omens and prognostics than any other nation; they keep written records of the observed results of any unusual phenomenon, so that they come to expect a similar consequence to follow a similar occurrence in the future. The art of divination is not attributed by them to any man, but only to certain gods: for instance, Heracles, Apollo, Athena, Artemis, Ares, and Zeus all have an oracle in the country, while the oracle of Leto in Buto is held in greater repute than any of them. The method of delivering the responses varies in the different shrines.

The practice of medicine they split up into separate parts, each doctor being responsible for the treatment of only one disease. There are, in consequence, innumerable doctors, some specializing in diseases of the eyes, others of the head, others of the teeth, others of the stomach, and so on; while others, again, deal with the sort of troubles which cannot be exactly localized. As regards mourning and funerals, when a distinguished man dies all the women of the household plaster their heads and faces with mud, then, leaving the body indoors, perambulate the town with the dead man's female relatives, their dresses fastened with a girdle, and beat their bared breasts. The men too, for their part, follow the same procedure, wearing a girdle and beating themselves like the women. The ceremony over, they take the body to be mummified.

Mummification is a distinct profession. The embalmers, when a body is brought to them, produce specimen models in wood, painted to resemble nature, and graded in quality; the best and most expensive kind is said to represent a being whose name I shrink from mentioning in this connexion[12]; the next best is somewhat inferior and cheaper, while the third sort is cheapest of all. After pointing out these differences in quality, they ask which of the three is required, and the kinsmen of the dead man, having agreed upon a price, go away and leave the embalmers to their work. The most perfect process is as follows: as much as possible of the brain is extracted through the nostrils with an iron hook, and what the hook cannot reach is rinsed out with drugs; next the flank is laid open with a flint knife and the whole contents of the abdomen removed; the cavity is then thoroughly cleansed and washed out, first with palm wine and again with an infusion of pounded spices. After that it is filled with pure bruised myrrh, cassia, and every other aromatic substance with the exception of frankincense, and sewn up again, after which the body is placed in natrum, covered entirely over, for seventy days — never longer. When this period, which must not be exceeded, is over, the body is washed and then wrapped from head to foot in linen cut into strips and smeared on the under side with gum, which is commonly used by the Egyptians instead of glue. In this condition the body is given back to the family, who have a wooden case made, shaped like the human figure, into which it is put. The case is then sealed up and stored in a sepulchral chamber, upright against the wall. When, for reasons of expense, the second quality is called for, the treatment is different: no incision is made and the intestines are not removed, but oil of cedar is injected with a syringe into the body through the anus which is afterwards stopped up to prevent the liquid from escaping. The body is then pickled in natrum for the prescribed number of days, on the last of which the oil is drained off. The effect of it is so powerful that as it leaves the body it brings with it the stomach and intestines in a liquid state, and as the flesh, too, is dissolved by the natrum, nothing of the body is left but the bones and skin. After this treatment it is returned to the family without further fuss.

The third method, used for embalming the bodies of the poor, is simply to clear out the intestines with a purge and keep the body seventy days in natrum. It is then given back to the family to be taken away.

When the wife of a distinguished man dies, or any woman who happens to be beautiful or well known, her body is not given to the embalmers immediately, but only after the lapse of three or four days. This is a precautionary measure to prevent the embalmers from violating the corpse, a thing which is said actually to have happened in the case of a woman who had just died. The culprit was given away by one of his fellow workmen. If anyone, either an Egyptian or a foreigner, is found drowned in the river or killed by a crocodile, there is the strongest obligation upon the people of the nearest town to have the body embalmed in the most elaborate manner and buried in a consecrated burial-place; no one is allowed to touch it except the priests of the Nile — not even relatives or friends; the priests alone prepare it for burial with their own hands and place it in the tomb, as if it were something more sacred than the body of a man.

The Egyptians are unwilling to adopt Greek customs, or, to speak generally, those of any other country. There is, however, one exception to this almost universal rule in the case of Chemmis, a large town near Neapolis in the district of Thebes. In this place there is a square of enclosed ground sacred to Perseus the son of Danae; palm trees grow round it, and there is a stone gateway of great size surmounted by two very large stone figures. Within the enclosure is a shrine containing a statue of Perseus. According to the local legend, Perseus is frequently to be seen in the neighbourhood, and also within the temple; sometimes a sandal which he has worn, three feet long, is found — a sign, they say, of the approach of a period of great prosperity for the whole of Egypt. In the worship of Perseus Greek ceremonies are used, athletic contests with all the usual events, and prizes of cattle, cloaks, and skins. When I asked why it was that Perseus revealed himself only to the people of Chemmis, and why they alone of the Egyptians celebrated games in his honour, the answer was that Perseus belonged by birth to their city; Danaus and Lynceus, they said, were Chemmites before they sailed to Greece, and from them they traced Perseus' descent. Further, when he came to Egypt from Libya with the Gorgon's head (which is the reason the Greeks also assign for his going there) he paid a visit to Chemmis, having previously learned the name of the place from his mother, and there acknowledged all his kinsmen. On his arrival he instructed them to celebrate games in his honour, and they accordingly did so.

一、导读

希罗多德，古希腊著名历史学家，约公元前484年出生于小亚细亚的希腊城邦哈里卡尔纳所斯（Halicarnassus），著有《历史》一书，被古罗马西塞罗（Cicero）称为“史学之父”。希罗多德的历史观、历史叙述方法对后世史学影响深远。但是，鉴于希罗多德的“有闻必录”以及《历史》中众多神话乃至“荒诞不经”的记述，又有后人称其为“谎言之父”。其实，“有闻必录”正是希罗多德对历史“探究”的一种客观态度，即他尽可能地将对同一历史事件的不同说法都记载下来，让读者进行“二次探究”，而不是像他的后继者修昔底德那样对所收集的材料进行考证、删减，最后只留给读者他认为是唯一正确的解释。因此，从历史写作方法和态度上看，希罗多德似乎比修昔底德更为客观、公正。希罗多德将历史写作或者研究理解为historia，即“探究”，这与司马迁“究天人之际”的著史目的有着异曲同工之妙。希罗多德的世界性眼光也同样令人赞叹，他在著作中对异族文化和习俗的理解与尊重超乎后人的想象，以至于有人称其为“亲蛮者”。当然，如何看待希罗多德对希腊和非希腊文明的态度，学界仍存有较大分歧。但不可否认的是，希罗多德的《历史》已被后世学者拿来作为分析希腊人建构蛮族“他者”形象和加强希腊人“自我”形象认同的重要依据。

希罗多德的《历史》本无分卷，亦无书名。希腊化时期，亚历山大里亚学者将希罗多德的著作整理成册，凡9卷，分别以古希腊9位缪斯女神的名称命名，并取书中“Historia”一词作为书名，即《历史》。尽管希罗多德在序言中开宗明义地指出，自己“探究”的目的是“为了保存人类的功业，使之不致由于年深日久而被人们遗忘，为了使希腊人和异邦人的那些值得赞叹的丰功伟绩不致失去它们的光彩，特别是为了把他们纷争的原因给记载下来”。但是，国内外学界对希罗多德《历史》所记载内容的理解仍然存有分歧：一种观点认为，《历史》是一部记载希腊和波斯战争的历史巨著，希罗多德《历史》商务印书馆版的副标题《希腊波斯战争史》即是最好的证明，但该书前半部分记载的是与战争毫无关系的内容；另一种观点认为，《历史》是一部记载波斯帝国兴起和对外扩张的历史巨著，作为全书主线，波斯帝国的兴起和对外扩张贯穿全书，并将众多纷繁复杂的内容统一起来。借用希罗多德的记述模式：关于《历史》一书内容的主要观点如上所述，至于哪种观点更有说服力，还要读者在阅读著作之后，根据自己的理解进行判断。

本篇英译本选自企鹅古典丛书（Penguin Classics）塞林科特译本（Herodotus, *The Histories*, trans., Aubrey de Selincourt, Penguin Books, 1972），内容选自第2卷对古代埃及风俗描述的部分，包括古埃及的生活习俗、

宗教习俗和丧葬习俗。此卷全部记述古代埃及的历史、习俗和文化，看似与全书其他部分脱节，学者也因此认为此卷可以独立成书。但是仔细阅读便不难发现，作者在第 2 卷的卷首和卷尾与前后卷做了完美的过渡与衔接。之所以选取第 2 卷古代埃及风俗部分，主要是因为：第一，此部分较好地体现了希罗多德的世界性眼光、历史记述方法和历史观；第二，此部分对埃及风俗的描述新颖、独特、生动、有趣，可读性强，是了解古代埃及习俗，比如丧葬习俗、木乃伊制作的重要资料。

二、注释

1. Selected from Hrodotus, *The Histories*, trans., Aubrey de Selincourt, Penguin Books, 1972.

2. Apis，汉译“阿匹斯”，是埃及最早将神性表现在动物身上的神祇。孟斐斯人多崇拜它，其象征丰饶及生产力，是一位戴有太阳盘及圣蛇的公牛神。目前在孟斐斯有神牛墓，所埋葬的就是这些阿匹斯圣牛。

3. 希罗多德在《历史》3.29 中对此进行了解释。

4. 安菲特律翁（Amphitryon），希腊神话中的底比斯将军，大力神赫拉克勒斯的养父，妻子是阿尔克墨涅（Alcmene）。

5. 所指阿马西斯二世（Amasis Ⅱ），古埃及第 26 王朝法老。波斯征服之前，他是埃及最后一位伟大的统治者。

6. 多多那（Dodona）位于希腊西北部伊庇鲁斯地区，古希腊著名的宙斯神谕所的所在地，以宙斯神谕所著称。多多那神谕的独特之处在于其神谕发布方式中最重要的元素——橡树，其神谕传达者——祭司的古怪行为，及问询时问题需刻在铅板或铅条上。

7. 古希腊女神阿尔忒弥斯（Artemis）相当于埃及的芭丝特（Bast）女神。芭丝特是埃及神话中猫首人身的女神，她的名字有时候也被拼为巴亚斯特（Baast）、巫巴丝特（Ubaste）。雅典娜（Athene）相当于古埃及涅伊特（Neith）女神，她是一位早期埃及神殿中的女神，塞易斯城的守护神。该城早在第一王朝起，就成为埃及尼罗河三角洲西部地区涅伊特的崇拜中心。它的古埃及名称叫扎乌（Zau）。太阳神（Sun）就是埃及神中的拉神（Ra）。战神阿瑞斯（Ares）就是埃及神中的塞特（Set）。

8. 古代埃及人认为动物是神的化身，是神在人间的代表，每一个动物都代表某一位神，如公羊代表阿蒙神，鹰代表天神荷鲁斯，猫代表女神巴斯泰托等。因此，在古代埃及人的观念中，动物是神圣的。

9. Lacedaemonian，汉译“拉西第梦人”，即斯巴达人。

10. Orphic，指希腊的奥菲斯秘仪。奥菲斯（Orpheus）是希腊传说中著名的吟唱诗人和预言者，被认为是奥菲斯宗教秘仪创始人。

11. Bacchic，指希腊的酒神崇拜仪式。虽然酒神（Dionysos）的起源古老，但其秘仪则晚至古风时代才兴起，而且有可能受到埃及宗教思想的影响。

12. 指古埃及奥西里斯神（Osiris）。

三、问题探讨

1. 结合节选材料，评价希罗多德的历史比较方法。

2. 结合节选材料，评述希罗多德的历史观。

四、参考文献

1. 黄洋：《希罗多德：历史学的开创与异域文明的话语》，《世界历史》2008年第4期。

2. 蒋保：《论希罗多德的埃及观》，《学海》2010年第5期。

3. 杨扬：《希罗多德“埃及卷”释读》，《西南大学学报》（社会科学版）2011年第5期。

4. Carolyn Dewald & John Marincola (ed.), *The Cambridge Companion to Herodotus*, Cambridge University Press, 2006.

5. Oswyn Murray & Alfonso Moreno (ed.), *A Commentary on Herodotus Books Ⅰ-Ⅳ*, Oxford University Press, 2007.

UNIT 3

PERICLES' FUNERAL ORATION[1]

Thucydides

In the same winter the Athenians, following their annual custom, gave a public funeral[2] for those who had been the first to die in the war. These funerals are held in the following way: two days before the ceremony the bones of the fallen are brought and put in a tent which has been erected, and people make whatever offerings they wish to their own dead. Then there is a funeral procession in which coffins of cypress wood are carried on wagons. There is one coffin for each tribe[3], which contains the bones of members of that tribe. One empty bier is decorated and carried in the procession: this is for the missing, whose bodies could not be recovered. Everyone who wishes to, both citizens and foreigners, can join in the procession, and the women who are related to the dead are there to make their laments at the tomb. The bones are laid in the public burial place, which is in the most beautiful quarter outside the city walls. Here the Athenians always bury those who have fallen in war. The only exception is those who died at Marathon[4], who, because their achievement was considered absolutely outstanding, were buried on the battlefield itself.

When the bones have been laid in the earth, a man chosen by the city for his intellectual gifts and for his general reputation makes an appropriate speech in praise of the dead, and after the speech all depart. This is the procedure at these burials, and all through the war, when the time came to do so, the Athenians followed this ancient custom. Now, at the burial of those who were the first to fall in the war Pericles, the son of Xanthippus, was chosen to make the speech. When the moment arrived, he came forward from the tomb and, standing on a high platform, so that he might be heard by as many people as possible in the crowd, he spoke as follows:

"Many of those who have spoken here in the past have praised the institution of this speech at the close of our ceremony. It seemed to them a mark of honour to our soldiers who have fallen in war that a speech should be made over them. I do not agree. These men have shown themselves valiant in action, and it would be enough, I think, for their glories to be proclaimed in action, as you have just seen it done at this funeral organized by the state. Our belief in the courage and manliness of so many should not be hazarded on the goodness or badness of one man's speech. Then it is not easy to speak with a proper sense of balance, when a man's listeners find it difficult to believe in the truth of what one is saying. The man who knows the facts and loves the dead may well think that an oration tells less than what he knows and what he would like to hear: others who do not know so much may feel envy for the dead, and think the orator over-praises them, when he speaks of exploits that are beyond their own capacities. Praise of other people is tolerable only up to a certain point, the point where one still believes that one could do oneself some of the things one is hearing about. Once you get beyond this point, you will find people becoming jealous and incredulous. However, the fact is that this institution was set up and approved by our forefathers, and it is my duty to follow the tradition and do my best to meet the wishes and the expectations of every one of you.

"I shall begin by speaking about our ancestors, since it is only right and proper on such an occasion to pay them the honour of recalling what they did. In this land of ours there have always been the same people living from generation to generation up till now, and they, by their courage and their virtues, have handed it on to us, a free country. They certainly deserve our praise. Even more so do our fathers deserve it. For to the inheritance they had received they added all the empire we have now, and it was not without blood and toil that they handed it down to us of the present generation. And then we ourselves, assembled here today, who are mostly in the prime of life, have, in most directions, added to the power of our empire and have organized our State in such a way that it is perfectly well able to look after itself both in peace and in war.

"I have no wish to make a long speech on subjects familiar to you all: so I shall say nothing about the warlike deeds by which we acquired our power or the battles in which we or our fathers gallantly resisted our enemies, Greek or foreign. What I want to do is, in the first place, to discuss the spirit in which we faced our trials and also our constitution and the way of life which has made us great. After that I shall speak in praise of the dead, believing that this kind of speech is not inappropriate to the present occasion, and that this whole assembly, of citizens and foreigners, may listen to it with advantage.

"Let me say that our system of government does not copy the institution of our neighbours. It is more the case of our being a model to others, than of our imitating anyone else. Our constitution is called democracy because power is in the hands not of a minority but of the whole people. When it is a question of settling private disputes, everyone is equal before the law; when it is a question of putting one person before another in positions of public responsibility, what counts is not membership of a particular class, but the actual ability which the man possesses. No one, so long as he has it in him to be of service to the state, is kept in political obscurity because of poverty. And, just as our political life is free and open, so is our day-to-day life in our relations with each other. We do not get into a state with our next-door neighbour if he enjoys himself in his own way, nor do we give him the kind of black looks which, though they do no real harm, still do hurt people's feelings. We are free and tolerant in our private lives; but in public affairs we keep to the law. This is because it commands our deep respect.

"We give our obedience to those whom we put in positions of authority, and we obey the laws themselves, especially those which are for the protection of the oppressed, and those unwritten laws which it is an acknowledged shame to break.

"And there is another point. When our work is over, we are in a position to enjoy all kinds of recreation for our spirits. There are various kinds of contests and sacrifices regularly throughout the year; in our own homes we find a beauty and a good taste which delight us every day and which drive away our cares. Then the greatness of our city brings it about that all the good things from all over the world flow in to us, so that to us it seems just as natural to enjoy foreign goods as our own local products.

"Then there is a great difference between us and our opponents, in our attitude towards military security. Here are some examples: Our city is open to the world, and we have no periodical deportations in order to prevent people observing or finding out secrets which might be of military advantage to the enemy. This is because we rely, not on secret weapons, but on our own real courage and loyalty. There is a difference, too, in our educational systems. The

Spartans, from their earliest boyhood, are submitted to the most laborious training in courage; we pass our lives without all these restrictions, and yet are just as ready to face the same dangers as they are. Here is a proof of this: When the Spartans invade our land, they do not come by themselves, but bring all their allies with them; whereas we, when we launch an attack abroad, do the job ourselves, and, though fighting on foreign soil, do not often fail to defeat opponents who are fighting for their own hearths and homes. As a matter of fact none of our enemies has ever yet been confronted with our total strength, because we have to divide our attention between our navy and the many missions on which our troops are sent on land. Yet, if our enemies engage a detachment of our forces and defeat it, they give themselves credit for having thrown back our entire army; or, if they lose, they claim that they were beaten by us in full strength. There are certain advantages, I think, in our way of meeting danger voluntarily, with an easy mind, instead of with a laborious training, with natural rather than with state-induced courage. We do not have to spend our time practising to meet sufferings which are still in the future; and when they are actually upon us we show ourselves just as brave as these others who are always in strict training. This is one point in which, I think, our city deserves to be admired. There are also others.

"Our love of what is beautiful does not lead to extravagance; our love of the things of the mind does not make us soft. We regard wealth as something to be properly used, rather than as something to boast about. As for poverty, no one need be ashamed to admit it: the real shame is in not taking practical measures to escape from it. Here each individual is interested not only in his own affairs but in the affairs of the state as well: even those who are mostly occupied with their own business are extremely well-informed on general politics — this is a peculiarity of ours: we do not say that a man who takes no interest politics is a man who minds his own business; we say that he has no business here at all. We Athenians, in our own persons, take our decisions on policy or submit them to proper discussions: for we do not think that there is an incompatibility between words and deeds; the worst thing is to rush into action before the consequences have been properly debated. And this is another point where we differ from other people. We are capable at the same time of taking risks and of estimating them beforehand. Others are brave out of ignorance; and, when they stop to think, they begin to fear. But the man who can most truly be accounted brave is he who best knows the meaning of what is sweet in life and of what is terrible, and then goes out undeterred to meet what is to come.

"Again, in questions of general good feeling there is a great contrast between us and most other people. We make friends by doing good to others, not to receiving good from them. This makes our friendship all the more reliable, since we want to keep alive the gratitude of those who are in our debt by showing continued goodwill to them: whereas the feelings of one who owes us something lack the same enthusiasm, since he knows that, when he repays our kindness, it will be more like paying back a debt than giving something spontaneously. We are unique in this. When we do kindnesses to others, we do not do them out of any calculations of profit or loss: we do them without afterthought, relying on our free liberality. Taking everything together then, I declare that our city is an education to Greece, and I declare that in my opinion each single one of our citizens, in all the manifold aspects of life, is able to show himself the rightful lord and owner of his own person, and do this, moreover, with exceptional grace and exceptional versatility. And to show that this is no empty boasting for the present occasion, but real tangible fact, you have only to consider the power which our city possesses and which has been won by those very qualities which I have mentioned. Athens, alone of the states we know, comes to her testing time in a greatness that surpasses what was imagined of her. In her case, and in her case alone, no invading enemy is ashamed at being defeated, and no subject can complain of being governed by people unfit for their responsibilities. Mighty indeed are the marks and monuments of our empire which we have left. Future ages will wonder at us, as the present age wonders at us now. We do not need the praises of a Homer, or of anyone else whose words may delight us for the moment, but whose estimation of facts will fall short of what is really true. For our adventurous spirit has forced an entry into every sea and into every land; and everywhere we have left behind us everlasting memorials of good done to our friends or suffering inflicted on our enemies.

"This, then, is the kind of city for which these men, who could not bear the thought of losing her, nobly fought and nobly died. It is only natural that every one of us who survive them should be willing to undergo hardships in her service. And it was for this reason that I have spoken at such length about our city, because I wanted to make it clear that for us there is more at stake than there is for others who lack our advantages; also I wanted my words of praise for the dead to be set in the bright light of evidence. And now the most important of these words has been spoken. I have sung the praises of our city; but it was the courage and gallantry of these men, and of people like them, which made her splendid. Nor would you find it true in the case of many of Greeks, as it is true of them, that no words can do more than justice to their deeds.

"To me it seems that the consummation which has overtaken these men shows us the meaning of manliness in its first revelation and in its final proof. Some of them, no doubt, had their faults; but what we ought to remember first is their gallant conduct against the enemy in defence of their native land. They have blotted out evil with good, and done more service to the commonwealth than they ever did harm in their private lives. No one of these men weakened because he wanted to go on enjoying his wealth: no one put off the awful day in the hope that he might live to escape his poverty and grow rich. More to be desired than such things, they chose to check the enemy's pride. This, to them, was a risk most glorious, and they accepted it, willing to strike down the enemy and relinquish everything else. As for success or failure, they left that in the doubtful hands of Hope, and when the reality of battle was before their faces, they put their trust in their own selves. In the fighting, they thought it more honourable to stand their ground and suffer death than to give in and save their lives. So they fled from the reproaches of men, abiding with life and limb the brunt of battle; and, in a small mount of time, the climax of their lives, a culmination of glory, not of fear, were swept away from us.

"So and such they were, these men — worthy of their city. We who remain behind may hope to be spared their fate, but must resolve to keep the same daring spirit against the foe. It is not simply a question of estimating the advantage in theory. I could tell you a long story (and you know is as well as I do) about what is to be gained by beating the enemy back. What I would prefer is that you should fix your eyes every day on the greatness of Athens as she really is, and should fall in love with her. When you realize her greatness, then reflect that what made her great was men with a spirit of adventure, men who knew their duty, men who were ashamed to fall below a certain standard. If they ever failed in an enterprise, they made up their minds that at any rate the city should not find their courage lacking to her, and they gave to her the best contribution that they could. They gave her their lives, to her and to all of us, and for their own selves they won praises that never grow old, the most splendid of sepulchres — not the sepulchre in which their bodies are laid, but where their glory remains eternal in men's minds, always there on the right occasion to stir other to speech or to action. For famous men have the whole earth as their memorial: it is not only the inscriptions on their graves in their own country that mark them out; no, in foreign lands also, not in any visible form but in people's hearts, their memory abides and grows. It is for you to try to be like them. Make up your minds that happiness depends on being free, and freedom depends on being courageous. Let there be no relaxation in face of the perils of the war. The people who have most excuse for despising death are not the wretched and unfortunate, who have no hope of doing well for themselves, but those who run the risk of a complete reversal in their lives, and who could feel the difference most intensely, if things went wrong for them. Any intelligent man would find a humiliation caused by his own slackness more painful to bear than death, when death comes to him unperceived, in battle, and in the confidence of his patriotism.

"For these reasons I shall not commiserate with those parents of the dead, who are present here. Instead I shall try to comfort them. They are well aware that they have grown up in a world where there are many changes and chances. But this is good fortune — for men to end their lives with honour, as these have done, and for you honourably to lament them: their life was set to a measure where death and happiness went hand in hand. I know that it is difficult to convince you of this. When you see other people happy you will often be reminded of what used to make you happy too. One does not feel sad at not having some good thing which is outside one's experience: real grief is felt at the loss of something which one is used to. All the same, those of you who are of the right age must bear up and take comfort in the thought of having more children. In your own homes these new children will prevent you from brooding over those who are no more, and they will be a help to the city, too, both in filling the empty places, and in assuring her security. For it is impossible for a man to put forward fair and honest views about our affairs if he has not, like everyone else, children whose lives may be at stake. As for those of you who are now too old to have children, I would ask you to count as gain the greater part of your life, in which you have been happy, and remember that what remains is not long, and let your hearts be lifted up at the thought of the fair fame of the dead. One's sense of honour is the only thing that does not grow old, and the last pleasure, when one is worn out with age, is not, as the poet said, making money, but having the respect of one's fellow men.

"As for those of you here who are sons of bothers of the dead, I can see a hard struggle in front of you. Everyone always speaks well of the dead, and, even if you rise to the greatest heights of heroism, it will be a hard thing for you to get the reputation of having come near, let alone equalled, their standard. When one is alive, one is always liable to the jealousy of one's competitors, but when one is out of the way, the honour one receives is sincere and unchallenged.

"Perhaps I should say a word or two on the duties of women to those among you who are now widowed. I can say all I have to say in a short word of advice. Your great glory is not to be inferior to what God has made you. And the greatest glory of a woman is to be least talked about by men, whether they are praising you or criticizing you. I have now, as the law demanded, said what I had to say. For the time being our offerings to the dead have been made, and for the future their children will be supported at the public expense by the city, until they come of age. This is the crown and prize which she offers, both to the dead and to their children, for the ordeals which they have faced. Where the rewards of valour are the greatest, there you will find also the best and bravest spirits among the people. And now, when you have mourned for your dear ones, you must depart."

一、导读

修昔底德，古希腊著名历史学家、政治哲学家，出生于约公元前460年，在伯罗奔尼撒战争期间担任将军之职。前424年，修昔底德受命率军救援被斯巴达军队围困的希腊北部城邦安菲波利斯（Amphipolis），但未获成功，修昔底德因此被雅典人处以流放之刑。流放期间，修昔底德潜心著述《伯罗奔尼撒战争史》。前404年战争结束，修昔底德得以重返雅典，但不久便去世。遗憾的是，他的巨著《伯罗奔尼撒战争史》未能完成，只写到公元前411年秋天。《伯罗奔尼撒战争史》奠定了西方政治军事史范型。此后，政治军事史成为西方史学的主流，一直到启蒙时期伏尔泰重回希罗多德创立的社会文化史范型。修昔底德对伯罗奔尼撒战争原因的分析更是被后世学者解读为“修昔底德陷阱”，成为国际关系领域中一个重要的概念和理论。

鉴于对史料搜集和因果分析的严谨态度，修昔底德被后世称为“科学历史”之父。他具有科学严谨的史学方法论，正如他在序言中所说：“对于这场战争的事件的叙述，我确定了一个原则：不听信道听途说，甚至不以我自己的一般印象为根据；我所描述的事件，不是我亲眼所见，就是我得知于目击者，而且经我尽量彻底核实过的。即便如此，要发现真实殊非易事：对于同一事件，就是得知于目击者也有不同的说法，他们或是偏袒这一方，或是偏袒那一方，或者是记忆不全。或许我的这部历史著作读来并不引人入胜，因为其中缺乏虚构的故事。不过，如果对那些想要清楚地了解过去的事件，或是将来亦会发生的类似事情（因为人性如此）的人来说，它还是有所帮助的话，我就心满意足了。我的著作不是用来迎合公众现时的口味，而是想垂诸永远的。”修昔底德的这一严谨的史学方法经由兰克学派继承和发扬，对西方现代史学产生了深远的影响。

然而，修昔底德战争史的客观性并非无可置疑，其主观性在著作中也有明显的体现。例如，他在著作中对雅典和斯巴达的叙述明显带有主观的喜好和偏见。在著名的伯里克利葬礼演说中，作者对雅典的喜好和赞美与对斯巴达的敌视和贬抑都流露于字里行间。在这里，修昔底德显然是把斯巴达作为雅典的对立面——“他者”来进行叙述的，从而体现出雅典“自我”形象的优越性。再比如，修昔底德在书中引用了大量的演说词。尽管如修昔底德本人所说“尽量保持演说原来的大意，同时使演说者说出我认为适合具体情形的话来”。但显然，他很难秉持客观的态度来处理这一类型的演说词。与希罗多德给读者呈现多种历史解释的“有闻必录”不同，修昔底德提供给读者的是经过他本人考证过的、自认正确的、唯一的历史解释。与希罗多德相比，修昔底德的历史记述方法似乎很“暴力”。因此，从这层意义上说，希罗多德的历史记述方法比修昔底德的更为客观。

本书选取的是伯里克利在公元前431年雅典为阵亡将士举行的公共葬礼上发表的著名演说。修昔底德很可能是聆听过这篇演说，但在相隔数十年之后，其记忆不可能十分确切。因此，学界认为，这篇演说同样是经过他本人加工而成的。其实，不论这篇演说词是否是修昔底德本人加工甚至杜撰，但不可否认的是，它毕竟是古代雅典人对自己城邦制度的评价，依然是我们了解和认识雅典城邦，尤其是雅典民主政治的重要资料。

二、注释

1. Selected from Thucydides, *History of the Peloponnesian War*, trans. Rec Warner, Penguin Books, 1954.

2. public funeral，即“公共葬礼”，是战争期间雅典城邦为战争中阵亡将士举行的年度国葬典礼。雅典公共葬礼起源于公元前5世纪末期，葬礼包括祭奠、游行、入殓（公墓）和演说几个部分。

3. tribe，希腊文 phyle，意为“部落”。克利斯提尼在其改革（前508年）中将雅典分为10个部落，它们是城邦的一级行政区划，而非原始形态的社会组织。

4. 这里指的是著名的马拉松战役。公元前490年，波斯国王大流士亲率大军入侵希腊，在雅典城东北的马拉松平原登陆。雅典军队（还有普拉提亚援军）在雅典将军米太亚德指挥下，以少胜多，击溃波斯军队。据说，胜利后，米太亚德派遣信使斐力庇第斯去雅典报告胜利的喜讯。当斐力庇第斯以最快的速度从马拉松跑到雅典中央广场，对雅典人说了一声“νενικήκαμεν”（我们胜利了）之后就倒在地上牺牲了。后来，人们为了纪念马拉松战役的胜利和表彰斐力庇第斯的功绩，1896年在雅典举行的第一届现代奥林匹克运动会上，增加了马拉松赛跑项目，把当年斐力庇第斯送信跑的里程——42.193千米作为赛跑的距离。1908年伦敦奥运会之后，国际田联将国际马拉松标准赛程定为42.195千米。

三、问题探讨

1. 结合伯里克利葬礼演说内容，谈谈古希腊人对雅典民主政治的理解。

2. 结合伯里克利葬礼演说内容，谈谈修昔底德对斯巴达“他者”形象的建构。

四、参考文献

1. 黄洋：《修昔底德的理性历史建构》，《历史教学》2007年第6期。

2. Thomas L. Pangle (ed.), *The Rebirth of Classical Political Rationalism:*

An Introduction to the Thought of Leo Strauss, University of Chicago Press, 1989.

3. Michael Grant, *Greek and Roman Historians: Information and Misinformation*, Routledge, 1995.

4. Jeremy Mynott (ed.), *Thucydides: The War of the Peloponnesians and Athenians*, Cambridge University Press, 2013.

5. Katherine Harloe, Neville Morley, *Thucydides and the Modern World: Reception, Reinterpretation and Influence from the Renaissance to the Present*, Cambridge University Press, 2012.

UNIT 4

THE RECONSTRUCTION OF ROME[1]

Livy

In Rome meanwhile the siege operations were more or less at a standstill; neither side showed any activity, and the Gaul's only anxiety seemed to be to prevent any of the Romans from slipping through their lines. It was in these circumstances that a young Roman solider performed a feat which won the admiration of friend and foe alike. There used to be an annual sacrifice on the Quirinal[2], and the duty of celebrating it belonged to the family of the Fabii. Determined not to allow the ceremony to lapse, Gaius Fabius Dorsuo risked his life to perform it: wearing a toga[3] girt up in ceremonial fashion and carrying the sacred vessels, he made his way down the slope of the Capitol[4] and through enemy pickets, ignoring challenges and threats, to the Quirinal, where with due solemnity, omitting nothing, he performed the rite, and with the same firm step, the same resolute face, returned by the same way to his companions on the Capitol, sure that the gods would favour one who had not neglected to serve them even for the fear of death. The Gauls did nothing to stop him; perhaps they were too much astonished by his incredible audacity, perhaps even touched (for the religious sentiment is strong in them) by a sort of awe.

The situation in Veii was now rapidly improving; the strength of the garrison as well as its confidence was increased by the accession not only of Romans who had been rendered homeless by the defeat and capture of the City, but also of numbers of volunteers from Latium who saw a chance of a share in the plunder; it was felt, therefore, that the time was ripe for an attempt to recover Rome. But who was to lead them? They had the body, but not, so to speak, the brains. Now no one could be in Veii without thinking of Camillus, and many of the troops there had already fought, and won, under Camillus's command; Caedicius[5], moreover, presented no obstacle, for though nothing on earth would make him resign his authority against his will, he was prepared on his own initiative to remember his rank and demand the appointment of a general. It was therefore unanimously resolved to send to Ardea[6] and invite Camillus[7] to undertake the command, but not before the Senate in Rome had been consulted — for even in their almost desperate plight they still preserved a proper respect for form and were unwilling to overstep their constitutional rights.

To get a message to the Senate meant passing at great risk through the Gallic outposts, and an enterprising young soldier named Pontius Cominus volunteered for the task. Floating on a life-buoy down the river to Rome, he took the shortest way to the Capitol up and over a bluff so steep that the Gauls had never thought of watching it; he was then taken to the magistrates, to whom he delivered the army's message. The Senate passed its resolution: "that Camillus" (it ran) "by vote of the curiate assembly[8], in accordance with the people's will, be forthwith named Dictator, and the soldiers have the commander whom they desire." Cominus hurried back to Veii by the same route, and a mission was at once dispatched to fetch Camillus from Ardea. It may be, however — and I myself prefer to believe — that Camillus did not leave Ardea until he knew that the Senate's resolution had been passed, as he could not change his place of residence without the people's authorization, and could not assume command of the army until he had been appointed Dictator. That would mean that the resolution was passed in the curiate assembly and that he was named Dictator in his absence.

During these transactions in Veii the Citadel in Rome passed through a brief period of extreme danger from an attempted surprise. It may be that the messenger from Veii had left footprints, and the Gauls had noticed them, or possibly they had observed, in the ordinary course of their duties, that the rocky ascent near the shrine of Carmenta[9] was easily practicable. In any case, one starlit night, they made the attempt. Having first sent an unarmed man to reconnoitre the route, they began the climb. It was something of a scramble: at the awkward spots a man would get a purchase for his feet on a comrade below him, then haul him up in his turn — weapons were passed up from hand to hand as the lie of the rocks allowed — until by pushing and pulling one another they reached the top. What is more, they accomplished the climb so quietly that the Romans on guard never heard a sound, and even the dogs — who are normally aroused by the least noise in the night — noticed nothing. It was the geese that saved them — Juno's sacred geese[10], which in spite of the dearth of provisions had not been killed. The cackling of the birds and the clapping of their wings awoke Marcus Manlius[11] — a distinguished officer who had been consul three years before — and he, seizing his sword and giving the alarm, hurried, without waiting for the support of his bewildered comrades, straight to the point of danger. One Gaul was already up, but Manlius with a blow from the boss of his shield toppled him headlong down the cliff. The falling body carried others with it; panic spread; many more who dropped their weapons to get a better grip of the rocks were killed by Manlius, and soon more Roman troops were on the scene, tumbling the climbers down with javelins and stones, until every man of them was dislodged and sent hurtling to the bottom of the cliff.

When the excitement had died down, the garrison was undisturbed for the remainder of the night — so far as the phrase can be used of men in such a situation, unable, as they were, to think even of the past peril without a shudder. At dawn next morning the bugle summoned all ranks to parade before the military tribunes, to be rewarded — or punished — for the events of the night before. Manlius, having been commended for his brave conduct, was given presents not only by the commanding officers but by the troops as well, every one of them agreeing to take to his house in the Citadel half a pound of flour and a gill of wine. That may sound a small thing, but in the light of the general scarcity the fact that the men in order to show their appreciation of a comrade were willing to go short of necessary supplies, was a signal proof of their affectionate regard. The sentries who had been on guard and had failed to observe the enemy's ascent were then called. It was the intention of Sulpicius[12], one of the officers in command, to punish all of them with death, in the "military manner"; but he was induced to change his mind by the unanimous protest of the troops, who insisted that one man only had been to blame. The rest were accordingly spared, and the single culprit, whose guilt was beyond doubt, was flung from the rock. Both verdict and punishment were universally approved. The memory of that night of peril led the Romans to keep a stricter watch; the Gauls, too, began to tighten their precautions, as it was common knowledge that messages were passing between Veii and Rome.

In both armies it was hunger that now caused more distress than anything else. The Gauls had disease as well to contend with, as the position they occupied on low ground between hills was an unhealthy one, and rendered more so by the parched conditions of the earth after the conflagrations, and the heat, and the choking clouds of ashes and dust whenever the wind blew. Such conditions were intolerable to a people accustomed to a wet, cold climate; the heat stifled them, infection spread, and they were soon dying like cattle. Before long the survivors had not the energy to bury the dead separately, but piled the corpses in heaps and burnt them. The spot where they burnt them came afterwards to be known as the Gallic Pyres[13].

About this time an armistice was agreed to and the commanders allowed the troops to communicate with each other. Gallic soldiers used frequently in talking to tell the Romans that they knew they were starving and ought therefore to surrender, and the story goes that the Romans, to make them believe that they were not, threw loaves of bread from various points in their lines down into the Gallic outposts. None the less the time soon came when hunger could no longer be either concealed or endured. Camillus was raising troops at Ardea, where after instructing his Master of Horse[14], Lucius Valerius, to bring up his men from Veii, he was busy training a force fit to deal with the Gauls on equal terms — while the beleaguered army on the Capitol waited and hoped. It was a terrible time: ordinary military duties were by now almost beyond their strength; they had survived all other ills that flesh is heir to, but one enemy — famine — which nature herself has made invincible, remained. Day after day they looked to see if help from Camillus was near; but at last when hope as well as food began to fail, and they were too weak to carry the weight of their equipment when they went on duty, they admitted that they must either surrender, or buy the enemy off on the best terms they could get — for the Gauls were already letting it be known pretty clearly that they would accept no very great sum to abandon the siege. The Senate[15] accordingly met, and the military tribunes were authorized to arrange the terms; Quintus Sulpicius conferred with the Gallic chieftain Brennus and together they agreed upon the price, one thousand pounds' weight of gold — the price of a nation soon to rule the world. Insult was added to what was already sufficiently disgraceful, for the weights which the Gauls brought for weighing the metal were heavier than standard, and when the Roman commander objected the insolent barbarian flung his sword into the scale, saying "Woe to the vanquished!"[16] — words intolerable to Roman ears.

Nevertheless it was neither God's purpose nor man's that the Romans — of all people — should owe their lives to a cash payment. The argument about the weights had unduly protracted the weighing-out of the gold, and it so happened that before it was finished and the infamous bargain completed, Camillus himself appeared upon the scene.

He ordered the gold to be removed and the Gauls to leave, and answered their indignant remonstrances by denying the existence of any valid agreement; such agreement as there was had, he pointed out, been entered into after his appointment as Dictator[17] and by an inferior magistrate acting without his instructions. The Gauls, therefore, must prepare to fight. He then ordered his troops to pile their baggage and get ready for action. "It is your duty," he said, "to recover your country not by gold but by the sword. You will be fighting with all you love before your eyes: the temples of the gods, your wives and children, the soil of your native land scarred with the ravages of war, and everything which honour and truth call upon you to defend, or recover, or avenge."

It was no place for military manoeuvre: the city was half in ruins and the ground, in any case, uneven and rough; but Camillus in his dispositions made the best of his opportunities, such as they were, and used all his experience to give the initial advantage to his own men. The Gauls were taken by surprise; arming themselves hurriedly, they attacked, but with more fire than judgement. Luck had turned at last; human skill, aided by the powers of heaven, was fighting on the side of Rome, and the invaders were scattered at the first encounter with as little effort as had gone to their victory on the Allia[18]. A second, and more regular, engagement was fought later eight miles out on the road to Gabbi, where the Gauls had reorganized, and resulted in another victory for Camillus. This time it was bloody and complete: the Gallic camp was taken, and the army annihilated. Camillus returned in triumph to Rome, his victorious troops roaring out their bawdy songs and saluting their commander by the well-merited titles of another Romulus[19], father of his country and second founder of Rome.

For Camillus it was not enough to have saved Rome from her enemies; for beyond doubt he saved her a second time now that the war was won by preventing the migration to Veii in spite of powerful opposition, both from the tribunes[20] who, since the havoc wrought by the fires, had been more urgently pressing it, and of the people themselves who were increasingly inclined to favour it, even without the tribunes' lead. It was that reason combined with strong pressure from the Senate to stand by his country at this moment of anxious indecision that determined Camillus not to resign the Dictatorship after the celebration of his triumph. His first act in accordance with his character as a man with the strictest sense of his religious duties, was to procure a decree of the Senate authorizing first, that all sacred buildings having been in possession of the enemy, should be restored and purified — together with a re-definition of their boundaries — and that the formula of purification should be sought in the *Sybilline Books*[21] by two officials appointed for the purpose; secondly, that a Treaty of Friendship and Hospitality should be made with the people of Caere[22] in recognition of the fact that they had given asylum to Roman priests and the sacred objects of Roman religion, thereby ensuring the continuity of religious observance and worship; thirdly, that the Capitoline Games[23] should be held, to celebrate the preservation in a time of peril, by Jupiter Greatest and Best, of his own temple and of the Citadel of Rome, the directors of the Games to be chosen by the Dictator Camillus from those who lived on the Capitol. Mention was also made of the need to expiate the guilt of ignoring the mysterious Voice which had been heard in the night prophesying disaster before the war, and for that purpose a shrine was to be built on the New Road, dedicated to the God of Utterance[24]; the gold which had been saved from the Gauls, together with what had been taken, during the alarm, from various temples and deposited in the shrine of Jupiter, as no one could now remember precisely where it belonged, was all to be considered sacred to Jupiter and placed underneath his throne. The public sense of what was fitting in this connection had already been notably exemplified; for when it was found that there was not enough gold in the treasury to pay the Gauls the agreed sum, contributions from the women had been accepted, to avoid touching what was consecrated. The women who had contributed were formally thanked and were further granted the privilege, hitherto confined to men, of having laudatory orations pronounced at their funerals.

Camillus felt that the demands of religion were now satisfied and that he had done all that could be done through the agency of the Senate. Only then, as the tribunes were still holding continual mass meetings at which they urged the abandonment of the ruins of Rome and the migration to Veii which stood, as it were, all ready to receive them, did he make his final appeal. Escorted by the whole body of senators, he came before the people, mounted the speaker's platform and delivered the following address:

"Men of Rome, these contentions with the tribunes are so little to my taste that all the time I was in Ardea the sole comfort of my bitter exile was the fact that I was well away from the scene of them, and because of these same wretched disputes I had intended never to return — no, not though Senate and people invited me home again a thousand times. What now has forced me to come back to you is the change not in my own feelings but in your situation: the question was no longer whether or not I personally should live in my native city, but whether the city should herself remain on the spot of earth which is her own. Even now I should gladly stand aloof and hold my tongue, were not the issue at stake a national issue, to shirk which, while life remains, is for any man a crime but for me worse than a crime — a sin. Why did we save Rome from the hands of our enemies, if we are to desert her now? When the victorious Gauls had the city in their power, the gods of Rome and the men of Rome still clung to the Capitol and the Citadel — and shall we now, in the hour of victory, voluntarily abandon even those strongholds which we held through the days of peril? Shall victory make Rome more desolate than defeat? Even were there no sacred cults coeval with Rome and handed down from generation to generation, so manifest at this time has been the power of God working for our deliverance that I, for one cannot believe that any man could slack his duties of worship and thanksgiving. Only consider the course of our history during these latter years: you will find that when we followed God's guidance all was well; when we scorned it, all was ill. Remember the war with Veii — so long, so hard — and how it ended only when we obeyed the divine injunction and drained the Alban Lake[25]. And what of this unprecedented calamity which has just befallen us? It never showed its ugly head till we disregarded the Voice from heaven warning us that the Gauls were coming — till our envoys violated the law of nations and we, who should have punished that crime, were again so careless of our duty to God as to let it pass. That is why we suffered defeat; that is why Rome was captured, and offered us again for gold; that is why we have been so punished by gods and men as to be an example to the world.

"Evil times came — and then we remembered our religion: we sought the protection of our gods on the Capitol, by the seat of Jupiter Greatest and Best;

having lost all we possessed, we buried our holy things, or took them away to other towns, where no enemy would see them; though abandoned by gods and men, we never ceased to worship. Therefore it is that heaven has given us back our city and restored to us victory and the old martial glory we had forfeited, turning the horror of defeat and death upon the enemy who, in his blind avarice for more gold, was disloyal to his compact and his plighted word. As you consider these manifest instances of the effect upon human destiny of obedience or of disobedience to the divine, can you not understand the heinousness of the sin which, though we have barely as yet won to shore from the shipwreck brought on us by our former guilt, we are preparing to commit? We have a city founded with all due rites of auspice and augury; not a stone of her streets but is permeated by our sense of the divine; for our annual sacrifices not the days only are fixed, but the places too, where they may be performed: men of Rome, would you desert your gods — the tutelary spirits which guards your families, and those the nation prays to as its saviours? Would you leave them all? Contrast this wicked thought with what Fabius did, that noble young soldier, only the other day during the siege — a deed which won the admiration of the enemy no less than your own — when braving the Gallic spears he made his way from the Citadel to the Quirinal, to celebrate there the annual sacrifice of his clan! Can you wish to abandon in time of peace our national ceremonies and our country's gods, when you allowed no interruption of family rites even in war? Are the pontiffs and flamens to care less for the religion of our country than one man has shown himself to care for the tutelary deity of his clan?

"It may be said perhaps that we shall perform these duties in Veii — or send our priests to perform them here. But in neither case could the proper sanctities be preserved. I cannot now make mention of all our gods, or of all our rites — but think, for instance, of Jupiter's Feast: how could his couch be decked anywhere but on the Capitol? What of Vesta's eternal fires, or of the image preserved in her shrine as a pledge of Rome's dominion? What of the sacred shields of Mars and of Quirinus, our Father? All these things you would leave behind on unconsecrated ground — sanctities as old as Rome, or older. How different we are from the men of long ago! Our fathers entrusted to us the celebration of certain sacrifices on the Alban Mount and in Lavinium: to transfer them — from enemy towns, as they were then — to Rome was felt to be impious — yet now you would take others of our own *into* an enemy town. How is that possible without sin? Remember, I beg you, how often some rite has to be performed afresh because by negligence or chance some portion of the ancient ritual has been omitted; why, only the other day, after the prodigy of the Alban Lake, it was the renewed, and perfect, performance of the holy ritual — that and nothing else — which saved our country in the struggle with Veii. Moreover, as if we still had some sense of the ancient pieties, we have given other men's deities a home amongst us, and instituted new cults of our town: Queen Juno was brought from Veii and given her temple on the Aventine — and what a day that was! Who can forget the crowds and the passionate joy of our women? We have agreed to build a shrine to the God of Utterance because of the celestial Voice which was heard in the New Road; to our other annual festivals we have added the Capitoline Games, and by the Senate's authority a new board has been set up to administer them: but what was the need of all these undertakings if we meant to leave Rome when the Gauls did — or if our remaining on the Capitol all those months of the siege was no wish of our own, but due simply to fear of the enemy?

"I speak of holy rites and holy places, but what of the priests? Surely it has occurred to you what sacrilege you are proposing to commit. The Vestal Virgins have their place — their *own* place, from which nothing but the capture of the City has ever moved them; the Flamen of Jupiter is forbidden by our religion to spend even one night outside the City Walls — yet you would make them, one and all, go and live for ever in Veii. Ah, Vesta! Shall thy Virgins desert thee? Shall the Flamen of Jupiter live abroad night after night and stain himself and our country with so deep a sin?

"Remember, too, our public functions nearly all of which we transact, after due ceremony, within the pomerium, and to what oblivion and neglect we are condemning them. The Meeting of the Curies, to deal with questions of war, the Meeting of the Centuries for the election of consuls or military tribunes — where with the proper rites can these be held but in the places tradition has made sacred? Either, I suppose, we shall transfer them to Veii, or else the people will come here, to a city deserted by gods and men, just to vote at elections — a convenient alternative indeed !

"Perhaps you will reply that, in spite of all I have said, to go is still a necessity: circumstances compel it — Rome is rubble and ashes, Veii stands unharmed: we cannot lay the burden of rebuilding upon our helpless and impoverished people. But I think you know even without my telling you that such an argument is only an attempt to justify yourselves, aware, as you are, that this question of migrating to Veii was discussed before the invasion, while every house, every temple and public building of Rome was still as perfect as on the day it was built. But oh! What a gulf there is, in this whole business, between the tribunes and me! As for them, they believe that even if the migration was inadvisable then, it is inescapable now; I, on the contrary — and do not be surprised till you understand my meaning — am convinced that even if it was right to consider going while Rome still stood, to abandon her ruins now would be grievously wrong. And why? Because then the reason for our going to live in a captured city would have been our victory — something for ourselves and our posterity to be proud of; but now such a removal is for us a wretched and shameful thing — the Gauls, not we, will glory in it, for it will be only too clear that we have not left our native city as conquerors, but lost it by defeat. The world will think that the rout on the Allia, the capture of Rome, and the siege of the Capitol have forced upon us the bitter necessity of deserting our beloved homes and of condemning ourselves to flee as exiles from a spot we had not the strength to defend. Must it be seen that Gauls could tumble Rome to the ground, while Romans are too weak to lift her up again? And suppose they come back, with a second army — for everyone knows that their numbers are almost beyond belief: suppose they want to settle here, in this city they captured and which you deserted — what could you do but let them? Or maybe your old enemies the Aequians or Volscians might take it into their heads to do the same — and how would you like to change nationalities with them? Surely you would rather Rome were your own wilderness than built again to house your enemies — a thing which in my view at least would be an outrage to the deepest feelings upon which patriotism rests. I cannot believe that you would commit so shameful a crime simply because you shrink from the labour of restoring these ruins; even if it were impossible to build here anything better or bigger than Romulus's Hut, surely it would be nobler to live like county shepherds amongst everything we hold sacred than to go into universal exile, deserting the gods of our hearths and homes. Those herdsmen long ago and that rabble of refugees, when there was nothing here but forest and swamp, made short work enough of building a new town — but we today: when the temples are sill standing and the Capitol and Citadel intact, cannot bring ourselves to rebuild what the fires have destroyed! Shall we refuse as a nation to do what any one of us would have done if his own house had been burned down?

"Suppose some fool, or some knave, should set Veii on fire — suppose the wind spread the flames and half the town were destroyed — what should we do then? Move on to Fidenae, or Gabii, or anywhere else we could find? So it seems — if indeed the soil of our native city and the earth we call our mother have so weak a hold upon us that our love of country is co-extensive with timber and stone. Men of Rome, I do not like to recall the wrong you did me, but I confess to you that whenever, in my absence, I thought of my country, what I saw in my mind's eye were these hills and plains, the Tiber and this beloved countryside, and the familiar sky under which I was born and bred. I can but hope that the love of these things will move you now to stay, and that the loss of them will not, in after years, tear your hearts with vain regret. Not without reason did gods and men choose this spot for the site of our City — the salubrious hills, the river to bring us produce from the inland regions and sea-borne commerce from abroad, the sea itself, near enough for convenience yet not so near as to bring danger from foreign fleets, our situation in the very heart of Italy — all these advantages make it of all places in the world the best for a city destined to grow great. The proof is the actual greatness — now — of a city which is still comparatively young; Rome, my friends, is 365 years old, and throughout those years you have been at war with many ancient peoples, yet — not to speak of single enemies — not the united strength of the powerful townships of the Aequians and Volscians, not the combined might of the armies and navies of Etruria, whose vast domains occupy the breadth of Italy from sea to sea, has ever been a match for you in war. What then in the devil's name makes you want to try elsewhere, when such has been your fortune here? Should you go, I grant you may take your brave hearts with you, but never the Luck of Rome. Here is the Capitol, where, in the days of old, the human head was found and men were told that on that spot would be the world's head and the seat of empire; here, when the Capitol was to be cleared of other shrines for the sake of Jupiter's temple, the two deities Juventas and Terminus refused, to the great joy of the men of those days, to be moved; here are the fires of Vesta, the sacred shields which fell from heaven, and all our gods who, if you stay, will assuredly bless your staying."

Camillus's oration is said to have moved his hearers, especially those parts of it which touched upon religion, but it was not decisive; what finally settled the matter was the chance remark of a centurion on duty. Soon after Camillus had ended, the Senate was holding a debate in the Curia Hostilia, and some soldiers returning from guard-duty happened to pass through the Forum; as they reached the Comitium, their centurion gave the order to halt, adding, "we might as well stop here." The words were heard in the Senate House; the senators hurried out exclaiming that they accepted the omen, and the crowd in the street signified its approval. The proposal for the migration was rejected, and the rebuilding of the city began.

The work of reconstruction was ill-planned. Tiles were supplied at the state's expense; permission to cut timber and quarry stone was granted without any restrictions except a guarantee that the particular structure should be completed within the year. All work was hurried and nobody bothered to see that the streets were straight; individual property rights were ignored, and buildings went up wherever there was room for them. This explains why the ancient sewers, which originally followed the line of the streets, now run in many places under private houses, and why the general lay-out of Rome is more like a squatter's settlement than a properly planned city.

一、导读

李维（Livy，公元前 64 年或公元前 59 年—公元 17 年）是古罗马著名的历史学家，著有《罗马建城以来的历史》（以下简称《罗马史》）。李维出生于意大利北部的帕塔维（Patavium），即现在的帕多瓦（Padua）。青少年时代的李维受到了良好的教育，系统学习过文学、修辞学、演说术等。公元前 29 年夏，李维从帕塔维迁居罗马。随后，李维结识奥古斯都（屋大维），两人关系甚密。据苏维托尼乌斯记载，李维奉奥古斯都之命教导他的外孙克劳狄一世，后来成为宫廷中著名的诗人和历史学家。李维虽然对新确立的元首制表示忠顺，但就李维本身而论，他思想保守，政治上拥护贵族共和制。李维撰写历史著作，是为了歌颂罗马人的光荣和伟大，宣扬罗马的爱国主义精神和传统习俗，这一点正好适应了奥古斯都统治的需要，因此他对李维的保守思想采取妥协的态度。李维于公元 14 年返回帕塔维，安度余生，死于公元 17 年。

李维以毕生精力从事巨著《罗马史》的写作，一直到公元 14 年奥古斯都去世之后才停笔，前后 40 余年。《罗马史》是一部卷帙浩繁、内容丰富的历史巨著，叙述内容从罗马建城开始（前 754 年）到德鲁斯之死（前 9 年），共有 142 卷。但目前这部历史著作存留下来的只有 35 卷，即第 1～10 卷以及第 21～45 卷。从严格意义上说，李维是一位历史编纂者和道德说教家。他在提及写作《罗马史》的目的时说："我想找到一种药，让我们的帝国返老还童，重新焕发青春的活力。这种能抗衰老的药就是我写的这部史书。当青年们看到我们的祖先是如何建功立业，如何享受元老院和人民赐予他们荣誉的时候，他们的心中必定会燃起不可遏止的豪情壮志，立誓今生即便不能超越古人，也要无愧于后世。他们更会从史书中汲取营养和经验，知道什么事能做，什么事不能做；怎样做才能善始善终，怎样做就会恶始恶终。"此外，李维经常编写一些书中人物的演说，其中有些明显地不符合历史事实。但是，这类演说辞使叙述显得生动，并且可以利用它们来对历史人物及其行动的原因加以说明和评论。尽管李维及其著作存在一些缺点和错误，但他仍不失为古代著名的历史学家。他的著作保存了丰富而宝贵的历史资料，在史学史上占有重要的地位。更为重要的是，在罗马早期历史的相关资料残缺不全、极其匮乏的情况下，李维在著作中对罗马早期历史保持了前后一贯的传统叙述。在这一方面，他独占鳌头，没有人能够取代他的地位。

本书选取的部分是第 5 卷第 46～55 章，主要记述公元前 390 年高卢人攻占、洗劫罗马后，罗马著名的政治家、军事将领卡米卢斯（Camillus）率军击溃高卢人，拯救了罗马，然后重建罗马的历史。文中记载的卡米卢斯反对罗马迁都维爱的演说较好地体现了李维的修辞学写作方法和优美的文笔。德国著名历史学家尼布尔盛赞道：“在任何拉丁或希腊的历史作品中，我们都找不到比这段更为动人的文字。”

二、注释

1. Selected from Livy, *The Early History of Rome*, trans. Aubrey de Selincourt, Penguin Books, 1960.

2. Quirinal，汉译“奎里纳尔”，是著名的“罗马七丘”之一。“罗马七丘”位于罗马心脏地带的台伯河东侧，其为罗马建城之初的重要宗教与政治中心，从南向北依次包括阿文蒂诺山（Aventine Hill）、凯里山（Caelian Hill）、帕拉蒂诺山（Palatine Hill）、卡皮托利诺山（Capitoline Hill）、埃斯奎利诺山（Esquiline Hill）、维米纳尔山（Viminal Hill）、奎里纳尔山（Quirinal Hill）等7个山丘。因此，罗马又称“七丘之城”。

3. toga，汉译“托加长袍”，是最能体现古罗马男子服饰特点的服装。它是一段呈半圆形的长约6米、最宽处约1.8米的羊毛制兼具披肩、饰带、围裙作用的服装。托加长袍也是罗马人的身份象征，只有男子才能穿着，而没有罗马公民权者是被禁止穿着托加长袍的。

4. Capitol，即朱庇特神庙。神庙位于罗马的卡皮托利诺山（Capitoline Hill），是古罗马最伟大的宗教庙宇。

5. Caedicius，卡迪西乌斯，公元前256年任罗马执政官。

6. Ardea，汉译“阿尔代亚”，古代罗马城市，公元前8世纪建城，距离罗马东南35千米。古罗马诗人维吉尔在著名史诗《阿涅阿斯记》中对阿尔代亚有所描述。

7. Camillus，卡米卢斯，古罗马共和时期著名的政治家，他5次当选为独裁官，4次举行凯旋仪式，被授予“第二罗马奠基人”的称号（罗慕洛斯是第一人）。第三次维爱战争中，他临危受命，率领罗马军队攻克维爱城，随后在政治斗争中失败被流放到阿尔代亚。公元前390年，高卢人攻陷罗马，卡米卢斯说服阿尔代亚的统治者和议员们，把役龄人员组织起来，在深夜突袭城外扎营的高卢军队，取得辉煌战果，并把高卢人最终赶出罗马，且开始了罗马重建。

8. curiate assembly，汉译“库利亚大会”，古罗马公民大会之一，起源于公元前11世纪至公元前6世纪的王政时代。库里亚大会有权决定战争，选举高级官员，通过或否决法律、法令及审判重大案件。

9. Carmenta，汉译“卡尔门塔”。在古罗马宗教神话中，卡尔门塔是司职生育和语言的女神，是母亲、儿童和助产婆的保护神。据说，卡尔门塔发明了拉丁字母。

10. Juno，汉译“朱诺”，罗马神话中的天后，婚姻和母性之神，罗马十二主神之一，朱庇特之妻，集美貌、温柔、慈爱于一身，是美丽孔雀的化身。据说，罗马人把鹅献给朱诺神庙。后来当高卢人进攻罗马的时候就演绎出白天鹅拯救罗马城的故事。

11. Marcus Manlius，马库斯·曼利乌斯，公元前 392 年任罗马执政官。公元前 390 年，高卢人进攻罗马，在朱诺神庙鹅的帮助下，他率军击退高卢人对罗马的夜袭。

12. Sulpicius，苏尔皮西乌斯，公元前 390 年，高卢进攻罗马时任罗马军队的指挥官。

13. Gallic Pyres，汉译“高卢火葬场”，即焚烧高卢人尸首的地方。

14. Master of Horse，汉译“骑兵长官”，古罗马共和国官职，由独裁官任命和罢免。独裁官不在的时候，骑兵长官可以代替其行使职权。

15. Senate，指古罗马“元老院”。

16. “Woe to the vanquished!”，拉丁文原文是“Vae victis”，意思是“被征服者就应该完全听命于征服者，而且也不应期望得到后者的一丝怜悯!”

17. Dictator，又称“Roman Dictator”，即汉译“独裁官”，是古罗马共和国时期非常任长官。当国家处于紧急状态时，经长老院提名，由执政官担任。独裁官手中的权力超越并且凌驾于一切之上，这一切包括行政、军事、立法、司法等大权。

18. Allia，汉译“阿里亚”，古罗马的一条河流的名称。公元前 390 年，高卢人和罗马人在台伯河与阿里亚河交汇处发生激战，结果罗马军队惨败，随后高卢人攻陷罗马城，历史学家称这次战役为阿里亚战役。

19. Romulus，罗慕路斯，罗马建城者和第一位国王。

20. tribunes，汉译“保民官”，是古罗马时期维护平民利益的一种特殊官职，产生于公元前 5 世纪初平民第一次分离运动获胜之后。保民官从平民会议中选出，最初为 2 人，后来增加到 10 人。保民官人身不受侵犯，享有否定罗马元老院决议的特殊权力。

21. *Sybilline Books*，汉译《西比尔预言集》，是古代意大利南部大希腊地区城市库迈（Cumae）女巫西尔比（Sibyl）写给罗马最后一位王塔克文（Tarquinius）的 9 卷本预言集，但是只有部分得以保存下来。

22. Caere，汉译“凯垒”，古罗马伊特鲁利亚（Etruria）地区南部的较大城市。

23. Capitoline Games，汉译“卡皮托利诺赛会”，是公元前 387 年罗马独裁官卡米卢斯为了纪念卡皮托利诺朱庇特神殿，同时也为了庆祝卡皮托利诺没有被高卢人占领而创立。赛会一年举行一次，每次持续 16 天，10 月 15 日开始。

24. the God of Utterance，汉译“辞令神”，拉丁文原文是 Aius Locutius，古罗马神祇之一。他曾预言公元前 4 世纪前后高卢人将入侵罗马城，但是并未能够引起罗马人的注意。

25. Alban Lake，汉译“阿尔巴湖”，火山喷发形成的一个小湖，位于罗马东南，距离罗马古城阿尔巴隆加（Alba Longa）不远。

三、问题探讨

1. 结合教材节选内容，谈谈李维的史学写作方法。
2. 结合教材节选内容，谈谈古罗马对古希腊史学的继承。

四、参考文献

1. 蔡丽娟：《李维史学研究》，商务印书馆 2014 年版。
2. ［意］马基雅维利：《论李维罗马史》，吕健忠译，商务印书馆 2013 年版。
3. J. D. Chaplin, *Livy's Exemplary History*, Oxford University Press, 2000.
4. G. B. Miles, *Livy: Reconstructing Early Rome*, Cornell University Press, 1995.
5. P. G. Walsh, *Livy: His Historical Aims and Methods*, Cambridge University Press, 1961.

UNIT 5

THE MAGNA CARTA, 1215[1]

John, by the grace of God, King of England, lord of Ireland, duke of Normandy and Aquitaine, and count of Anjou, to the archbishops, bishops, abbots, earls[2], barons, justiciars, foresters, sheriffs, stewards, servants, and to all his bailiffs and faithful subjects, greetings. Know that we, out of reverence for God and for the salvation of our soul and those of all our ancestors and heirs, for the honour of God and the exaltation of holy church, and for the reform of our realm, on the advice of our venerable fathers, Stephen, archbishop of Canterbury, primate of all England and cardinal of the holy Roman Church, Henry archbishop of Dublin, William of London, Peter of Winchester, Jocelyn of Bath and Glastonbury, Hugh of Lincoln, Walter of Worcester, William of Coventry and Benedict of Rochester, bishops, of master Pandulf, subdeacon and member of the household of the lord pope, of brother Aymeric, master of the order of Knights Templar in England, and of the noble men William Marshal earl of Pembroke, William earl of Salisbury, William earl of Warenne, William earl of Arundel, Alan of Galloway constable of Scotland, Warin fitz Gerold, Peter fitz Herbert, Hubert de Burgh seneschal of Poitou, Hugh de Neville, Matthew fitz Herbert, Thomas Basset, Alan Basset, Philip de Aubeney, Robert of Ropsley, John Marshal, John fitz Hugh, and others, our faithful subjects:

1. In the first place have granted to God, and by this our present charter confirmed for us and our heirs for ever that the English church shall be free, and shall have its rights undiminished and its liberties unimpaired; and it is our will that it be thus observed; which is evident from the fact that, before the quarrel between us and our barons began, we willingly and spontaneously granted and by our charter confirmed the freedom of elections which is reckoned most important and very essential to the English church, and obtained confirmation of it from the lord pope Innocent III; the which we will observe and we wish our heirs to

observe it in good faith for ever. We have also granted to all free men of our kingdom, for ourselves and our heirs for ever, all the liberties written below, to be had and held by them and their heirs of us and our heirs.

2. If any of our earls or barons or others holding of us in chief by knight service dies, and at his death his heir be of full age and owe relief he shall have his inheritance on payment of the old relief, namely the heir or heirs of an earl £100 for a whole earl's barony, the heir or heirs of a baron £100 for a whole barony, the heir or heirs of a knight 100s, at most, for a whole knight's fee; and he who owes less shall give less according to the ancient usage of fiefs.

3. If, however, the heir of any such be under age and a ward, he shall have his inheritance when he comes of age without paying relief and without making fine.

4. The guardian of the land of such an heir who is under age shall take from the land of the heir no more than reasonable revenues, reasonable customary dues and reasonable services, and that without destruction and waste of men or goods; and if we commit the wardship of the land of any such to a sheriff, or to any other who is answerable to us for its revenues, and he destroys or wastes what he has wardship of, we will take compensation from him and the land shall be committed to two lawful and discreet men of that fief, who shall be answerable for the revenues to us or to him to whom we have assigned them; and if we give or sell to anyone the wardship of any such land and he causes destruction or waste therein, he shall lose that wardship, and it shall be transferred to two lawful and discreet men of that fief, who shall similarly be answerable to us as is aforesaid.

5. Moreover, so long as he has the wardship of the land, the guardian shall keep in repair the houses, parks, preserves, ponds, mills and other things pertaining to the land out of the revenues from it; and he shall restore to the heir when he comes of age his land fully stocked with ploughs and the means of husbandry according to what the season of husbandry requires and the revenues of the land can reasonably bear.

6. Heirs shall be married without disparagement, yet so that before the marriage is contracted those nearest in blood to the heir shall have notice.

7. A widow shall have her marriage portion[3] and inheritance forthwith and without difficulty after the death of her husband; nor shall she pay anything to have her dower[4] or her marriage portion or the inheritance which she and her husband held on the day of her husband's death; and she may remain in her

husband's house for forty days after his death, within which time her dower shall be assigned to her.

8. No widow shall be forced to marry so long as she wishes to live without a husband, provided that she gives security not to marry without our consent if she holds of us, or without the consent of her lord of whom she holds, if she holds of another.

9. Neither we nor our bailiffs will seize for any debt any land or rent, so long as the chattels of the debtor are sufficient to repay the debt; nor will those who have gone surety for the debtor be distrained so long as the principal debtor is himself able to pay the debt; and if the principal debtor fails to pay the debt, having nothing wherewith to pay it, then shall the sureties answer for the debt; and they shall, if they wish, have the lands and rents of the debtor until they are reimbursed for the debt which they have paid for him, unless the principal debtor can show that he has discharged his obligation in the matter to the said sureties.

10. If anyone who has borrowed from the Jews any sum, great or small, dies before it is repaid, the debt shall not bear interest as long as the heir is under age, of whomsoever he holds; and if the debt falls into our hands, we will not take anything except the principal mentioned in the bond.

11. And if anyone dies indebted to the Jews, his wife shall have her dower and pay nothing of that debt; and if the dead man leaves children who are under age, they shall be provided with necessaries befitting the holding of the deceased; and the debt shall be paid out of the residue, reserving, however, service due to lords of the land; debts owing to others than Jews shall be dealt with in like manner.

12. No scutage or aid shall be imposed in our kingdom unless by common counsel of our kingdom, except for ransoming our person, for making our eldest son a knight, and for once marrying our eldest daughter; and for these only a reasonable aid shall be levied. Be it done in like manner concerning aids from the city of London.

13. And the city of London shall have all its ancient liberties and free customs as well by land as by water. Furthermore, we will and grant that all other cities, boroughs, towns, and ports shall have all their liberties and free customs.

14. And to obtain the common counsel of the kingdom about the assessing of an aid (except in the three cases aforesaid) or of a scutage, we will cause to be summoned the archbishops, bishops, abbots, earls and greater barons,

individually by our letters — and, in addition, we will cause to be summoned generally through our sheriffs and bailiffs all those holding of us in chief — for a fixed date, namely, after the expiry of at least forty days, and to a fixed place; and in all letters of such summons we will specify the reason for the summons. And when the summons has thus been made, the business shall proceed on the day appointed, according to the counsel of those present, though not all have come who were summoned.

15. We will not in future grant any one the right to take an aid from his free men, except for ransoming his person, for making his eldest son a knight and for once marrying his eldest daughter, and for these only a reasonable aid shall be levied.

16. No one shall be compelled to do greater service for a knight's fee or for any other free holding than is due from it.

17. Common pleas shall not follow our court, but shall be held in some fixed place.

18. Recognitions of *novel disseisin*, of *mort d'ancester*, and of *darrein presentment*[5], shall not be held elsewhere than in the counties to which they relate, and in this manner we, or, if we should be out of the realm, our chief justiciar, will send two justices through each county four times a year, who, with four knights of each county chosen by the county, shall hold the said assizes in the county and on the day and in the place of meeting of the county court.

19. And if the said assizes cannot all be held on the day of the county court, there shall stay behind as many of the knights and freeholders who were present at the county court on that day as are necessary for the sufficient making of judgments, according to the amount of business to be done.

20. A free man shall not be amerced for a trivial offence except in accordance with the degree of the offence, and for a grave offence he shall be amerced in accordance with its gravity, yet saving his way of living; and a merchant in the same way, saving his stock-in-trade; and a villein shall be amerced in the same way, saving his means of livelihood — if they have fallen into our mercy: and none of the aforesaid amercements shall be imposed except by the oath of good men of the neighbourhood.

21. Earls and barons shall not be amerced except by their peers, and only in accordance with the degree of the offence.

22. No clerk shall be amerced in respect of his lay holding except after the manner of the others aforesaid and not according to the amount of his ecclesiastical benefice.

23. No vill or individual shall be compelled to make bridges at river banks, except those who from of old are legally bound to do so.

24. No sheriff, constable, coroners, or others of our bailiffs, shall hold pleas of our crown[6].

25. All counties, hundreds, wapentakes and trithings shall be at the old rents without any additional payment, except our demesne manors.

26. If anyone holding a lay fief of us dies and our sheriff or bailiff shows our letters patent of summons for a debt that the deceased owed us, it shall be lawful for our sheriff or bailiff to attach and make a list of chattels of the deceased found upon the lay fief to the value of that debt under the supervision of law-worthy men, provided that none of the chattels shall be removed until the debt which is manifest has been paid to us in full; and the residue shall be left to the executors for carrying out the will of the deceased. And if nothing is owing to us from him, all the chattels shall accrue to the deceased, saving to his wife and children their reasonable shares.

27. If any free man dies without leaving a will, his chattels shall be distributed by his nearest kinsfolk and friends under the supervision of the church, saving to every one the debts which the deceased owed him.

28. No constable or other bailiff of ours shall take anyone's corn or other chattels unless he pays on the spot in cash for them or can delay payment by arrangement with the seller.

29. No constable shall compel any knight to give money instead of castle-guard if he is willing to do the guard himself or through another good man, if for some good reason he cannot do it himself; and if we lead or send him on military service, he shall be excused guard in proportion to the time that because of us he has been on service.

30. No sheriff, or bailiff of ours, or anyone else shall take the horses or carts of any free man for transport work save with the agreement of that freeman.

31. Neither we nor our bailiffs will take, for castles or other works of ours, timber which is not ours, except with the agreement of him whose timber it is.

32. We will not hold for more than a year and a day the lands of those

convicted of felony, and then the lands shall be handed over to the lords of the fiefs.

33. Henceforth all fish-weirs shall be cleared completely from the Thames and the Medway and throughout all England, except along the sea coast.

34. The writ called *Praecipe*[7] shall not in future be issued to anyone in respect of any holding whereby a free man may lose his court.

35. Let there be one measure for wine throughout our kingdom, and one measure for ale, and one measure for corn, namely "the London quarter"; and one width for cloths whether dyed, russet or halberget[8], namely two ells within the selvedges. Let it be the same with weights as with measures.

36. Nothing shall be given or taken in future for the writ of inquisition of life or limbs: instead it shall be granted free of charge and not refused.

37. If anyone holds of us by fee-farm, by socage, or by burgage, and holds land of another by knight service, we will not, by reason of that fee-farm, socage, or burgage, have the wardship of his heir or of land of his that is of the fief of the other; nor will we have custody of the fee-farm, socage, or burgage, unless such fee-farm owes knight service. We will not have custody of anyone's heir or land which he holds of another by knight service by reason of any petty serjeanty which he holds of us by the service of rendering to us knives or arrows or the like.

38. No bailiff shall in future put anyone to trial upon his own bare word, without reliable witnesses produced for this purpose.

39. No free man shall be arrested or imprisoned or disseised or outlawed or exiled or in any way victimised, neither will we attack him or send anyone to attack him, except by the lawful judgment of his peers or by the law of the land.

40. To no one will we sell, to no one will we refuse or delay right or justice.

41. All merchants shall be able to go out of and come into England safely and securely and stay and travel throughout England, as well by land as by water, for buying and selling by the ancient and right customs free from all evil tolls, except in time of war and if they are of the land that is at war with us. And if such are found in our land at the beginning of a war, they shall be attached, without injury to their persons or goods, until we, or our chief justiciar, know how merchants of our land are treated who were found in the land at war with us when war broke out; and if ours are safe there, the others shall be safe in our land.

42. It shall be lawful in future for anyone, without prejudicing the allegiance due to us, to leave our kingdom and return safely and securely by land and water, save, in the public interest, for a short period in time of war — except for those imprisoned or outlawed in accordance with the law of the kingdom and natives of a land that is at war with us and merchants (who shall be treated as aforesaid).

43. If anyone who holds of some escheat such as the honour of Wallingford, Nottingham, Boulogne, Lancaster, or of other escheats which are in our hands and are baronies dies, his heir shall give no other relief and do no other service to us than he would have done to the baron if that barony had been in the baron's hands; and we will hold it in the same manner in which the baron held it.

44. Men who live outside the forest need not henceforth come before our justices of the forest upon a general summons, unless they are impleaded or are sureties for any person or persons who are attached for forest offences.

45. We will not make justices, constables, sheriffs or bailiffs save of such as know the law of the kingdom and mean to observe it well.

46. All barons who have founded abbeys for which they have charters of the kings of England or ancient tenure shall have the custody of them during vacancies, as they ought to have.

47. All forests that have been made forest in our time shall be immediately disafforested; and so be it done with river-banks that have been made preserves by us in our time.

48. All evil customs connected with forests and warrens, foresters and warreners, sheriffs and their officials, river-banks and their wardens shall immediately be inquired into in each county by twelve sworn knights of the same county who are to be chosen by good men of the same county, and within forty days of the completion of the inquiry shall be utterly abolished by them so as never to be restored, provided that we, or our justiciar if we are not in England, know of it first.

49. We will immediately return all hostages and charters given to us by Englishmen, as security for peace or faithful service.

50. We will remove completely from office the relations of Gerard de Athée so that in future they shall have no office in England, namely Engelard de Cigogné, Peter and Guy and Andrew de Chanceaux, Guy de Cigogné, Geoffrey de Martigny and his brothers, Philip Marc and his brothers and his nephew

Geoffrey, and all their following.

51. As soon as peace is restored, we will remove from the kingdom all foreign knights, cross-bowmen, serjeants, and mercenaries, who have come with horses and arms to the detriment of the kingdom.

52. If anyone has been disseised of or kept out of his lands, castles, franchises or his right by us without the legal judgment of his peers, we will immediately restore them to him: and if a dispute arises over this, then let it be decided by the judgment of the twenty-five barons who are mentioned below in the clause for securing the peace[9]: for all the things, however, which anyone has been disseised or kept out of without the lawful judgment of his peers by king Henry, our father, or by king Richard, our brother, which we have in our hand or are held by others, to whom we are bound to warrant them, we will have the usual period of respite of crusaders, excepting those things about which a plea was started or an inquest made by our command before we took the cross; when however we return from our pilgrimage, or if by any chance we do not go on it, we will at once do full justice therein.

53. We will have the same respite, and in the same manner, in the doing of justice in the matter of the disafforesting or retaining of the forests which Henry our father or Richard our brother afforested, and in the matter of the wardship of lands which are of the fief of another, wardships of which sort we have hitherto had by reason of a fief which anyone held of us by knight service, and in the matter of abbeys founded on the fief of another, not on a fief of our own, in which the lord of the fief claims he has a right; and when we have returned, or if we do not set out on our pilgrimage, we will at once do full justice to those who complain of these things.

54. No one shall be arrested or imprisoned upon the appeal of a woman for the death of anyone except her husband.

55. All fines made with us unjustly and against the law of the land, and all amercements imposed unjustly and against the law of the land, shall be entirely remitted, or else let them be settled by the judgment of the twenty-five barons who are mentioned below in the clause for securing the peace, or by the judgment of the majority of the same, along with the aforesaid Stephen, archbishop of Canterbury, if he can be present, and such others as he may wish to associate with himself for this purpose, and if he cannot be present the business shall

nevertheless proceed without him, provided that if any one or more of the aforesaid twenty-five barons are in a like suit, they shall be removed from the judgment of the case in question, and others chosen, sworn and put in their place by the rest of the same twenty-five for this case only.

56. If we have disseised or kept out Welshmen from lands or liberties or other things without the legal judgment of their peers in England or in Wales, they shall be immediately restored to them; and if a dispute arises over this, then let it be decided in the March by the judgment of their peers — for holdings in England according to the law of England, for holdings in Wales according to the law of Wales, and for holdings in the March according to the law of the March. Welshmen shall do the same to us and ours.

57. For all the things, however, which any Welshman was disseised of or kept out of without the lawful judgment of his peers by king Henry, our father, or king Richard, our brother, which we have in our hand or which are held by others, to whom we are bound to warrant them, we will have the usual period of respite of crusaders, excepting those things about which a plea was started or an inquest made by our command before we took the cross; when however we return, or if by any chance we do not set out on our pilgrimage, we will at once do full justice to them in accordance with the laws of the Welsh and the foresaid regions[10].

58. We will give back at once the son of Llywelyn and all the hostages from Wales and the charters that were handed over to us as security for peace.

59. We will act toward Alexander, king of the Scots, concerning the return of his sisters and hostages and concerning his franchises and his right in the same manner in which we act towards our other barons of England, unless it ought to be otherwise by the charters which we have from William his father, formerly king of the Scots, and this shall be determined by the judgment of his peers in our court.

60. All these aforesaid customs and liberties which we have granted to be observed in our kingdom as far as it pertains to us towards our men, all of our kingdom, clerks as well as laymen, shall observe as far as it pertains to them towards their men.

61. Since, moreover, for God and the betterment of our kingdom and for the better allaying of the discord that has arisen between us and our barons we have

granted all these things aforesaid, wishing them to enjoy the use of them unimpaired and unshaken for ever, we give and grant them the under-written security, namely, that the barons shall choose any twenty-five barons of the kingdom they wish, who must with all their might observe, hold and cause to be observed, the peace and liberties which we have granted and confirmed to them by this present charter of ours, so that if we, or our justiciar, or our bailiffs or any one of our servants offend in any way against anyone or transgress any of the articles of the peace or the security and the offence be notified to four of the aforesaid twenty-five barons, those four barons shall come to us, or to our justiciar if we are out of the kingdom, and, laying the transgression before us, shall petition us to have that transgression corrected without delay. And if we do not correct the transgression, or if we are out of the kingdom, if our justiciar does not correct it, within forty days, reckoning from the time it was brought to our notice or to that of our justiciar if we were out of the kingdom, the aforesaid four barons shall refer that case to the rest of the twenty-five barons and those twenty-five barons together with the community of the whole land shall distrain and distress us in every way they can, namely, by seizing castles, lands, possessions, and in such other ways as they can, saving our person and the persons of our queen and our children, until, in their opinion, amends have been made; and when amends have been made, they shall obey us as they did before. And let anyone in the land who wishes take an oath to obey the orders of the said twenty-five barons for the execution of all the aforesaid matters, and with them to distress us as much as he can, and we publicly and freely give anyone leave to take the oath who wishes to take it and we will never prohibit anyone from taking it. Indeed, all those in the land who are unwilling of themselves and of their own accord to take an oath to the twenty-five barons to help them to distrain and distress us, we will make them take the oath as aforesaid at our command. And if any of the twenty-five barons dies or leaves the country or is in any other way prevented from carrying out the things aforesaid, the rest of the aforesaid twenty-five barons shall choose as they think fit another one in his place, and he shall take the oath like the rest. In all matters the execution of which is committed to these twenty-five barons, if it should happen that these twenty-five are present yet disagree among themselves about anything, or if some of those summoned will not or cannot be present, that shall be held as fixed and established which the majority of those present ordained or commanded, exactly as if all the twenty-five had consented to it; and the said twenty-five shall swear that they will faithfully observe all the things aforesaid and will do all they can to get them observed. And we will procure nothing from anyone, either personally or through anyone else, whereby any of these concessions and liberties might be revoked or diminished; and if any such thing is procured, let it be void and null, and we will never use it either personally or through another.

62. And we have fully remitted and pardoned to everyone all the ill-will, indignation and rancour that have arisen between us and our men, clergy and laity, from the time of the quarrel. Furthermore, we have fully remitted to all, clergy and laity, and as far as pertains to us have completely forgiven, all trespasses occasioned by the same quarrel between Easter in the sixteenth year of our reign and the restoration of peace. And, besides, we have caused to be made for them letters testimonial patent of the lord Stephen archbishop of Canterbury, of the lord Henry archbishop of Dublin and of the aforementioned bishops and of master Pandulf about this security and the aforementioned concessions.

63. Wherefore we wish and firmly enjoin that the English church shall be free, and that the men in our kingdom shall have and hold all the aforesaid liberties, rights and concessions well and peacefully, freely and quietly, fully and completely, for themselves and their heirs from us and our heirs, in all matters and in all places for ever, as is aforesaid. An oath, moreover, has been taken, as well on our part as on the part of the barons, that all these things aforesaid shall be observed in good faith and without evil disposition. Witness the above-mentioned and many others. Given by our hand in the meadow which is called Runnymede between Windsor and Staines on the fifteenth day of June, in the seventeenth year of our reign.

一、导读

1215 年 6 月 19 日，英国国王约翰在贵族的武力胁迫下签署了一份封建性政治文件《大宪章》。该文件一方面迫使国王承认封臣的各项权利，以保障教俗贵族的财产和人身安全；另一方面又详细地规定了国王在封建规则下行使职权的范围，以维护封建传统习俗，防止国王滥用权力。《大宪章》在很大程度上彰显出“王在法下”“权利平等”和“民主协商”等宪政精神，开辟了英国政治秩序从专制、强权向法理化、制度化过渡的道路。

1215 年签署的《大宪章》共有 63 条，由于其起草过程较为仓促，因此各条款并没有完全按照逻辑顺序进行安排。大体来看，《大宪章》的内容可以归纳为 5 个方面：

第一，保护教会的自由权。《大宪章》第 1 条规定，教会的权利和自由不受国王侵犯。第 22 条规定，神职人员犯罪应根据其财产比例而非财产价值予以罚款，不得苛刻征收。

第二，维护世俗贵族的财产和人身安全。第 2 条、第 3 条规定，贵族因服军役而去世后，其子女只需按照旧时习俗缴纳继承金便可享有地产，不受额外的封建剥削。第 7～8 条规定，保护寡妇对亡夫遗产和继承物的占有权。第 30～32 条规定，国王不得恶意侵占贵族土地，不得强取臣民的马匹、车辆和木材等。第 39 条规定，不经合法裁决，贵族不得被监禁、剥夺财产或放逐。

第三，限制国王滥用权力，禁止强征重税和劳役。第 15 条规定，国王不得征收超过合理数额的贡金，也不得征收传统贡金之外的其他贡金。第 23 条规定，国王不得强征臣民修筑河堤和桥梁等。第 29 条规定，骑士自愿守城时，国王不得额外征收守城费。

第四，保护商人和城市的利益。第 13 条规定，伦敦及其他城市、市镇以及港口均享有惯常的自由权与自由习惯。第 41 条规定，除战时或敌对国家商人外，其他商人均有自由进出、居住于英格兰的权利。

第五，监督国王遵守《大宪章》。第 14 条规定，国王征收协助金和免役税需要召集会议，获得教俗贵族的同意。第 61 条规定，贵族组成 25 人委员会监督国王及其官员，纠正其违法行为。

近代以来，学者对《大宪章》历史意义的界定尚存在一定的争议。以斯塔布斯为代表的“宪政主义史学派”极力颂扬 1215 年贵族反叛国王的行为具有民主斗争的性质，将《大宪章》视为英国历史上最伟大的一个奠基性文件；“法律史学派”代表性人物梅特兰对《大宪章》的评价较为客观，他认为《大宪章》并没有提出新鲜的内容，只是复制了以往的法律习惯，以成文法的形式来规范国王的作为；也有学者通过对法律文本的分析指出，《大宪章》本身是一个倒退性的文件，如爱德华·詹克斯就认为，《大宪章》具有浓厚的封建政治文件色彩，因过于强调封建法则和贵族利益而一度成为英国宪政发展的绊脚石。

本书认为，考察《大宪章》的影响力不应摆脱不同历史时期的社会背景。从整个历史发展的进程看，《大宪章》对世界政治史和法律史的积极影响是有目共睹的。《大宪章》不但为英国议会以及君主立宪制度的确立提供了法理依据，还为后世资产阶级阐发和诠释现代民主政治理论提供了思想资源。因此，将《大宪章》视为英国宪法的基石是合情合理的。直到800多年后的今天，《大宪章》依然是英国宪政体系中举足轻重的部分。

二、注释

1. Selected from Harry Rothwell (ed.), *English Historical Documents* 1189 - 1327, Eyre & Spottiswoode, 1975.

2. earl，通常是指英国的伯爵；count，通常指法、德等欧洲大陆国家的伯爵。

3. marriage portion，即嫁妆。

4. dower，寡妇产，或称亡夫遗产，指在中世纪英格兰，一旦丈夫去世，妻子享有丈夫生前所有地产的三分之一来维持生活。

5. *darrein presentment*，法律术语，是指强占土地、收回遗产及最后控诉等案件。

6. crown，最初是指国王（或女王）所佩戴的王冠，后来主要指佩戴王冠的国王（或女王）本人及其君主的身份。此处的crown可翻译为王权或国王。

7. *praecipe*，是一种原令状，责令司法行政官员命令被告做某事或说明他为什么不做某事，此处是指强制转移土地争执令状。

8. halberget，锁子甲。

9.《大宪章》第61条中对“二十五人男爵”有更为详细的解释。

10.《大宪章》第56、57条主要适用于威尔士，而第52条的规定主要适用于英格兰。

三、问题探讨

1. 从文本看，《大宪章》保护教会和世俗贵族哪些方面的权利？普通民众能否从《大宪章》中获得现实利益？

2.《大宪章》中哪些条款是用来限制王权的？限制了国王的哪些方面的权力？

四、参考文献

1. 孟广林：《英国“宪政王权”论稿：从〈大宪章〉到“玫瑰战争”》，人民出版社 2017 年版。

2. 齐延平：《自由大宪章研究》，中国政法大学出版社 2007 年版。

3. [英] 詹姆斯 · C. 霍尔特：《大宪章》，毕竞悦等译，北京大学出版社 2008 年版。

4. [英] 丹 · 琼斯：《分裂的王国：约翰、男爵和〈大宪章〉》，周文佳译，中信出版社 2017 年版。

5. Zbigniew Rau, *Magna Carta*, Routledge, 2016.

UNIT 6

THE GOLDEN BULL OF CHARLES Ⅳ[1]

PART Ⅰ[2]

CHAPTER Ⅰ　ESCORT AND SAFE-CONDUCT FOR THE ELECTORS

1. We decree and determine by this imperial edict that, whenever the electoral princes are summoned according to the ancient and praiseworthy custom to meet and elect a king of the Romans and future emperor, each one of them shall be bound to furnish on demand an escort and safe-conduct to his fellow electors or their representatives, within his own lands and as much farther as he can, for the journey to and from the city where the election is to be held. Any electoral prince who refuses to furnish escort and safe-conduct shall be liable to the penalties for perjury and to the loss of his electoral vote for that occasion.

2. We decree and command also that all other princes who hold fiefs from the empire by whatever title, and all counts, barons, knights, clients, nobles, commoners, citizens, and all corporations of towns, cities, and territories of the empire, shall furnish escort and safe-conduct for this occasion to every electoral prince or his representatives, on demand, within their own lands and as much farther as they can. Violators of this decree shall be punished as follows: Princes, counts, barons, knights, clients and all others of noble rank, shall suffer the penalties of perjury, and shall lose the fiefs which they hold of the emperor or any other lord, and all their other possessions; citizens and corporations shall also suffer the penalty for perjury, shall be deprived of all the rights, liberties, privileges, and graces which they have received from the empire, and shall incur the ban of the empire against their persons and property. Those whom we deprive of their rights for this offence may be attacked by any

man without appealing to a magistrate, and without danger of reprisal, for they are rebels against the state and the empire, and have attacked the honor and security of the prince, and are convicted of faithlessness and perfidy.

3. We also command that the citizens and corporations of cities shall furnish supplies to the electoral princes and their representatives on demand at the regular price and without fraud, whenever they arrive at, or depart from, the city on their way to or from the election; those who violate this decree shall suffer the penalties described in the preceding paragraph for citizens and corporations. If any prince, count, baron, knight, client, noble, commoner, citizen, or city shall attack or molest in person or goods any of the electoral princes or their representatives, on their way to or from an election, whether they have safe-conduct or not, he and his accomplices shall incur the penalties above described, according to his position and rank.

4. If there should arise any enmity or hostility between two electoral princes, it shall not be allowed to interfere with the safe-conduct which each is bound to furnish to the other on the occasion of the election, under penalty of being declared guilty of perjury, and being deprived of his vote for that occasion, as described above.

5. If any other princes, counts, barons, knights, clients, nobles, commoners, citizens, or cities are at war with any electoral prince or princes, they shall nonetheless be bound to furnish to them and their representatives escort and safe-conduct for the journey to and from the election, under the same penalties. In order to render the observance of the above demands more certain, we desire and instruct all electoral and other princes, and all counts, barons, nobles, cities, and corporations to bind themselves by oaths and written promises to observe them. If anyone refuses to do this, he shall incur the penalties above described, according to his rank and station.

6. If any electoral prince violates any of the above or following laws of the empire, he shall be excluded by his fellow electors from their body, and shall be deprived of his vote and his electoral dignity, and of his right to hold fiefs of the empire. If any other prince of any rank or station, or any count, baron, or noble who holds fiefs of the empire, or any of their successors to their fiefs, is guilty of a similar crime, he shall not be invested with the fiefs which he holds of the empire, nor be able to receive a fief from any other lord, and he shall incur the

above penalties, according to his rank.

7. The above rules apply to escorts and safe-conduct in general, but we have thought it well to indicate also the neighboring lands which should furnish escort and safe-conduct in each separate case to each elector.

8. To the king of Bohemia, the chief cup-bearer of the empire, the following should furnish escort and safe-conduct: the archbishop of Mainz, the bishops of Bamberg and Würzburg, the burggrave of Nürnberg, etc.

9. To the archbishop of Cologne, archchancellor of the empire for Italy, the archbishops of Mainz and Trier, the count palatine of the Rhine, the landgrave of Hesse, etc.

10. To the archbishop of Trier, archchancellor of the empire for Gaul and the kingdom of Arles, the archbishop of Mainz, the count palatine of the Rhine, etc.

11. To the count palatine of the Rhine, the archbishop of Mainz.

12. To the duke of Saxony, archmarshall[3] of the empire, the king of Bohemia, the archbishops of Mainz and Magdeburg, the bishops of Bamberg and Würzburg, the margrave of Meissen, the landgrave of Hesse, the abbots of Fulda and Hersfeld, the burggrave[4] of Nürnberg, etc. These shall also furnish escort and safe-conduct to the margrave of Brandenburg, the archchamberlain of the empire.

13. We wish and command that each electoral prince should give due notice to those from whom he intends to require safe-conduct, of his journey and of the route by which he intends to go; and he should make a formal demand upon such persons for safe-conduct, in order that they may be able to make fitting preparations.

14. The above decrees concerning safe-conduct are to be understood to mean that any person, whether expressly named or not, from whom safe-conduct is demanded on the occasion of the election, must furnish it in good faith within his own lands, and as much farther as he can, under the penalties described above.

15. It shall be the duty of the archbishop of Mainz to send notice of the approaching election to each of the electoral princes by his messenger bearing letters patent, containing the following: first, the date on which the letter should reach the prince to whom it is directed; then the command to the electoral prince to come or send his representatives to Frankfort on the Main, three months from that date, such representatives being duly accredited by letters bearing the great seal of the prince, and giving them full power to vote for the king of the Romans

and future emperor. The form of the letter of notification and of the credentials of the representatives are appended to this document, and we hereby command that these forms be used without change.

16. When the news of the death of the king of the Romans has been received at Mainz, within one month from the date of receiving it the archbishop of Mainz shall send notices of the death and of the approaching election to all the electoral princes. But if the archbishop neglects or refuses to send such notices, the electoral princes are commanded on their fidelity to assemble on their own motion and without summons at the city of Frankfort[5] within three months from the death of the emperor, for the purpose of electing a king of the Romans and future emperor.

17. Each electoral prince or his representatives may bring with him to Frankfort at the time of the election a retinue of 200 horsemen, of whom not more than 50 shall be armed.

18. If any electoral prince, duly summoned to the election, fails to come or to send representatives with credentials containing full authority, or if he or his representatives withdraws from the place of the election before the election has been completed, without leaving behind substitutes fully accredited and empowered, he shall lose his vote in that election.

...

CHAPTER Ⅱ THE ELECTION OF THE KING OF THE ROMANS

1. (Mass shall be celebrated on the day after the arrival of electors. The archbishop of Mainz administers this oath, which the other electors repeat:)

2. "I, archbishop of Mainz[6], archchancellor of the empire for Germany, electoral prince, swear on the holy gospels here before me, and by the faith which I owe to God and to the holy Roman empire, that with the aid of God, and according to my best judgment and knowledge, I will cast my vote, in this election of the king of the Romans and future emperor, for a person fitted to rule the Christian people. I will give my voice and vote freely, uninfluenced by any agreement, price, bribe, promise, or anything of the sort, by whatever name it may be called. So help me God and all the saints."

3. After the electors have taken this oath, they shall proceed to the election, and shall not depart from Frankfort until the majority have elected a king of the

Romans and future emperor, to be ruler of the world and of the Christian people. If they have not come to a decision within thirty days from the day on which they took the above oath, after that they shall live upon bread and water and shall not leave the city until the election has been decided.

4. Such an election shall be as valid as if all the princes had agreed unanimously and without difference upon a candidate. If any one of the princes or his representatives has been hindered or delayed for a time, but arrives before the election is over, he shall be admitted and shall take part in the election at the stage which had been reached at the time of his arrival. According to the ancient and approved custom, the king of the Romans elect, immediately after his election and before he takes up any other business of the empire, shall confirm and approve by sealed letters for each and all of the electoral princes, ecclesiastical and secular, the privileges, charters, rights, liberties, concessions, ancient customs, and dignities, and whatever else the princes held and possessed from the empire at the time of the election; and he shall renew the confirmation and approval when he becomes emperor. The original confirmation shall be made by him as king, and the renewal as emperor. It is his duty to do this graciously and in good faith, and not to hinder the princes in the exercise of their rights.

5. In the case where three of the electors vote for a fourth elector prince, his vote shall have the same value as that of the others to make a majority and decide the election.

CHAPTER Ⅲ THE LOCATION OF THE SEATS OF THE ARCHBISHOPS OF TRIER, COLOGNE, AND MAINZ

In the name of the holy and undivided Trinity, amen. Charles by the grace of God emperor of the Romans, Augustus, and king of Bohemia ... To prevent any dispute arising between the archbishops of Trier, Mainz, and Cologne, electoral princes of the empire, as to their priority and rank in the diet[7], it has been decided and is hereby decreed with the advice and consent of all the electoral princes, ecclesiastical and secular, that the archbishop of Trier shall have the seat directly opposite and facing the emperor; that the archbishop of Mainz shall have the seat at the right of the emperor when the diet is held in the diocese or province of Mainz, or anywhere in Germany except in the diocese of Cologne; that the archbishop of Cologne shall have the seat at the right of the emperor when the diet is held in the diocese or province of Cologne, or anywhere in Gaul or Italy. This applies to all public ceremonies: court sessions, conferring of fiefs, banquets, councils, and all occasions on which the princes meet with the emperor for the transaction of imperial business. This order of seating shall be observed by the successors of the present archbishops of Cologne, Trier, and Mainz, and shall never be questioned.

CHAPTER Ⅳ THE LOCATION OF THE SEATS OF THE ELECTORAL PRINCES

1. In the imperial diet, at the council-board, table, and all other places where the emperor or king of the Romans meets with the electoral princes, the seats shall be arranged as follows: On the right of the emperor, first, the archbishop of Mainz, or of Cologne, according to the province in which the meeting is held, as arranged above; second, the king of Bohemia, because he is a crowned and anointed prince; third, the count palatine of the Rhine; on the left of the emperor, first, the archbishop of Cologne, or of Mainz; second, the duke of Saxony; third, the margrave of Brandenburg.

2. When the imperial throne becomes vacant, the archbishop of Mainz shall have the authority, which he has had from of old, to call the other electors together for the election. It shall be his peculiar right also, when the electors have convened for the election, to collect the votes, asking each of the electors separately in the following order: first, the archbishop of Trier, who shall have the right to the first vote, as he has had from of old; then the archbishop of Cologne, who has the office of first placing the crown upon the head of the king of the Romans; then the king of Bohemia, who has the priority among the secular princes, because of his royal title; fourth, the count palatine of the Rhine; fifth, the duke of Saxony; sixth, the margrave of Brandenburg. Then the princes shall ask the archbishop of Mainz in turn to declare his choice and vote. At the diet, the margrave of Brandenburg shall offer water to the emperor or king, to wash his hands; the king of Bohemia shall have the right to offer him the cup first, although, by reason of his royal dignity, he shall not be bound to do this unless he desires; the count palatine of the Rhine shall offer him food; and the duke of Saxony shall act as his marshal in the accustomed manner.

CHAPTER Ⅴ THE RIGHTS OF THE COUNT PALATINE AND OF THE DUKE OF SAXONY

1. During the vacancy of the empire, the count palatine of the Rhine, archseneschal[8] of the empire, by reason of his principality and office, shall exercise the authority of the future king of the Romans in the Rhine lands, in Suabia; and in the region of the Frankish law; this includes the right to present to ecclesiastical benefices, to collect revenues and incomes, to invest with fiefs, and to receive the oath of fidelity in the name of the emperor. All of these acts, however, must be confirmed and renewed by the king of the Romans after he is elected. The count palatine shall not have the right to invest the princes of the empire with fiefs which are called *Fahnlehen*[9], the investiture and conferring of which is reserved to the king of the Romans in person. The count palatine is expressly forbidden to alienate or mortgage the imperial lands during the period of his administration. The duke of Saxony, archmarshal of the holy empire, shall exercise the same authority during the vacancy of the empire for the region of the Saxon law, under the same conditions as expressed above.

2. The emperor or king of the Romans must appear before the count palatine of the Rhine, when he ia cited by anyone, but the count palatine shall try such cases only at the imperial diet when the emperor or king is present.

CHAPTER Ⅶ THE SUCCESSION OF THE ELECTORAL PRINCES

1. ... It is known and recognized throughout the world, that the king of Bohemia, the count palatine of the Rhine, the duke of Saxony, and the margrave of Brandenburg, by virtue of the principalities which they possess, have the right to vote in the election of the king of the Romans along with their coelectors, the ecclesiastical princes, and that they with the ecclesiastical princes are the true and legal electoral princes of the holy empire. In order to prevent disputes arising among the sons of these secular electoral princes in regard to the electoral authority and vote, which would be productive of delays dangerous to the state and other evils, we have fixed the succession by the present law which shall be valid forever. On the death of one of the secular electoral princes his right, voice, and vote in the election shall descend to his first-born son who is a layman; if the son has died before this, to the son's first-born son who is a layman. If the first-

born lay son of the elector has died without legitimate lay sons, by virtue of the present law the succession shall go to the elector's next oldest lay son and then to his heirs, and so on according to the law of primogeniture. In case the heir is under age the paternal uncle of the heir shall act as guardian and administrator until the heir comes of age, which shall be, in the case of electoral princes, at eighteen years. Then the guardian shall immediately surrender to him the electoral vote and authority and all the possessions of the electorate.

2. When any electorate falls vacant for lack of heirs, the emperor or king of the Romans shall have the power to dispose of it, as if it reverted to the empire, saving the rights, privileges, and customs of the kingdom of Bohemia, according to which the inhabitants of that kingdom have the right to elect their king in case of a vacancy.

CHAPTER Ⅷ THE IMMUNITY OF THE KINGDOM OF BOHEMIA AND ITS INHABITANTS

Our predecessors, the emperors and kings of the Romans, have conceded to our ancestors, the kings of Bohemia, and to the kingdom and crown ...that no prince, baron, noble, knight, client, citizen, or other person of the kingdom, of any station, dignity, rank, or condition, should be cited, haled, or summoned before any tribunal outside of the kingdom, or before any judge except the king of Bohemia and the judges of his court. We hereby renew and confirm this privilege, custom, and concession by our royal authority and power, and decree that no one of the aforesaid, prince, baron, noble, knight, client, citizen, or peasant, or any other person, shall be required to appear or answer before any tribunal outside of the kingdom of Bohemia, in any case, civil, criminal, or mixed.

...

CHAPTER Ⅸ MINES OF GOLD, SILVER, AND OTHER METALS

We decree, by this present law, that our successors, the kings of Bohemia, and all the electoral princes, ecclesiastical and secular, shall hold and possess with full rights, all mines of gold, silver, tin, copper, iron, lead, or other metals, and all salt works, both those already discovered and those which shall be discovered in the future, situated within their lands, domains, and dependencies. They shall also have authority to tax Jews, the right to collect tolls already in force and all other rights which they or their predecessors have possessed to the present day.

CHAPTER COINAGE

1. We also decree that our successors, the future kings of Bohemia, shall possess and exercise in peace the rights of coinage of gold and silver, in all parts of their dominions and of the lands belonging to their subjects, in such form and manner as they may determine: a right which is known to have belonged to our predecessors, the former kings of Bohemia.

2. We also grant to the future kings of Bohemia forever the right to buy, purchase, or receive as gift or in payment, any lands, castles, possessions, or goods from any princes, magnates, counts, or other persons; such lands and property to remain, however, in their former legal status, and to pay the customary dues and services to the empire.

3. We extend this right by the present law to all the electoral princes, ecclesiastical and secular, and to their legal heirs, under the same conditions and form.

CHAPTER Ⅺ THE IMMUNITIES OF THE PRINCES

1. We decree also that no count, baron, noble, vassal, burggrave[10], knight, client, citizen, burgher, or other subject of the churches of Cologne, Mainz, or Trier, of whatever status, condition or rank, shall be cited, haled, or summoned to any authority before any tribunal outside of the territories, boundaries, and limits of these churches and their dependencies, or before any judge, except the archbishops and their judges. ...We refuse to hear appeals based upon the authority of others over the subjects of these princes; if these princes are accused by their subjects of injustice, appeal shall lie to the imperial diet, and shall be heard there and nowhere else.

...

2. We extend this right by the present law to the secular electoral princes, the count palatine of the Rhine, the duke of Saxony, and the margrave of Brandenburg, and to their heirs, successors, and subjects forever.

CHAPTER Ⅻ ASSEMBLIES OF THE PRINCES

...It has been decided in the general diet held at Nürnburg with the electoral princes, ecclesiastical and secular, and other princes and magnates, by their advice and with their consent, that in the future, the electoral princes shall meet every year in some city of the empire four weeks after Easter; this year they are to meet at that date in the imperial city of Metz[11]; on that occasion, and on every meeting thereafter, the place of assembling for the following year shall be fixed by us with the advice and consent of the princes. This ordinance shall remain in force as long as it shall be pleasing to us and to the princes; and as long as it is in effect, we shall furnish the princes with safe-conduct for that assembly, going, staying, and returning.

...

CHAPTER XIII THE REVOCATION OF PRIVILEGES

We hereby decree and determine that the liberties, jurisdiction, rights, honors, and authority of the electoral princes, ecclesiastical or secular, or of any one of them, ought not to be and shall not be in any way diminished by any privileges or charters of rights, graces, immunities, customs, etc., granted or to be granted by us or our predecessors to any person of whatsoever rank, station, or dignity, or to any city, town or territory, even if it is expressly stated in such privileges and charters that they are not revocable. In so far as any such privileges do diminish the liberties, jurisdiction, rights, honors, or authority of the said electoral princes, we hereby revoke them and decree by our imperial authority that they are to be regarded as revoked and void.

CHAPTER XIV THE FORFEITING OF FIEFS

In many regions it is becoming the practice for vassals and feudatories to renounce and resign verbally and without due notice the fiefs and benefices which they hold of their lords, and then to declare themselves free from their allegiance and to seize the fiefs under pretext of war. Therefore we decree hereby that such renunciation shall not be valid unless it is genuine and made with the condition that the fiefs and benefices shall revert immediately to the lords from whom they are held; those who have renounced their allegiance shall never disturb or molest their lords in the possession of these fiefs. Any subject violating this decree shall lose his fiefs and benefices, shall be branded with infamy, and placed under the imperial ban; no one shall ever give him a fief or a benefice, and any grant or investiture made to him shall be void.

CHAPTER XV CONSPIRACIES

We reprobate, condemn, and declare void all detestable and illegal conspiracies, confederations, and societies, which are or shall be made by cities or by persons of any rank or station, under color of any pretext whatever, inside or outside of cities, between city and city, person and person, or city and person, without the consent of the lords of the persons or territories; for it is well known that such conspiracies are declared illegal and void by the laws of our predecessors, the august emperors. We except from this condemnation such confederations and leagues as are entered into by princes, cities, and others for the preservation of the peace of their lands; these shall remain in force until we have decreed otherwise. If any person shall violate this decree and the ancient laws against conspiracies, besides incurring the regular penalties he shall be branded with infamy and shall be fined ten pounds of gold; cities and corporations guilty of a similar crime shall be fined 100 pounds of gold, half of which shall go to the imperial treasury, and half to the lord of the district, and they shall be deprived of the liberties and privileges which they have received from the empire.

CHAPTER XVI PFAHLBURGHERS[12]

The complaint has frequently been made of late that certain citizens and subjects of princes, barons, and other lords, in order to escape from their proper subjection, have had themselves received as citizens in other cities, and thus, while dwelling in the lands, cities, towns, or regions of the lords whom they have deserted, they claim to enjoy the liberty and immunity of the other cities, and to be freed from the lord's authority, because of that citizenship; these are the persons who are called in the vulgar tongue in Germany "pfahlburghers". Now since fraud and deceit cannot constitute a legal defense for any one, we hereby decree by our imperial authority and by the advice of the electoral princes, ecclesiastical and secular, that from this day forth within all the lands of the empire such citizens shall not enjoy the rights and liberties of the cities, unless they have actually moved into them and established their homes there, making their real residence and domicile in the cities and bearing their share of the debts, burdens, and municipal taxes. If any such persons are or shall be admitted into cities contrary to this edict, the admission shall be void of effect, and the persons shall not profit by the laws and liberties of those cities, in spite of any laws, privileges, and customs to the contrary, all of which, as far as they contradict this decree, we declare to be void; and the lords shall retain their rights over the persons and goods of their subjects who have deserted them in this manner. Those who receive the subjects of other lords on these terms contrary to our law, and who do not drive them away within one month after receiving notice of their presence, shall be fined for each such violation, 100 pounds of gold, half of which shall go to the imperial treasury and half to the lords of the deserters.

CHAPTER XVII RENUNCIATION OF ALLEGIANCE

If any person renounces his allegiance or alliance without due notice and in a place where he does not have his residence, even if he thinks he has just grounds, we declare that he shall not have the right to inflict injury or violence upon those from whom he has in this manner withdrawn. And since fraud and deceit cannot constitute legal defence, we hereby declare that renunciation of this sort from the society or association of any lord or person shall not be valid, and may not be used as pretext for making war, unless the renunciation has been announced to those who are concerned personally or publicly in the place where they have their regular residence, three full days before, and the notification can be proved by good witnesses. Whoever shall make war on another without making renunciation in this form, shall be branded with infamy, just as if he had never made any renunciation, and he shall be punished as a traitor by all judges. We forbid and condemn also all unjust wars and strife, all unjust burning, wasting, and rapine, all unusual and unjust tolls and exactions for safe-conduct, under penalties fixed by the laws of the empire.

CHAPTER XVIII FORM OF THE LETTER OF NOTIFICATION

"To you, the illustrious and magnificent margrave of Brandenburg, archchamberlain of the holy empire, our fellow-elector and dear friend, we give notice by these presents of the approaching election of the king of the Romans, and we summon you according to the duty of your office to come to that election at the regular place within three months from ________ ________ (date)[13], or to send one or more representatives or agents with sufficient authority, in order to consider with your fellow-electors and agree upon the choice of a king of the

Romans and future emperor; to remain there until the election is completed; and to do such other things as are required by the laws of the empire in this matter. Otherwise, in spite of your absence, we shall proceed with our fellow-electors to carry out the aforesaid business, as the authority of the imperial laws empowers us."

CHAPTER XIX FORM OF THE CREDENTIALS FOR REPRESENTATIVES OR AGENTS OF THE ELECTORAL PRINCES, SENT IN THEIR BEHALF TO THE ELECTION

We (name), by the grace of God (title), (office) of the holy empire. Be it known to all by these presents ...that we have constituted our faithful subjects (names) our true, legal, and special representatives and agents, to treat with our fellow-princes and electors, ecclesiastical and secular, and to agree and decide with them concerning a suitable person to be elected king of the Romans; to be present, deliberate, name, consent to, and elect the king of the Romans and future emperor in our name and for us; and to take the necessary, due, and accustomed oaths upon our soul, in regard to the aforesaid things; to appoint substitutes to do any and all things which may be necessary, useful, or convenient to the aforesaid consideration, nomination, deliberation, and election, and to do anything which we would be able to do if we were present in person at the election, even if these things be special and peculiar things not mentioned specifically. in the above. We will accept and ratify everything done by the aforesaid representatives or their substitutes.

CHAPTER XX THIS UNITY OF THE ELECTORAL PRINCIPALITIES

It is known that the right of voting for the king of the Romans and future emperor inheres in certain principalities, the possessors of which have also the other offices, rights, and dignities belonging to these principalities. We decree, therefore, by the present law that the electoral vote and other offices, dignities, and appurtenances shall always be so united and conjoined that the possessor of one of these principalities shall possess and enjoy the electoral vote and all the offices, dignities, and appurtenances belonging to it, that he shall be regarded as electoral prince, that he and no other shall be accepted by the other electoral princes and admitted to participation in the election and all other acts which regard the honor and advantage of the holy empire, and that no one of these rights, which are and ought to be inseparable, shall ever be taken from him. And if through error or by any other means any decision or sentence is issued by any judge against the present law, it shall be void.

CHAPTER XXI THE PRECEDENCE AMONG THE ARCHBISHOPS

We have defined above the location of the seats of the ecclesiastical electors in the council, at the table, and on other occasions, when the emperor meets with the electoral princes, but we have thought it well to indicate also the order of precedence in procession and march. Therefore we decree by the present imperial edict that whenever the emperor or king of the Romans meets with the electoral princes, and the insignia are borne before him in procession, the archbishop of Trier shall march directly before the emperor or king, no one being between them except the bearers of the insignia; and when the emperor or king marches without the insignia the archbishop shall immediately precede him. The other two archbishops [of Mainz and Cologne] shall march on either side of the archbishop of Trier, their position on the right or the left being determined by the region in which the ceremony is held, as described above.

CHAPTER XXII THE ORDER OF PRECEDENCE AMONG THE SECULAR ELECTORAL PRINCES, AND THE BEARERS OF THE INSIGNIA

We also determine by the present decree the precedence among the secular electoral princes as follows: When the electoral princes march in procession with the emperor or king of the Romans in any of the ceremonies of the imperial diet and the insignia are borne before him, the duke of Saxony shall precede the emperor or king, marching between him and the archbishop of Trier, and bearing the imperial or royal sword; the count palatine of the Rhine shall march at the right of the duke of Saxony with the imperial globe, and the margrave of Brandenburg at the left with the sceptre; the king of Bohemia shall follow immediately behind the emperor or king.

CHAPTER XXIII BENEDICTIONS OF THE ARCHBISHOPS IN THE PRESENCE OF THE EMPEROR

When the mass is celebrated in the presence of the emperor or king, the archbishops of Mainz, Trier, and Cologne, or any two of them, being present, the archbishops shall perform the services on the different days in turn in the order of their consecration, each one on his day officiating in the confession which is said before the mass, in the presenting of the gospel to be kissed, in the giving of peace after the *Agnus Dei*[14], in the benedictions after the mass and before meals, and in returning thanks after meals. Each archbishop on his day should invite the other archbishops to participate in the services, to set a good example to men by honoring one another.

PART Ⅱ[15]

CHAPTER XXⅣ

If any person shall have joined in a conspiracy or taken oath to join in a conspiracy with any other persons, princes, knights, or private persons, to slay one of the electoral princes of the holy empire, he shall be judged guilty of offence against the majesty of the emperor, and shall be executed, and all his goods shall be forfeited to the royal treasury; for we regard the electoral princes as members of our own body, and visit offences against them with the same severity as against ourself. [The rest of the chapter is devoted to the effects of the confiscation and attainder upon children and heirs of criminals, etc.]

CHAPTER XXⅤ

If it is proper that the integrity of the ordinary principalities should be preserved, for the better securing of justice and peace for the subjects, it is even more important that the great principalities of the electoral princes should be kept intact in their domains, honors, and rights. Therefore we determine and decree by this imperial edict that the lands, districts, fiefs, and other possessions of the great principalities, namely, the kingdom of Bohemia, the palatinate of the Rhine, the duchy of Saxony, and the mark of Brandenburg, should never under any circumstances be separated, divided, or dismembered. In order that they may be preserved in their integrity, the first-born son in each case shall succeed to them, and shall exercise ownership and dominion in them, unless he be incapacitated for ruling by reason of imbecility, or other notorious defect. In that case, he shall not be allowed to inherit, but the succession shall go to the nearest male lay heir on the paternal side.

CHAPTER XXVI

1. On the day of the imperial diet, all the electoral princes shall proceed to the imperial palace about the first hour, and shall assist the emperor or king in donning the insignia; then they shall proceed on horseback to the place of the diet with the emperor or king, preserving the order of precedence indicated above. The archchancellor of the kingdom in which the diet is held shall bear the seals of the empire or kingdom upon a silver staff; the secular princes shall bear the sceptre, globe, and sword, as indicated above; the German and Lombard crowns shall be borne, in this order, by princes of inferior rank named for this office by the emperor, immediately before the archbishop of Trier, who precedes the emperor, now wearing the imperial crown.

2. The empress or queen, clad in her insignia, shall also proceed to the place of the diet with her officials and ladies, taking her place behind the emperor or king and behind the king of Bohemia, who follows immediately after the emperor or king.

CHAPTER XXVII THE OFFICE OF THE ELECTORAL PRINCES AT THE DIET

1. After the emperor or king is seated on his throne, the duke of Saxony shall appear before the place of the diet on horseback with a silver staff and a silver measure, each of the value of twelve marks in silver, and shall fill his measure with oats from a heap that has been placed before the building in which the diet is held. This heap of oats shall be as high as the breast of the horse on which he rides. He shall then give this measure of oats to the first servant that approaches. Then he shall thrust his staff into the heap of oats and go away, and the vice-marshal, the count of Pappenheim, or in his absence the marshal of the court, shall distribute the oats. After the emperor or king has taken his place at the table the ecclesiastical electors, supported by other prelates, shall stand before the table and one of them shall pronounce the blessing, according to the

order of precedence established above; after the benediction the chancellor of the court shall present the seals to the archbishops, and they shall bear them to the emperor, all three touching with their hands the staff on which they are suspended, the archchancellor of the kingdom in which the diet is held marching in the middle and the other two on either side of him. They shall lay the seals reverently before the emperor or king, who shall immediately return them to the archbishops. The archchancellor of the kingdom in which the diet is held shall wear the great seal of the empire about his neck during the dinner and until he returns to his abode. The staff, which shall be of silver of the value of twelve marks, and the seals, shall be handed over to the chancellor of the court. The archbishop who bears the great seal shall return this also to the chancellor of the court by one of his own servants, mounted on a horse which shall be presented to the chancellor of the court as a perquisite of his office and as a token of the love of the archchancellor.

2. The margrave of Brandenburg, the archchamberlain of the empire, shall approach on horseback, bearing water in silver basins of the value of twelve marks, and a beautifully embroidered napkin, and shall dismount and offer the emperor or king water to wash his hands.

3. The count palatine of the Rhine shall approach on horseback, bearing four silver dishes, each of the value of three marks, filled with food, and shall dismount and carry them in and place them on the table before the emperor or king.

4. Then the king of Bohemia, the archcupbearer of the empire, shall ride up, bearing a silver cup or goblet, of the value of twelve marks, filled with wine and water mixed, and shall dismount and offer the goblet to the emperor or king to drink.

5. When the offices have been performed by the secular electoral princes, the vice-marshal, the count of Falkenstein, shall receive the horse and the silver basins of the margrave of Brandenburg; the master of the kitchen, the count of Nortemberg, shall receive the horse and the dishes of the count palatine of the Rhine; the vice-cupbearer, the count of Limburg, shall receive the horse and the goblet of the king of Bohemia; the vice-marshal, the count of Pappenheim, shall receive the horse, the staff, and the measure of the duke of Saxony. If these officials are not present, the ordinary officials of the court shall receive these gifts

in their places.

CHAPTER XXIX

We have learned from records and traditions, that it has been the custom in the past to hold the election of the king of the Romans in Frankfort, the coronation in Aachen, and the first diet in Nürnberg; therefore we decree that in the future these ceremonies shall be held in these places, unless there shall be some legitimate obstacle.

...

一、导读

1356年1月和12月，神圣罗马帝国皇帝查理四世（1347—1378年在位）分别在纽伦堡和梅斯帝国会议上颁布了诏书，从法律上肯定了大贵族分裂割据的合法性。因为诏书上加盖了黄金印玺，故而被称为《黄金诏书》（或称《金玺诏书》）。从14世纪到19世纪，《黄金诏书》成为神圣罗马帝国的“帝国基本法”。它一方面体现了教俗大贵族采取措施削弱皇权、维持德意志分裂局面的决心；另一方面也反映出《大宪章》模式之外，西欧国家另一宪政传统的形成及其发展特点，为认识德国式宪政发展提供了一个视角。

除序言外，《黄金诏书》共有31章，主要涉及皇帝选举法和规定诸侯权限等内容。诏书规定，皇帝由7个选帝侯（美因茨大主教、科隆大主教、特里尔大主教、波希米亚王、莱茵的巴拉丁伯爵、萨克森公爵和勃兰登堡的边地伯爵）在法兰克福选举产生。选举会议由美因茨大主教召集并主持，帝位加冕礼在亚琛举行，德意志国王即是神圣罗马帝国皇帝，不再需要罗马教皇的承认。诏书还规定，世俗选帝侯由长子继承、男性相续，领地不可分割；选帝侯拥有特恩权，在领地内政治独立，拥有征税、铸币、盐和铁矿开采等国家主权，掌握最高司法裁判权；未经特别许可，不准城市结盟，不准封臣反抗领主；皇帝赐给城市或者任何人的权力不得损害选帝侯的“自由、司法权、权力、荣誉和领地”，否则被视为无效；不经领主许可，禁止城市之间缔结同盟或者条约，领主的附庸逃亡到城市，限期一个月送还，否则将被罚款；选帝侯还拥有监督帝国的职权。

目前，国内外学者对《黄金诏书》的研究还比较薄弱。即便在德语学术界，相关研究也多以文本翻译和评注为主，专题性的学术研究论著并不多见。从现有的学术成果看，学者们普遍认可《黄金诏书》削弱了皇权、加剧了德意志的政治分裂、确定了德意志诸侯分立体制这一观点。不过，部分学者也注意到《黄金诏书》的积极影响，具体体现在：

其一，通过《黄金诏书》，德意志在一定程度上摆脱了教皇的干涉与影响，建立起较为稳定的国王选举制度，有利于维护帝国国内的和平秩序。

其二，《黄金诏书》对中世纪德意志的法律与习惯进行了梳理，在西欧第一次试图将多数原则作为一个基本的选举观念，从而体现出诸侯对中央皇权取得胜利的宪政进程。

本书的英译本节选自奥利弗·泰切尔主编的《中世纪历史文献》。该版本对《黄金诏书》进行了适当删减，只保留了那些具有重要历史影响力的条文。

二、注释

1. Selected from Oliver J. Thatcher (ed.), *A Source Book for Medieval History*, New Charles Scribner's Son, 1905.

2.《黄金诏书》第一部分，1356年1月10日颁布于纽伦堡。

3. archmarshall，即执政官。

4. burggrave，即城堡及其领地的领主。

5. 法兰克福（Frankfort）之所以被定为选举皇帝的地点，是因为从东法兰克时代开始，德意志便形成了在该市选举国王和进行加冕仪式的传统。

6. 选举团抵达法兰克福后，应在第二天举行弥撒和宣誓仪式，美因茨大主教主持该仪式。

7. 宴会中选帝侯的座次体现其政治地位的高低，因此该条款对选帝侯的座次进行了非常明确的规定。

8. archseneschal，即大管家。

9. *Fahnlehen*，即旗帜采邑，是指一种免除了封建义务、可以终身使用的土地。

10. burggrave，即国王或君主在城市的官方代表。

11. 查理四世通过该条款规定了选帝侯定期年会制度，他希望能够利用该制度形成帝国事务的咨询委员会。然而，该规定并未引起选帝侯的重视，在后来没有得到执行，成为一纸空文。

12. Pfahlburghers，是指摆脱了封建义务的城市自由人。

13. 此处由告示发布者添加当时的发布日期。

14. *Agnus Dei*，即天主教弥撒歌曲《羔羊颂》。

15.《黄金诏书》第二部分，1356年12月25日颁布于梅斯。

三、问题探讨

1.《黄金诏书》对皇帝的选举程序进行了哪些方面的规定？这些规定能否保证选举的公平与公正性？

2.《黄金诏书》赋予了选帝侯哪些方面的特权？这些特权为什么会导致中世纪德意志的分裂割据？

四、参考文献

1. 王银宏：《1356年〈金玺诏书〉与德意志国王选举制度》，《史学月刊》2016年第7期。

2.［英］詹姆斯·布赖斯：《神圣罗马帝国》，孙秉董等译，商务印书馆 1998 年版。

3.［美］史蒂文·奥茨门特：《德国史》，邢来顺等译，中国大百科全书出版社 2009 年版。

4.［德］格隆曼等：《德意志史第 1 卷：古代和中世纪》，张载扬等译，商务印书馆 1999 年版。

5. Heinz H. F. Eulau, "Theories of Federalism under the Holy Roman Empire", *The American Political Science Review*, Vol. 35, No. 4 (Aug. , 1941), pp. 643 - 664.

UNIT 7

SPEECH OF POPE URBAN Ⅱ AT THE COUNCIL OF CLERMONT[1]

In the year of our Lord's Incarnation one thousand and ninety-five, a great council was convened within the bounds of Gaul, in Auvergne, in the city which is called Clermont. Over this Pope Urban Ⅱ presided, with the Roman bishops and cardinals. This council was a famous one on account of the concourse of both French and German bishops, and of princes as well. Having arranged the matters relating to the Church, the lord Pope went forth into a certain spacious plain, for no building was large enough to hold all the people. The Pope then, with sweet and persuasive eloquence, addressed those present in words something like the following, saying:

"Oh, race of Franks, race beyond the mountains[2], race beloved and chosen by God (as is clear from many of your works), set apart from all other nations by the situation of your country, as well as by your Catholic faith and the honor you render to the holy Church: to you our discourse is addressed, and for you our exhortations are intended. We wish you to know what a serious matter has led us to your country, for it is the imminent peril threatening you and all the faithful that has brought us hither.

...

"On whom, therefore, rests the labor of avenging these wrongs and of recovering this territory, if not upon you — you, upon whom, above all other nations, God has conferred remarkable glory in arms, great courage, bodily activity, and strength to humble the heads of those who resist you? Let the deeds of your ancestors encourage you and incite your minds to manly achievements...

"But if you are hindered by love of children, parents, or wife, remember what the Lord says in the Gospel, 'He that loveth father or mother more than me is not worthy of me'. 'Every one that hath forsaken houses, or brethren, or sisters, or father, or mother, or wife, or children, or lands, for my name's sake, shall receive an hundred-fold, and shall inherit everlasting life'. Let none of your possessions restrain you, nor anxiety for your family affairs. For this land which you inhabit, shut in on all sides by the seas and surrounded by the mountain peaks, is too narrow for your large population; nor does it abound in wealth; and it furnishes scarcely food enough for its cultivators. Hence it is that you murder and devour one another, that you wage war, and that very many among you perish in civil strife.

"Let hatred, therefore, depart from among you; let your quarrels end; let wars cease; and let all dissensions and controversies slumber. Enter upon the road of the Holy Sepulcher; wrest that land from the wicked race, and subject it to yourselves. That land which, as the Scripture says, 'floweth with milk and honey' was given by God into the power of the children of Israel. Jerusalem is the center of the earth; the land is fruitful above all others, like another paradise of delights. This spot the Redeemer of mankind has made illustrious by His advent, has beautified by His sojourn, has consecrated by His passion, has redeemed by His death, has glorified by His burial.

"This royal city, however, situated at the center of the earth, is now held captive by the enemies of Christ ... She seeks, therefore, and desires to be liberated, and ceases not to implore you to come to her aid. From you especially she asks succor, because, as we have already said, God has conferred upon you, above all other nations, great glory in arms. Accordingly, undertake this journey eagerly for the remission of your sins, with the assurance of the reward of imperishable glory in the kingdom of heaven."

...

"Most beloved brethren, today is manifest in you what the Lord says in the Gospel, 'Where two or three are gathered together in my name, there am I in the midst of them'. For unless God had been present in your spirits, all of you would not have uttered the same cry; since, although the cry issued from numerous mouths, yet the origin of the cry was one. Therefore I say to you that God, who implanted this in your breasts, has drawn it forth from you. Let that, then, be your war cry in battle, because it is given to you by God. When an armed attack is made upon the enemy, let this one cry be raised by all the soldiers of God: 'It is the will of God! It is the will of God!'[3]

"And we neither command nor advise that the old or feeble, or those incapable of bearing arms, undertake this journey. Nor ought women to set out at all without their husbands, or brothers, or legal guardians. For such are more of a hindrance than aid, more of a burden than an advantage. Let the rich aid the needy; and according to their wealth let them take with them experienced soldiers. The priests and other clerks [clergy], whether secular or regular, are not to go without the consent of their bishop; for this journey would profit them nothing if they went without permission. Also, it is not fitting that laymen should enter upon the pilgrimage without the blessing of their priests.

"Whoever, therefore, shall decide upon this holy pilgrimage, and shall make his vow to God to that effect, and shall offer himself to Him for sacrifice, as a living victim, holy and acceptable to God, shall wear the sign of the cross of the Lord on his forehead or on his breast. When he shall return from his journey, having fulfilled his vow, let him place the cross on his back between his shoulders. Thus shall ye, indeed, by this twofold action, fulfill the precept of the Lord, as He commands in the Gospel, 'He that taketh not his cross, and followeth after me, is not worthy of me'".

一、导读

1095年11月，罗马教皇乌尔班二世（1088—1099年在位）在法国南部城市克勒芒召开宗教会议，发表了《十字军东征演讲》。聆听演讲的除了天主教僧侣外，还有封建主、商人和普通民众。演讲中，乌尔班二世号召东征耶路撒冷。他宣称在东方有大量的战利品，将给予参加东征的人免除或者延期偿还债务的优待，并许诺参加东征的农奴可以获得自由。历时近200年（1096—1293）的十字军东征由此拉开序幕。

自11世纪以来，无论是教会还是世俗组织都留下了大量关于十字军东征的资料，其中乌尔班二世的《十字军东征演讲》无疑是流传最为广泛的文献。在20世纪之前，西方学者并不重视对这类文献进行深入挖掘研究。他们在论著中热衷于歌颂宗教和民族主义，弘扬所谓的十字军精神，先入为主地将十字军东征看作是欧洲白人基督教徒的胜利。但随着20世纪以来全球化进程的加快，以及大量档案资料被引入学术研究领域，西方学界才开始站在人类文明史的高度重新审视十字军东征对东西方文明产生的影响。此时，学者们除了敢于批判十字军东征的各种负面影响外，还十分注意该运动对东西方文化交流产生的促进作用。英国史学家屈勒味林（G. M. Trevelyan）在其著作《英国史》中就曾对十字军东征评价道：如果野蛮的欧洲在中世纪后期依然像东征之前那样闭关自守，那么中世纪后期的社会剧变以及文艺复兴都将无从谈起。

目前所见，该演讲共有4个版本的原始文献存世，每个版本的内容差异并不大。本书的英译本选自弗雷德里克·奥斯丁主编的《中世纪史文献》，该版本的作者是兰斯教职人员罗伯特（Robert the Monk, a resident of Rheims）。

二、注释

1. Selected from Frederic Austin Ogg (ed.), *A Source Book of Medieval History*, American Book Company, 1907.

2. the mountains，指阿尔卑斯山。

3. 教皇为了使战争拥有“合法性”，故在此处为战争披上一层宗教外衣，认为“东征”是上帝的意愿，读者对此要有正确的认识。

三、问题探讨

1. 结合教材节选内容，谈谈在十字军东征之前西欧面临着哪些社会问题？

2. 乌尔班二世在演讲中一再强调十字军东征的“正义性”，这些所谓的“正义性”主要体现在哪些方面？试评价之。

四、参考文献

1. 赵立行：《西欧社会变动与十字军东征的进程》，《复旦学报》（社会科学版）2002 年第 4 期。

2. [法] 阿敏·马洛夫：《阿拉伯人眼中的十字军东征》，彭广恺译，（台湾）河中文化实业有限公司 2011 年版。

3. [英] 海伦·尼克尔森：《十字军》，刘晶波译，上海社会科学院出版社 2013 年版。

4. [英] 乔纳森·赖利-史密斯：《十字军史》，欧阳敏译，商务印书馆 2016 年版。

5. Vladimir P. Goss (ed.), *The Meeting of Two Worlds: Cultural Exchange between East and West during the Period of the Crusades*, Medieval Institute Publications, 1986.

UNIT 8

LONDON CRAFT GUILD ORDINANCES[1]

ORDINANCE OF THE PEPPERERS OF SOPER LANE[2]

These are the points which the good folks of Soper lane, of the trade of Peppers, with the assent of Sir Stephen de Abyndone, mayor of London, John de Gisors, Nicholas of Faringdon, and other aldermen, have made for the common profit of all the people of the land..., on [May 5,] the Wednesday next after the feast of St. Philip and St. James, in the 9th year of the reign of King Edward.

In the first place, that no one of the trade, or other person in his name or for him, shall mix any manner of wares, that is to say, shall put old things with new, or new things with old, by reason whereof the good thing may be impaired by the old; nor yet things of one price, or of one sort, with other things of another price, or of another sort.

Also, that no person shall dub any manner of wares; that is to say, by putting in a thing that was in another bale, and then dressing the bale up again in another manner than the form in which it was first bought, so as to make the ends of the bale contain better things than the remainder within the bale, by reason whereof the buyer may be deceived, and so lose his goods.

Also, that no one shall moisten any manner of merchandise, such as saffron, alum, ginger, cloves, and such manner of things as may admit of being moistened; that is to say, by steeping the ginger, or turning the saffron out of the sack and then anointing it, or bathing it in water, by reason whereof any manner of weight may be increased, or any deterioration arise to the merchandise.

Also, that every vendor shall give to his buyer the thing that is on sale by the hundredweight of 112 pounds to the hundred, 15 ounces to every pound; save only, things that are confected, or things powdered. And such things confected and powdered are to be sold by the 12 ounces, the same as always has been the custom.

Also, that all their weights shall agree, the one with the other.

ARTICLES OF THE GIRDLERS[3]

Unto the mayor, aldermen, and chamberlain, of the city of London, pray the good folks, the girdlers [that is, beltmakers] of the same city, that certain defaults which they find in their trade may be amended, and by certain folks of the trade be regulated; the same persons before you to be sworn to do the same.

In the first place, that no man of the trade shall work any manner of tissue of silk, or of wool, or of linen thread, if the tissue be not of such length and assize as was wont to be used heretofor, that is to say, 6 quarters.

Also, that no man of the said trade shall garnish, or cause to be garnished, girdles or garters, with any but pure metal, such as latten [that is, a copper alloy], or else with iron or steel...

Also, that no tissue of silk or wool, or of thread or leather, that is in breadth of sixth size, fifth, third, or double size, shall be garnished, unless it have a double point in the buckle, and in the tongue; as also, the bars with a double point down to the rowel below; that is to say, as well with reference to close-harness, as other [work]...

Also, that no man of the trade shall take an apprentice, unless he be free of the city; and if he be free, that he shall take no one for less than seven years.

Also, that no strange man shall be admitted to work in the trade, if he will not be an apprentice in the trade, or buy his freedom.

Also, that no man of the trade shall work on Saturday, or on the eve of a double feast, after None has been rung.

Also, that no man of the trade shall work in such trade at either roset or tirlet [that is, types of straps].

Also, that no man of the trade shall keep his shop open on Sundays, or on double feasts, to sell his wares. But if any strange person, passing by chance through the city upon any feast day, shall have occasion in a hurry to buy anything touching the said trade, it shall be fully lawful for a man of the same trade, whosoever he may be, to sell to him within his own house whatever he shall wish to buy; but without opening his shop.

Also, that no one of the trade shall set any woman to work, other than his wedded wife or his daughter.

Also, that no one of the said trade shall dare to work by night at the said trade, on the pain hereafter written.

Also, that no man from henceforth shall make a girdle of any worse leather than ox leather.

And hereupon, it is ordained by the mayor and aldermen, with the assent of all the good folks of the said trade, that if anyone of the trade shall be found by the men so sworn acting against the ordinances aforesaid, or any one point of them, the first time, he shall be amerced in 40 pence, the second time half a mark, the third time 10 shillings, the fourth time one mark, and the fifth time 20 shillings, to the use of the chamber. And such girdles as shall be found to have been falsely made, against the points aforesaid, by the sworn men before mentioned, shall be burnt.

ARTICLES OF THE SPURRIERS[4]

In the first place, that no one of the trade of spurriers shall work longer than from the beginning of the day until curfew rung out at the church of St. Sepulcher, outside Newgate, by reason that no man can work so neatly by night as by day. And many persons of the said trade, who compass how to practise deception in their work, desire to work by night rather than by day: and then they introduce false iron, and iron that has been cracked, for tin, and also, they put gilt on false copper, and cracked. And further, many of the said trade are wandering about all day, without working at all at their trade; and then, when they have become drunk and frantic, they take to their work, to the annoyance of the sick and of all their neighbourhood, as well by reason of the broils that arise between them and the strange folks who are dwelling among them. And then they blow up their fires so vigorously, that their forges begin all at once to blaze, to the great peril of themselves and of all the neighbourhood around. And then too, all the neighbors are much in dread of the sparks, which so vigorously issue forth in all directions from the mouths of the chimneys in their forges. By reason whereof, it seems unto them that working by night [should be ended,] in order to avoid such false work and such perils; and therefore, the mayor and aldermen do will, by assent of the good folks of the said trade, and for the common profit, that from henceforth such time for working, and such false work made in the trade, shall be forbidden. And if any person shall be found in the said trade to do to the contrary hereof, let him be amerced, the first time in 40d., one half thereof to go to the use of the chamber of the guildhall of London, and the other half to the use of the said trade; the second time, in half a mark, and the third time, in 10s., to the use of the same chamber and trade; and the fourth time, let him forswear the trade forever.

Also, that no one of the said trade shall keep a house or shop to carry on his business, unless he is free of the city; and that no one shall cause to be sold, or exposed for sale, any manner of old spurs for new ones; or shall garnish them, or change them for new ones.

Also, that no one of the said trade shall take an apprentice for a term of less than seven years; and such apprentice shall be enrolled, according to the usages of the said city...

Also, that no one of the said trade shall receive the apprentice, serving-man, or journeyman of another in the same trade, during the term agreed between his master and him, on the pain aforesaid.

Also, that no alien of another country, or foreigner of this country, shall follow or use the said trade, unless he is enfranchised before the mayor, aldermen, and chamberlain; and that, by witness and surety of the good folks of the said trade, who will undertake for him as to his loyalty and his good behavior.

Also, that no one of the said trade shall work on Saturdays, after Nones has been rung out in the city; and not from that hour until the Monday morning following.

ORDINANCES OF THE WHITE TAWYERS[5]

In honour of God, of Our Lady, and of all saints, and for the nurture of tranquility and peace among the good folks the megucers, called "white tawyers" [that is, processors of animal hides] the folks of the same trade have, by assent of Richard Lacer, mayor, and of the aldermen, ordained the points underwritten.

In the first place, they have ordained that they will find a wax candle, to burn before Our Lady in the church of All Hallows, near London Wall.

Also, that each person of the said trade shall put in the box such sum as he shall think fit, in aid of maintaining the candle.

Also, if by chance anyone of the said trade shall fall into poverty, whether through old age, or because he cannot labour or work, and have nothing with which to help himself, he shall have every week from the said box 7d[6] for his support, if he be a man of good repute. And after his decease, if he have a wife, a woman of good repute, she shall have weekly for her support 7d. from the said box, so long as she shall behave herself well, and keep single.

And that no stranger shall work in the said trade, or keep house [for the same] in the city, if he be not an apprentice, or a man admitted to the franchise of the said city.

And that no one shall take the serving-man of another to work with him, during his term, unless it be with the permission of his master.

And if anyone of the said trade shall have work in his house that he cannot complete, or if for want of assistance such work shall be in danger of being lost, those of the said trade shall aid him, that so the said work shall be not lost.

And if anyone of the said trade shall depart this life, and have not wherewithal to be buried, he shall be buried at the expense of their common box; and when anyone of the said trade shall die, all those of the said trade shall go to the vigil, and make offering on the morrow.

And if any serving-man shall conduct himself in any other manner than properly towards his master, and act rebelliously towards him, no one of the said trade shall set him to work, until he shall have made amends before the mayor and aldermen; and before them such contempt shall be redressed.

And that no one of the said trade shall behave himself the more thoughtlessly, in the way of speaking or acting amiss, by reason of the points aforesaid; and if anyone shall do to the contrary thereof, he shall not follow the said trade until he shall have reasonably made amends.

And if anyone of the said trade shall do to the contrary of any point of the ordinances aforesaid, and be convicted thereof by good men of the said trade, he shall pay to the chamber of the guildhall of London, the first time 2s., the second time 40d., the third time half a mark, and the fourth time 10s., and shall forswear the trade.

[Ordinances added in 1376:]

Also, that the good folks of the same trade shall once in the year be assembled in a certain place, convenient thereto, there to choose two men of the most loyal and befitting of the said trade, to be overseers of work and all other things touching the trade, for that year. These persons shall be presented to the mayor and aldermen for the time being, and sworn before them diligently to enquire and make search, and loyally to present to the said mayor and aldermen such defaults as they shall find touching the said trade, without sparing anyone for friendship or for hatred, or in any other manner. And if anyone of the said trade shall be found rebellious against the said overseers, so as not to let them properly make their search and assay, as they ought to do, or if he shall absent himself from the meeting aforesaid, without reasonable cause, after due warning by the said overseers, he shall pay to the chamber, upon the first default, 40d.; and on the second like default, half a mark; and on the third, one mark; and on the fourth, 20s., and shall forswear the trade for ever.

Also, that if the overseers shall be found lax and negligent about their duty, or partial to any person, for gift or for friendship, maintaining him or voluntarily permitting him [to continue] in his default, and shall not present him to the mayor and aldermen, as before stated, they are to incur the penalty aforesaid.

...And if it shall be found that through laxity or negligence of the said governors such assemblies are not held, each of the said overseers is to incur the said penalty.

Also, that all skins falsely and deceitfully wrought in their trade, which the said overseers shall find on sale in the hands of any person, citizen or foreigner, within the franchise, shall be forfeited to the said chamber, and the worker thereof amerced in manner aforesaid.

Also, that no one who has not been an apprentice, and has not finished his term of apprenticeship in the said trade, shall be made free of the same trade; unless it be attested by the overseers for the time being, or by four persons of the said trade, that such person is able, and sufficiently skilled to be made free of the same.

Also, that no one of the said trade shall induce the servant of another to work with him in the same trade, until he has made a proper fine with his first master, at the discretion of the said overseers, or of four reputable men of the said trade...

Also, that no one shall take for working in the said trade more than they were wont heretofore; that is to say, for [tawing] ten Scottish stags, half a mark; for ten Irish stags, half a mark; for ten Spanish stags, 10s.; for the hundred of goatskins, 20s.; the hundred of roe-leather, 16s.; for the hundred skins of young female deer, 8s.; and for the hundred of kidskins, 8s.

ORDINANCES OF THE FARRIERS[7]

...To Henry Pycard, mayor, and the aldermen of the city of London, the good folks, the master farriers of the same city, show that whereas many offenses and great damages had been committed, against the persons of the court, and the commonalty of the same city and of all the realm, by people not wise therein, who kept forges in the said city, and intermeddled with works of farriery, which they did not understand how to bring to good end, by reason whereof, many horses had been lost, to the great damage of the people. ...therefore, the said mayor doth will and doth grant, by assent of the good folks of the said trade, that all those who shall be found or proved to be making false work in shoes or nails, or works of false metal, shall pay 40 pence, the first time, to the chamber of the guildhall; the second time, half a mark; the third time, 13s. 4d. ; the fourth time, they shall forswear the said trade within the city for ever. And that no one from henceforth shall take any forge in the said city, until he shall have been admitted by the masters of the said trade, so as to be known as able and skilled in his trade, to the profit of the commonalty of the said city, and of all the realm.

And also, it is agreed between the said masters and the good folks of the said trade, that they will well and loyally advise all those who shall ask counsel of them, as well in the purchase of horses as in their cure; and that this they will not fail to do for any brokerage or gifts, whereby the said trade may be scandalized.

...

And that no one of the said trade shall commence or undertake any great cure, if he does not reasonably see at the beginning that the same cure will be brought to good end. And that if any person shall undertake any great cure, and shall fear in his conscience that the same will take a disastrous turn, then, in such case, he shall come before the masters and other wise men of the said trade, to ask their counsel and aid, for the saving of the horse, and for the profit of him to whom the horse belongs, and the honour of the trade. And if the contrary thereof shall in any manner be found, or it shall be proved against any person, that through conceit, or through negligence, he has let the same horse perish, then he shall be accused thereof before the mayor and aldermen, and be punished at their discretion, in the way of making restitution for same horse to the person to whom the same belongs.

And also, it is agreed between the said masters and the good folks of the said trade, that they shall not take from henceforth more than they were wont to take before the time of the pestilence; that is to say, for a shoe of 6 nails 1 d.; for a shoe of 8 nails 2d.; and for taking off a shoe of 6 nails or 8 nails, one halfpenny; for putting on the shoe of a courser, 2d.; the shoe of a charger, 3d.; and for taking off the shoe of a courser or charger, one penny; which points aforesaid the said masters and good folks of the said trade agree well and lawfully to keep and perform, to the best of their power, and have sworn thereto on the Holy Evangelists.

And also, it is agreed between the said masters and the good folks of the said trade, that no one of them shall commence or follow the trade or work of a smith, or any other than the trade which they follow, and by which they live, that is to say, horse-shoeing and farriery of horses. And further, that no one of them shall withdraw, take, or set to work, any smith, or any servants of smiths, or any serving-man of any other trade, if he be not a skilful man, and well versed in horse-shoeing and farriery; whereby the said trade might be slandered, and the commonalty deceived or damaged.

...

ORDINANCES OF THE COURT-HAND WRITERS, OR SCRIVENERS[8]

Unto the honourable lords, the mayor and aldermen of the city of London, the writers of court-hand of the same city pray that, whereas their craft is very much in request in the same city, and it is especially requisite that it should be ruled and followed lawfully and wisely and by persons instructed therein, and seeing that, for want of good rule, many mischiefs and defaults are, and have been oftentimes, committed in the said craft, by those who resort from divers countries unto the said city, both chaplains and others, who have no knowledge of the customs, franchises, and usages of the city, and who cause themselves to be called "scriveners", and undertake to make wills, deeds, and all other things touching the said craft; the fact being that they are foreigners and unknown, and also are less skilled than the aforesaid scriveners who are free of the said city, and who for long have been versed in their craft, and have largely given of their means for their instruction and freedom therein: to the great damage and disinheritance of many persons, as well of the said city as of many countries of the realm, and to the great damage and scandal of all the good and lawful men of the said craft — therefore the good scriveners pray that it may please your honorable and discreet lordships, to grant unto them, and to establish for the common profit of the said city, and of many other countries, and for the well-being and amendment of their condition, that they, and their successors for all time, may be ruled and may enjoy their franchise in their degree in manner as other folks of divers trades of the said city are ruled and do enjoy their franchise, in their degree; according to the points that follow.

In the first place, they pray that no person shall be suffered to keep shop of the said craft in thecity, or in the suburb thereof, if he be not free of the city, made free in the same craft, and that, by men of the craft.

Also, that no one shall be admitted to such freedom, if he be not first examined and found able by those of the same craft who shall, for the time being, by you and your successors be assigned and deputed to do the same, and to be wardens of the said craft.

Also, that every scrivener of the said city, and of the suburb thereof, shall put his name to the deeds which he makes, that it may be known who has made the same.

Also, that every one who shall act against this ordinance and enactment, shall pay to the chamber the first time 40d.; the second time, half a mark; and the third time, 10s.

Also, that these articles shall be enrolled in the said chamber, as being firm and established for ever.

ORDINANCES OF THE FULLERS[9]

To the honorable lords, and gracious, the mayor and aldermen of the city of London, pray very humbly, and with all their heart, John Oliscompe, Geoffrey Suttone, and John Swift, for themselves and all other fullers, and all other good folks of the same trade, in the city of London, that whereas the said trade has for a long time past used urine in the fulling of cloths, by reason whereof the said trade has been and is always being reproved by many folks of the said city, and certain persons of the trade of dyers say that no cloth can be either properly fulled or dyed, when such urine is put thereupon in fulling: and the said trade of fullers is of good desire that no urine shall be put upon any cloth in fulling, that so they may avoid reproach and for the profit of all the commonalty: may it please your very gracious lordships, that the said point be accepted before you, and enrolled: that no one of the said trade of fullers shall dare to allow urine any longer to be used from henceforth in their trade, on pain of paying 100s. to the chamber of the guildhall.

And that it be ordained, that no one in the said trade of fullers shall be allowed from henceforth to work within the city, if he be not free of the same.

Also, the said fullers do pray, that, whereas the hurers [that is, makers of shaggy fur caps] of the said city are wont to full their caps in the mills at Wandsworth, Old Ford, Stratford, and Enefield, where the said fullers full their cloths, it may please your very benign lordships, that the said hurers shall not be allowed from henceforth to full in the said mills; having regard that the said fullers cannot there full their cloths, by reason that when the caps are mixed with their cloths in fulling, such caps crush and tear the cloths, to the great damage and loss, as well of the said fullers, as of all the community.

ORDINANCES OF THE CHEESEMONGERS[10]

To the honourable lords, the mayor, recorder, and aldermen of London, pray the cheesemongers of London, that whereas our said lord the mayor has told them heretofore to devise and ordain how the price of cheese and of butter may be amended, the said cheesemongers therefore, by their common assent, have well considered how the said price may be well amended; if our said lord the mayor, and his good council, will put their hand to, confirm, and enroll the points underwritten.

First, that foreigners who come to the city with cheese and butter for sale, in carts and upon horses, shall be charged to bring their wares into the market of the Ledenhall, or the market between St. Nicholas Shambles and Newgate, and nowhere else, before noon rung at such place where the purchase shall be made: and shall be charged that they shall not put away in houses or in rooms, privily or openly, either after noon rung or before, any cheese or butter, on pain of forfeiting the same that shall be so put away.

Also, whereas those who carry or bring cheese or butter to the city by water, do sell it in secret to huckster and to others, against the ancient usage...: they do pray that from henceforth all such dealers shall be charged to bring such cheese or butter to the markets aforesaid, and there sell the same; on pain of forfeiting the thing to be sold, and also on pain of imprisonment, and of making fine at the will and ordinance of our said lord the mayor.

Also, diverse hucksters of cheese, from Ham, Hackney, and the suburbs of London, are wont to go to diverse markets, and to buy up such wares in order to make a profit, when the wares ought to come to the hands of the working-men in London; and such hucksters then bring the same into London, and go about through diverse streets in the said city, and sell it, to the great damage of the commonalty, saying and affirming that it is the produce of their own cattle, and of their own making; they do pray therefore that from henceforth such forestallers, regrators, and hucksters, and all other vendors of cheese or of butter, foreigners or freemen, shall be charged to sell the same at one of the said markets, on the pain aforesaid.

Also, whereas strangers do come and bring to the city cheese of Wales, called "talgar"[11], and house the same in Fleet Street and in Holborn, and other places, both within the city as without, and there sell it in secret, against the ancient custom, in manner aforesaid; ... [the cheesemongers ask] that they may be charged to bring their wares to the said markets, in form and on the pain aforesaid.

...

Also, that the good folks of the said trade shall be charged every year, at the feast of St. Michael [September 29], to choose two of the most able men to oversee as to the points aforesaid, that they are well kept and observed in manner before stated. And that the persons so chosen shall have power to seize such manner of merchandise, so forfeitable, and to present the same before the mayor; in amendment of the price aforesaid, to the great profit of the commonalty in time to come.

...

一、导读

行会是中世纪和近代早期西欧重要的社会经济组织，在长达几个世纪中控制着城市的经济活动。英语中行会“guild”一词来源于盎格鲁-撒克逊语“gild”或“geld”，原意为“贡”或“税”，即每个成员需要缴纳一定的会费才可以加入，后来逐步发展成为同一行业从业者为了共同利益，相互援助而自愿组成的协会或公会。其目的是规范本行业内部的事务，维护其共同利益。按照行会的从业特点，中世纪行会可以分为商人行会和手工业行会。商人行会是行会发展的第一个阶段，主要存在于12—13世纪。手工业行会在13世纪后期取代了商人行会成为城市经济生活的主导，将行会带入第二个发展阶段，其在14世纪达到鼎盛，15世纪开始衰落，并逐步被近代化的工会所取代。

从目前掌握的行会文献内容看，中世纪行会章程明确而详细地规定了行会成员的义务和责任，其中关于产品质量和生产数量的规定内容较多，目的是确保生产出优质产品，减少竞争，为行会获得良好声誉。其约束会员的惯常方法通常包括以下几个方面：

第一，严格控制行会会员的生产数量和工作时间等，不允许超量生产。

第二，禁止使用惯例以外的生产工具或方法，严格控制商品的原材料、工艺和质地等。

第三，规定帮工或学徒的学习时间，防止会员数量过多而加剧内部竞争。

第四，规定销售时间和地点，严格控制销售价格，禁止会员降价销售，防止出现价格上的竞争。

第五，控制制造工艺和质量标准，禁止生产和销售质量低劣的商品。

第六，对于违反行规的行为进行严厉的经济惩罚，严重者可能要面临法律起诉等。

手工业行会是小商品经济时代的特殊产物。追求“平均主义”和社会稳定是其制定章程的主要出发点，然而它们有悖于近代资本主义商品经济发展的要求。行会试图通过统一价格来阻止从业者之间的竞争，却挫伤了广大手工业者生产的积极性，导致生产过程墨守成规、缺乏生机。行会试图通过统一质量标准来抑制投机行为，维护工匠们的社会声誉，却阻碍了新工艺和新工具的发明与推广。行会还试图通过垄断经营和限制从业者数量来保证利润率，却扼杀了扩大生产规模的可能性，最终阻碍了近代城市经济的发展。不过，中世纪行会也有其积极的一面，其催生出的合作经营思想、互助思想、“工匠精神”等都为现当代的职业协会、同业公会发展提供了重要的参考。

本文献选自1868年出版的《13—15世纪伦敦和伦敦生活》，主要包括14世纪伦敦地区胡椒商、腰带匠、马刺匠、鞣白皮匠、蹄铁匠、法律从业者、漂洗匠和干酪匠等 8 个手工业行会的章程。这些内容可以全面呈现中世纪行会的经济活动和制度管理的特点。

二、注释

1. Selected from Emilie Amt (ed.), *Medieval England 1000 - 1500*, Broadview Press, 1985.

2. Soper Lane，即索珀巷，伦敦圣潘克拉斯（St Pancras）地区的一个教区，起源于中世纪时期，1666 年毁于伦敦大火，此后并未重建。本文献的索珀巷胡椒商行会章程制定于 1316 年。

3. Girdlers，即腰带匠、腰带匠行会。本章程制定于 1344 年。

4. Spurriers，即马刺匠、马刺匠行会。本章程制定于 1345 年。

5. White Tawyers，即鞣白皮匠、鞣白皮匠行会。本章程制定于 1346 年。

6. 英国旧制货币单位为英镑（缩写为 s)、先令（缩写为 p)、便士（缩写为 d)。其中，1 英镑为 20 先令，1 先令为 12 便士。

7. Farriers，即蹄铁匠、蹄铁匠行会。本章程制定于 1356 年。

8. Scriveners，即法律文书和公证人，或其成立的行会。本章程制定于 1373 年。

9. Fullers，即漂洗匠、漂洗匠行会。本章程制定于 1376 年。

10. Cheesemongers，即干酪商、干酪商行会。本章程制定于 1377 年。

11. talgar，即塔尔加尔，一种威尔士干酪。

三、问题探讨

1. 以上文献中提到的手工业行会规章制度是如何限制生产和销售规模扩大的？对违反规定的工匠又是怎样进行惩罚的？

2. 中世纪行会制定的规章制度中，哪些条款对产品质量进行了规定？提高产品质量是这些规章制度制定的主要目的吗？

四、参考文献

1. 金志霖：《英国行会史》，上海社会科学院出版社 1996 年版。

2. ［法］布罗代尔：《十五至十八世纪的物质文明、经济和资本主义》，顾良译，生活·读书·新知三联书店 1993 年版。

3. ［英］M. M. 波斯坦、爱德华·米勒：《剑桥欧洲经济史》（第二卷），钟和等译，经济科学出版社 2004 年版。

4. Daniel Detzer, *Handicraft and Guilds in the Late Medieval Cities*, Grin Verlag, 1988.

5. Joan Jovinelly, *The Crafts and Culture of a Medieval Guild*, Rosen Publishing Group, 2006.

UNIT 9

PEACETREATIES OF WESTPHALIA[1]

(A) Peace Treaty of Osnabrück between Emperor Ferdinand Ⅲ and Queen Christina of Sweden and their respective allies, Osnabrück (October 14/24, 1648)

In the Name of the most Holy and Indivisible Trinity. Amen.

Let it be known to each and every one whom it concerns or whom it could in any manner concern: that after the differences and troubles which began several years ago in the Roman Empire had increased to such a degree that not only all Germany, but likewise several neighboring kingdoms, especially Sweden and France, were thus involved, and from which arose a long and cruel war [...], at last, through God's grace, it happened that both sides turned their thoughts towards a universal peace [...] and to this end appointed by common consent the 11th day of July (N. S.) or the 1st day of July (O. S.) 1643[2] as the starting date for an assembly or congress of plenipotentiaries[3] at Osnabrück and at Münster in Westphalia. Thus the ambassadors and plenipotentiaries of both sides appeared at the established time and place [...]. Having prayed for God's help and duly exchanged their credentials (exact copies of which are appended to this instrument), they mutually, in the presence of and with the consent and approval of the electors, princes, and estates of the Holy Roman Empire, also for the glory of God and the security of Christendom, agreed to the following articles of peace and friendship.

Article Ⅰ

[*Establishment of Peace*.] A Christian, universal, and perpetual peace and a true and sincere friendship shall be established between His Holy Imperial Majesty, the House of Austria, and all its allies and adherents and their heirs and successors (principally the Catholic King of Spain and the electors, princes, and estates of the Empire), on the one side, and Her Holy Royal Majesty and the kingdom of Sweden, and all her allies and adherents and their heirs and successors (principally the Most Christian King [of France] and the respective electors, princes, and estates of the Empire), on the other side. This [peace] shall be sincerely and earnestly preserved and upheld, so that each party may promote the benefit, honor, and advantage of the other, whereby the fruits of this peace and friendship shall flourish and bloom again reciprocally between the entire [Holy] Roman Empire and the kingdom of Sweden.

Article Ⅱ

[*Cessation of Hostilities; Amnesty*.] That there be, on both sides, a perpetual oblivion and amnesty for all hostile acts committed since the beginning of these troubles in whatever place or manner, by one party or the other, [...] [so] that all injuries, acts of violence, hostility, damage, and expense, which either side has inflicted on the other, both before and during the war, are — without any regard to persons or things through spoken word, writings, or actions — to be forgotten, to the degree that anything one party could allege of the other on this account is to be buried in perpetual oblivion.

Article Ⅲ

1. [*Restoration of Rulers' Rights*.] According to this foundation of a general and unlimited amnesty, each and every elector of the Holy Roman Empire, the princes and estates therein included, the nobility that hold [fiefs] immediately of the Empire, their vassals, subjects, citizens and inhabitants [...] shall be fully re-established on both sides, in the same estate as to both spiritual and temporal rights, which they enjoyed or could by right enjoy before those troubles, notwithstanding all the changes made to the contrary, which shall be annulled and remain void. [...]

Article Ⅳ

5. [*New Palatine Electorate*.][4] Concerning the Palatine House, emperor and Empire consent, in the interests of public peace, that, by virtue of this agreement, an eighth electorate shall be created, which Charles Louis, Count Palatine of the Rhine, and his heirs and agnates of the Rudolphine line shall in the future enjoy in accordance with the rule of succession set forth in the Golden Bull. Beyond this investiture, however, neither Charles Louis nor his successors shall possess any right over that which has been granted (together with the electoral dignity) to the elector of Bavaria and the entire Wilhelmine line.

6. [*Restoration of the Lower/Rhine Palatinate*.] In addition, the entire Lower Palatinate, each and every ecclesiastical and secular property, right, and appurtenance, which the electors and princes Palatine enjoyed before the troubles of Bohemia, also all the documents, registers, accounts, and other acts depending thereupon, shall be fully restored to him, making void whatever has been done to the contrary. The emperor shall ensure that neither the Catholic King [of Spain] nor any other current possessor of any part of this property shall oppose in any way this restitution. [...]

51. [*Resettlement of Belligerents*.] Finally, each and every military officer and soldier, counselor and official, civil and ecclesiastical, of whatever title and condition, who have engaged themselves on either side to fight with sword or pen for them or their allies and adherents [...] shall be resettled, as regards their persons and their goods, in the same state of life, reputation and honor, conscience and liberty, rights and privileges they enjoyed or could have enjoyed before the said hostilities. [...] All of this shall apply equally to those who are not subjects or vassals of his Imperial Majesty or of the House of Austria. [...]

53. [*Restoration of Confiscated Properties*.] As to what concerns their properties, if they have been lost by confiscation, or in any other manner, before [the owners] declared for Sweden or France [...], those properties shall remain lost and confiscated for the benefit of their current possessors.

Article V

[*Regulation of Confessional Relations*.] Now, whereas the grievances that have arisen among the electors, princes, and estates of the Empire, whether of one confession or the other, have mainly been the cause and occasion of the present war, the following is agreed to and settled:

1. [*Treaty of Passau* 1552 *and Religious Peace of Augsburg* 1555.] The treaty signed at Passau in 1552 and the Religious Peace [of Augsburg], which followed in 1555, the articles of which were unanimously accepted and approved [in 1566, etc.] by the emperor and the electors, princes, and estates of both religions, shall be faithfully and inviolably observed in all their points and articles.

[*Contested Articles of the Religious Peace*.] Whatever this treaty says, based on a common decision by the [confessional] parties, about formerly contested articles shall be regarded, both in the courts and elsewhere, as a permanent explanation of the Religious Peace until the day when, through God's grace, an agreement about religion is established. Any challenge or protest raised at any time by anyone, be he clergyman or layman, whether within or outside the Empire, shall be declared by the force of this present treaty to be null and void.

[*Equality of Religions among Imperial Estates*.] In all other matters, there shall be a precise and mutual equality among the electors, princes, and estates of both religions, to the degree that this provision conforms to the Empire's constitution, the Imperial laws, and this treaty. [...] On this basis, all violence and force between the two [confessional] parties is forever forbidden. [...]

14. [*Determining the Date for Ecclesiastical Lands of Imperial Subjects*.] As to the ecclesiastical goods immediate to the Empire [...], whoever possessed them on January 1, 1624, whether they are Catholic estates or of the Augsburg Confession, the adherent of that religion shall possess them all, peaceably and without disturbance, until We have arrived, by the grace of God, at an agreement about the religious disputes. [...] And if the religious differences cannot be overcome, which God forbid, the present convention shall have the weight of a perpetual law, and the peace shall last forever.

15. [*Ecclesiastical Reservation*.] If a Catholic archbishop, bishop, or prelate, or an adherent of the Augsburg Confession who is chosen or postulated to be an archbishop, bishop, or prelate, should happen to change his religion (acting either alone or conjointly with his prebendaries and canons, whether one or more or altogether), or if any other ecclesiastics should change their religion in the future, they all shall immediately forfeit their right, though without damage to their honor or reputation, and shall without any delay or any challenge whatsoever relinquish the [offices'] possessions and revenues. Furthermore, the chapter or others who are legally entitled shall have the right to elect or request another person of the same religion to whom, by virtue of this act, the benefice shall belong. He shall, however, forsake the fruits and revenues which the archbishop, bishop, or prelate, etc., who changed his religion, received and consumed in the meantime. [...]

25. [*Benchmark for Ecclesiastical Lands not Immediate to the Empire*.] [...] All mediate ecclesiastical properties, [...] as well as the revenues and rights, however named, that the electors, princes, and estates of the Augsburg Confession possessed on January 1, 1624, shall be one and all possessed [...]

until the religious differences are terminated by a general, amicable agreement. All claims to the contrary shall be ignored. [...]

26. [*Restoration of the Monasteries*.] The Catholics shall likewise possess all the mediate monasteries, foundations, and colleges, which they actually possessed on January 1, 1624, even if such are situated in the lands and jurisdiction of estates adherent to the Augsburg Confession. Such properties shall not be transferred, however, to a religious order other than the one to which they were first donated. [...] In all the foundations, collegiate churches, monasteries, and hospitals where Catholics and those of the Augsburg Confession have lived among one another, they shall henceforth live in the same proportions that existed on January 1, 1624, and the exercise of religion shall remain the same as it was in each place in the said year and day, without disturbance from one side or the other. [...]

28. [*Religious Rights of Imperial Nobility*.] With regard to the free and immediate nobles, who collectively and individually hold [fiefs] immediately of the Empire, and each and all of their members, subjects, and feudal and allodial goods and possessions, [...] they shall, by virtue of the religious peace and the present agreement, have the same rights that the aforementioned electors, princes, and estates enjoy in matters of religion and the advantages arising therefrom. [...] Moreover, all who have been molested [in these rights] shall have them entirely restored. [...]

31. [*Toleration of Protestant Subjects*.] Yet notwithstanding this rule, the vassals and subjects of the Catholic states that have had the public or private exercise of the religion of the Augsburg Confession in 1624 or any part of that year, either by a particular agreement and privilege, by long usage, or by the sole observance of the said religion only for that year, shall retain the same for the future with all the appurtenances and dependencies they have or can prove were possessed in the said year. [...]

34. [*Toleration of Non-Conforming Subjects*.] It has also been agreed that those adherents of the Augsburg Confession who are subjects of the Catholics, and the Catholic subjects of the estates of the Augsburg Confession who had no public or private exercise of their religion at any time in the year 1624, and who at some time following the peace's publication shall profess and embrace a religion different from that of the lord of their territory, shall be patiently

tolerated and have liberty of conscience, and shall not be hindered in attending their devotions held privately in their homes. They shall not be prohibited from participating in the public exercise of religion in their vicinities as often as they wish, nor prohibited from sending their children to foreign schools of their own confession, nor from having them instructed at home by private teachers. Yet the said freeholders, vassals, and subjects shall perform their duty in all other things with due obedience and submission, and without any disturbance or commotion.

35. [*Guarantee of Properties of Non-Conforming Subjects.*] Subjects — whether Catholic or of the Augsburg Confession — shall not be condemned anywhere on account of their religion nor excluded from the communities of merchants, artisans, or companies nor deprived of successions, legacies, hospitals, lazar houses, or alms houses and other privileges or rights, including the use of churchyards and the honor of burial. Nothing more shall be exacted from them for the costs of their funerals than the dues usually paid for graves in parish churches. In these and all other similar things, they shall be treated in the same manner as brethren and sisters with equal justice and protection.

36. [*Toleration of Subjects Who Convert to a Different Religion.*] If a subject who possessed [the right to] neither public nor private exercise of his religion in the year 1624, or who changes his religion after the publication of the peace, shall have a mind to change his religion or be willing to change his abode or be ordered by the lord of the manor to emigrate, then he shall be free to sell his properties or to have them administered by his relations, to visit them freely without any letters of passport, and to do this as often as is required to prosecute his affairs, conduct legal business, and pay his debts. [...]

52. [*Religious Conflicts Settled by Negotiation, Not Majority Rule.*] In religious and all other affairs in which the estates cannot be considered as one body, and when the Catholic estates and those of the Augsburg Confession are divided into two parties, the dispute is to be decided by amicable agreement alone, and neither side is to be bound by a majority vote.

The issue of decision by majority vote on taxation matters, however, which the present assembly could not decide, is referred to the next session of the Diet.

Article VI

[*The Swiss Confederation's Relationship to the Empire.*] His Imperial Majesty has sought counsel from the Imperial estates concerning the complaints that were made in the presence of his plenipotentiaries and deputies in the present assembly in the name of the city of Basel and of all Switzerland, touching certain procedures and executory orders issued from the Imperial Chamber [Court] against the said city, the other united Swiss cantons, and their citizens and subjects, who had asked the estates of the Empire for counsel and advice. His Majesty declared, by a particular decree of May 14, 1647, that the said city of Basel and the other Swiss cantons possess full liberty and are exempt from the Empire and in no way subject to the tribunals and sentences of the said Empire. It has therefore been decided that this same decree shall be incorporated into this public peace treaty and be regarded as valid and lasting. Therefore, all suits and the confiscations at any time occasioned by them shall be void and invalid.

Article Ⅶ

1. [*Toleration of the Reformed Faith as a Third Imperial Confession*.] It has likewise been decided unanimously by His Imperial Majesty and all the Imperial estates that the same right or advantage, which the other Imperial constitutions [...] and especially the Religious Peace grant to the Catholic estates and subjects, and to those of the Augsburg Confession, also ought to be granted to those who call themselves the Reformed. [...] [*There follow rules, adapted from Article Ⅴ, for conversions between the Reformed and the Lutherans*.]

2. [*Restrictions on Toleration in Public Offices*.] If, in the event of such a change, any community embraces the religion of its lord and wishes, at its own expense, to adopt the exercise of the religion to which its prince or lord adheres, he shall be free to grant them their wish without prejudice to the rest. This grant may not be revoked by his successors. Some persons, however, may not adhere to any religion but that which is generally professed in that place at that time. They include members of a consistory, ecclesiastical visitors[5], and professors of theology and philosophy in schools and universities. [...]

Beyond the religions stipulated, no other shall be accepted or tolerated in the Holy Roman Empire.

Article Ⅷ

1. [*Rights of Territorial Rulers*.] In order to prevent all future disputes over the political order, each and every elector, prince, and estate of the [Holy] Roman Empire shall, by virtue of this treaty, be established and confirmed in their possession of all their ancient rights, prerogatives, liberties, privileges, the

free exercise of their territorial rights, both spiritual and temporal, their seigneuries, and their regalian rights. In the possession of all these things, they may not, by virtue of the present transaction, be molested at any time, in any manner, or under any pretext whatsoever.

2. [*Rights of Imperial Estates; Foreign Alliances*.] They shall enjoy without contradiction the right of suffrage in all deliberations affecting the affairs of the Empire, especially with respect to interpreting the laws, declaring war, imposing taxes, raising levies and quartering soldiers, building for the public use new fortresses in the lands of the estates, and reinforcing old garrisons, making peace and alliances, and treating other such affairs. None of these or similar things shall be done or afterward approved except with the freely given advice and consent of all the Imperial estates:

First of all, each Imperial estate shall freely and forever enjoy the right of making alliances with other estates or with foreigners for its own preservation and security, always provided that such alliances not be made against the emperor, the Empire, the public peace, or this treaty. And in every case, they must be made without any prejudice to the oath that binds each of them to the emperor and the Empire.

3. [*The Imperial Diet*.][6] Within six months from the date of this treaty's ratification, the Imperial estates shall assemble at an Imperial Diet, and again thereafter as often as the public interest and necessity shall require. At the first Diet, they shall correct especially the faults of preceding assemblies' decisions. Among the objects of correction should be the manner of electing the King of the Romans, the Imperial capitulation (which ought to be reduced to terms that cannot subsequently be altered), the manner and order for placing one or more of the estates under the ban of the Empire, besides what has been formerly declared in the Imperial constitutions. They shall also treat there the re-establishment of the Imperial Circles[7], the renewal of the Imperial matricula[8], the means of inserting in it the names of such that have been taken out, moderating and lowering the taxes of the Empire, the reformation of policy and law of the fees that are paid to the Imperial Chamber Court, the best manner of forming and instructing the ordinary deputies according to the necessity and advantage of the commonwealth, the true business and duty of the directors of the colleges of the Empire, and other such affairs which cannot be specified here.

4. [*Imperial Free Cities*.] The Imperial Free Cities shall have a valid voice in the general and particular diets, equal to those of the other Imperial estates. Their regalian rights, annual revenues, and liberties and privileges of confiscation and imposing duties may not be touched or meddled with. The same applies to any other rights that they have legally obtained from the emperor and the Empire, or which they have possessed and exercised by a long usage before these present troubles, together with full jurisdiction within their walls and territories. Whatever has been done or attempted to the contrary up till now, namely through reprisals, arrests, stopping up of passages, and other prejudicial acts by private authority during the war, under any pretext whatsoever, or which may afterwards be done or executed without any pretended formality of law, shall remain for all future time null and void and forbidden. For the rest, in the future, all laudable customs, constitutions, and fundamental laws of the Holy Roman Empire shall be strictly kept and observed, and all the confusions and disorders that have crept in during the war shall be abolished. [...]

Article X

1. [*Reparations for the Queen of Sweden*.] Furthermore, since the most Serene Queen of Sweden has demanded that she should be compensated for the restitution of the places occupied by her during this war, and that the Empire's Public Peace be adequately restored, His Imperial Majesty, with the consent of the electors, princes, and Imperial estates and especially of those [directly] concerned, yields to the said most Serene Queen, her heirs and successors, the kings and the kingdom of Sweden, by virtue of the present treaty, the following provinces in full right as a perpetual and immediate fief of the Empire:

2. [*Hither Pomerania and Other Lands to Sweden*.] First, all of Hither Pomerania [...] together with the island of Rügen. [...] In addition, in Further Pomerania, the towns of Stettin, Gartz, Damm, Gollnow, and the island of Wollin, together with the Oder River and the arm of the sea commonly called *das frische Haff*. Likewise the three mouths of the Peene, Swiene, and Divenow [rivers] and the adjacent land on both sides beginning at the royal [Swedish] territory and extending to the Baltic Sea. [...] [*The precise boundaries are to be determined by commissioners appointed for this task*.]

6. [*Port Cities to the Queen of Sweden*.] Second, the emperor, with the consent of the whole Empire, also yields to the Most Serene Queen and her heirs

and successors, the kings and the kingdom of Sweden, as a perpetual and immediate fief of the Empire, the town and port of Wismar together with the fortress of Walfisch and also the bailiwick of Poel (except the villages of Seedorf, Weidendorf, Brandenhusen, and Wangern which belong to the hospital of the Holy Ghost in Lübeck) and that of Neukloster. [...]

7. [*Ecclesiastical Lands to the Queen of Sweden*.] Third, [...] the archbishopric of Bremen and the bishopric of Verden together with the town and bailiwick of Wildeshausen and the whole right that had belonged to the late archbishops of Bremen over the chapter and diocese of Hamburg. [...]

8. [*The City of Bremen to Retain Its Freedoms*.] The town of Bremen, its territory and subjects shall be left without any trouble or hindrance in their present state, their freedoms, and their rights and privileges in ecclesiastical and political matters. [...]

9. [*The Queen of Sweden as Imperial Estate*.] Fourth, the emperor and the Empire receive, based on the account of all the aforesaid provinces and fiefs, the Most Serene Queen and her successors to the crown of Sweden as an immediate Imperial estate. Therefore, the aforesaid queen and the said kings shall henceforth be summoned to the Imperial Diets, along with the other Imperial estates, under the titles of dukes of Bremen, Verden, and Pomerania as well as [the titles] of princes of Rügen and lords of Wismar. [...]

Article XVI

1. [*Enforcement of the Peace*.] As soon as the peace treaty shall have been signed and sealed by the plenipotentiaries and ambassadors, all acts of hostility shall cease, and whatever things have been agreed above shall at the same time be executed and performed on both sides. [...] [*The subsequent paragraphs concern the publication of the peace, the release of prisoners, and the withdrawal of garrisons. The estates of seven Imperial Circles are required to pay* 5,000,000 *Thalers in return for the queen's withdrawal of the Swedish armies from their lands*.]

18. [*Retention of Present Holdings*.] It shall not, for the future or at present, be a detriment to or prejudice against any town that has been taken and kept by one party or the other. [...]

19. [*Dispersal of Armies*.] Finally, the troops and armies of all those who are making war in the Empire shall be disbanded and discharged, and each party shall keep up only as many men in his own dominion as he judges necessary for

his security.

Article XVIII

2. [*The Peace as Imperial Law.*] For the greater strength and security of these articles, the present treaty shall serve as a perpetual law and established sanction of the Empire to be inserted, like other fundamental laws and constitutions of the Empire, into the acts of the next Imperial Diet and into the emperor's electoral capitulation. They shall bind no less the absent than the present, the ecclesiastics as well as the laity, whether Imperial estates or not. They shall be a prescribed rule to be followed for all time by the emperor's councilors and officials, as well as those of other lords, also by all judges and officers of courts of justice.

3. [*Invulnerability of the Peace to Other Laws.*] It never shall be alleged, allowed, or admitted that against this treaty and its clauses and articles, no challenge may be raised on the basis of any law, canon or civil law [...] or agreement, much less on that of the edict of 1629 or the transaction of Prague with its appendices or the concordats with the popes or the interims of the year 1548 or any other temporal or ecclesiastical decree. [...] All exceptions, no matter what basis is alleged, shall equally be invalid. The same applies to all exceptions taken, no matter what they assert or allege. [...]

5. [*Universal Duty to Defend the Peace.*] The peace herein concluded shall remain in force, and all parties in this transaction shall be obliged to defend and protect all and every article of this peace against everyone without distinction of religion. [...]

6. [*Redress for Injured Parties.*] If, nevertheless, for the space of three years the differences cannot be terminated by any of these means, all and every one of those concerned in this treaty shall be obliged to aid the injured party with word and deed, once the party has demonstrated that peaceful means will be successful. [...]

7. [*Prohibition of the Use of Force of Arms to Settle Conflicts.*] No Imperial estate shall be permitted to pursue its rights by force of arms. [...]

(B) Treaty between Emperor Ferdinand III and the King of France, Louis XIV, and their respective allies, Münster (October 14/24, 1648)

In the name of the most Holy and Indivisible Trinity.

Be it known to all and to everyone whom it concerns in any way. Once the strife and hostilities that had been stirred up in the [Holy] Roman Empire increased to such a degree that not only all Germany but also the neighboring kingdoms, especially France, were drawn into them. The ensuing long and cruel war involved, on one side, [...] [Emperor] Ferdinand Ⅱ [...] with his allies and supporters, and, on the other, [...] King Louis ⅩⅢ of France [...] with his allies and supporters. And after their deaths, [it continued] between Ferdinand Ⅲ [...] and King Louis ⅩⅢ and their respective allies and supporters. There ensued a great spilling of Christian blood and the devastation of many provinces. At last it has happened that by the grace of God and the good offices of the Serene Republic of Venice, which during this sad time, when all Christendom has been embroiled in war, has never ceased to counsel for peace and the public good. Finally, thoughts of universal peace have become espoused on both sides. For this purpose and by mutual agreement between the two parties made at Hamburg on December 25/15, 1641, it was decided to hold an assembly of ambassadors, who should gather at Münster and Osnabrück in Westphalia on July 11/1, 1643.

3. [*Peace among the Emperor, the French King, and the Imperial Estates.*] And that a reciprocal amity between the emperor, the Most Christian King, the electors, princes, and estates of the Empire may be maintained so much more firmly and sincerely (to say nothing at present of the article of security, which will be mentioned hereafter), the one shall never assist the present or future enemies of the other under any title or pretence whatsoever, either with arms, money, soldiers, or any sort of ammunition, nor shall anyone who is a member of this pacification suffer any enemy's troops to retire through or sojourn in his country.

[*Burgundian Circle.*] The Burgundian Circle shall be and continue to be a member of the Empire after the disputes between France and Spain comprehended in this treaty shall be terminated. Nevertheless, neither the emperor nor any of the estates of the Empire shall meddle in the current wars between them.

[*Future Conflicts between the Empire and the French Kingdom.*] If, in the future, any dispute arises between these two kingdoms, the reciprocal obligation named above of not aiding each other's enemies shall always continue firm between the Empire and the kingdom of France, yet the estates shall be free to provide help to this kingdom or that outside the boundaries of the [Holy] Roman Empire but still according to the constitutions of the Empire.

4. [*Lorraine.*] The controversy affecting Lorraine shall be referred to arbitrators nominated by both sides or it shall be terminated by a treaty between France and Spain or some other friendly means. [...]

69. [*Protection of the Peace.*] And that the said peace and amity between the emperor and the Most Christian King may be the more corroborated and the public safety better provided for, it has been agreed with the consent, advice, and will of the electors, princes, and estates of the Empire for the benefit of peace.

70. [*Prince-bishoprics of Metz, Toul, and Verdun.*] First, that the chief dominion, right of sovereignty, and all other rights upon the bishoprics of Metz, Toul, and Verdun, and over the cities of that name and their dioceses, particularly over Moyenvick, in the same manner as they formerly belonged to the emperor, shall for the future appertain to the crown of France and shall be irrevocably incorporated with that forever except the right of the metropolitan, which belongs to the archbishopric of Trier.

71. [*Restoration of the Prince-bishop of Verdun.*] Lord Francis, duke of Lorraine, shall be restored to the possession of the bishopric of Verdun as the lawful bishop there. [...]

72. [*Pinerolo.*] Second, the emperor and Empire resign and transfer to the Most Christian King and his successors the right of direct lordship and sovereignty, and all that has belonged or might belong to him and the Holy Roman Empire up to now in Pinerolo.

73. [*Cession of Austrian Rights in Alsace and Breisach.*] Third, the emperor on his own behalf and behalf of the whole most serene House of Austria and also of the Empire resigns all rights, properties, domains, possessions, and jurisdictions, which have up to now belonged to him, the Empire, and the family of Austria, over the city of Breisach, the landgraviate of Upper and Lower Alsace, Sundgau, and the provincial lordship of ten Imperial cities situated in Alsace, namely, Hagenau, Colmar, Schlettstadt, Weissenburg, Landau, Oberehnheim, Rosheim, Münster im St. Gregoriental, Kaysersberg, Türkheim, and of all the villages and other rights which depend on the said landgraviates. One and all there are made over to the Most Christian King and the kingdom of France in the same manner as the city of Breisach [...] nevertheless, with the privileges and liberties granted to the said town formerly by the House of Austria.

74. [*Permanent Transfer of Alsatian Lands to the French Kingdom.*]

Likewise, the said landgraviates of both Alsace and Sundgau and also the Imperial protectorate over the ten [Imperial] cities nominated, and their dependencies as well, all the vassals, subjects, people, towns, boroughs, castles, houses, fortresses, woods, coppices, gold, silver, and other mineral mines, rivers, brooks, pastures, and all the rights, regalia, and appurtenances, without any reserve, shall belong to the Most Christian King and the crown of France and shall be forever incorporated with the kingdom of France with all manner of jurisdiction and sovereignty, without any contradiction from the emperor, the Empire, the House of Austria, or any other. [...]

75. [*Protection of the Catholic Religion in Alsace*.] The Most Christian King shall, nevertheless, be obliged to preserve in each and every one of these districts the Catholic religion as maintained under the princes of Austria and to abolish all innovations that crept in during the war.

76. [*Castle Philippsburg*.][9] Fourth, by the consent of the emperor and the whole Empire, the Most Christian King and his successors shall have perpetual right to keep a garrison in the castle of Philippsburg but limited to such a number of soldiers that they do not give their neighbors a well-founded cause for suspicion, and [this garrison] shall be maintained exclusively at the expense of the crown of France. The passage also shall be open by land and water into the Empire for the king to send soldiers, convoys, and bring necessary things there whenever and as often as it is necessary. [...]

87. [*Liberties of the Prince-bishops of Strasbourg and Basel*.] The Most Christian King shall be bound to leave not only the bishops of Strasbourg and Basel with the city of Strasbourg but also the other estates or orders in the one and the other Alsace that depend immediately upon the [Holy] Roman Empire [...] in the same liberty and possession of the immediacy of the Empire they have enjoyed up to now, in such a way that he cannot pretend any royal superiority over them. [...]

88. [*French Compensation to the Habsburg Ruler*.] Likewise the most Christian King, in compensation for the things made over to him, shall pay the said archduke, Ferdinand Charles, three million French livres on St. John the Baptist's Day [24/14 June] in the following years: 1649, 1650, 1651, [that is] paying each year one third each of the said sum at Basel in good money to the archduke or his deputies. [...]

一、导读

《威斯特伐利亚和约》是1648年神圣罗马帝国皇帝与法国、瑞典以及神圣罗马帝国境内的诸侯邦国签订的条约。《威斯特伐利亚和约》由两个条约构成：一是《威斯特伐利亚和约——神圣罗马帝国皇帝和法兰西国王以及他们各自的同盟者之间的和平条约》，即《明斯特条约》，由序文和128则条款组成；另一是《威斯特伐利亚和约——神圣罗马帝国皇帝和瑞典女王以及他们各自的同盟者之间的和平条约》，即《奥斯纳布鲁克条约》，由序文和17则条款组成。《威斯特伐利亚和约》主要涉及宗教、领土变更、神圣罗马帝国内的邦国权力，以及其他有关战后处理问题。

在宗教事务方面，和约肯定了1555年《奥格斯堡条约》“教随国定”原则的有效性，神圣罗马帝国内各诸侯邦国可自行决定官方宗教，臣民不愿改宗者限期迁出；加尔文教被授予合法地位；和约规定居住在教派混合的自治市的居民可以在不制造任何骚乱或破坏的情况下自由地从事各自的教派活动；和约还有利于天主教徒和新教徒在帝国议会以及帝国其他重要决策机构中实现地位平等。

在领土方面，合约重新确定了当时欧洲的领土变更和划分：瑞典长期以来对波罗的海地区的领土要求在《奥斯纳布鲁克条约》中得以实现，并通过法律条款加以确认；法国国王则对神圣罗马帝国让与的土地拥有绝对的所有权和权威；就德意志境内的诸侯来说，巴拉丁公国被一分为二，信奉天主教的巴伐利亚公爵得到上巴拉丁，并列为神圣罗马帝国第八选帝侯，信奉新教的下巴拉丁维持独立。

在邦国权力方面，合约削弱了哈布斯堡家族对神圣罗马帝国内各诸侯邦国的控制。根据和约，德意志境内的诸侯们获得了独立的领地统治权。《明斯特条约》确认了诸侯自古以来就享有的权利和特权，并不受到任何人干涉，尤其是在宣战、媾和、课税和征兵等涉及帝国事务的重大问题上，邦国都享有投票权，帝国皇帝却无权决定。

《威斯特伐利亚和约》在国际关系理论和国际关系史上具有革命性的意义。在国际关系理论上，国家主权原则在合约中得到体现：以国际会议的方式来解决国家争端；国际法承认的宣告方式被首次明确表达出来，如和约承认瑞士与荷兰独立；确立了主权平等原则和互不干涉原则等。在国际关系史上，该和约奠定了17—18世纪国际关系的基础，被视为近代国际关系的开端。

此外，《威斯特伐利亚和约》在欧洲近代史上具有非常重要的意义，它划定了欧洲大陆各国的国界，改变了欧洲政治力量对比。同时，和约作为欧洲近代早期第一个多边条约，是在主权国家的基础上建立欧洲大陆外交秩序的第一次成功尝试，打破了罗马天主教一统天下的状态，破除了教皇神权下的世界主权论。

二、注释

1. Selected from Tryntje Helfferich (ed.), *The Thirty Years' War: A Documentary History*, Hackett, 2009.

2. N. S.: New Style，指格里高利历，即新历；O. S.: Old Style，指罗马儒略历，即旧历。1582—1752 年，这两种历法同时使用，新教徒使用罗马儒略历，而天主教徒则使用格里高利历，两者相差 10 天。根据罗马儒略历，《威斯特伐利亚条约》在 1684 年 10 月 14 日签订，而根据格里高利历，其签订日期则在 1648 年 10 月 24 日。

3. plenipotentiaries，"全权代表"之意。

4. *New Palatine Electorate*，即新巴拉丁选帝侯。13 世纪，巴伐利亚维特尔斯巴赫王朝分为两大主要支系：巴拉丁支系（Palatine，即文中 Rudolphine line 鲁道夫支系）和巴伐利亚支系（Bavarian，即文中 Wilhelmine line 威廉支系），两大支系共同享有"莱茵巴拉丁伯爵"和"巴伐利亚公爵"称号。宗教改革时，维特尔斯巴赫家族的两个支系在宗教问题上分道扬镳，巴伐利亚支系仍坚持他们传统的天主教信仰，而巴拉丁支系则成了加尔文宗的信徒。在"三十年战争"中双方分别加入不同阵营，并且巴拉丁选帝侯在战争初期担任新教阵营的领袖。"三十年战争"后，由于在战争中忠于神圣罗马帝国皇帝，巴伐利亚公爵被封为第八大选帝侯。

5. ecclesiastical visitors，文中意思为负责探访和纠正当地牧师和教会的神职人员。

6. Imperial Diet，即帝国议会。

7. Imperial Circles，指 1495—1512 年创建的 12 个帝国行政区。

8. Imperial matricula，指帝国税收。

9. *Castle Philippsburg*，即菲利普斯堡，在 1632 年之前被称作乌登海姆（Undenheim），位于莱茵河右岸卡尔斯鲁厄的北部，与第 73 条款中的布赖萨赫一样都划给了法国。

三、问题探讨

1. 结合材料阐述《威斯特伐利亚和约》确立的国家主权原则。
2. 分析《威斯特伐利亚和约》在世界近代历史发展进程中的意义和影响。

四、参考文献

1. 王绳祖：《国际关系史》（第一卷），世界知识出版社 1995 年版。
2. Andreas Osiander, "Sovereignty, International Relations, and the

Westphalian Myth", *International Organization*, vol. 55, 2001.

3. Evan Luard, *The Balance of Power: The System of International Relations*, 1648 - 1815, Macmillan, 1992.

4. Ronald G. Asch, *The Thirty Years' War: The Holy Roman Empire and Europe*, 1618 - 1648, St Martin's Press, 1997.

5. William P. Guthruie, *The Later Thirty Years' War: From the Battle of Wittstock to the Treaty of Westphalia*, Greenwood Press, 2003.

UNIT 10

BILL OF RIGHTS[1]

Whereas the Lords Spiritual and Temporal and Commons assembled at Westminster, lawfully, fully and freely representing all the estates of the people of this realm, did upon the thirteenth day of February in the year of our Lord one thousand six hundred eighty-eight [old style date] present unto their Majesties, then called and known by the names and style of William and Mary, prince and princess of Orange, being present in their proper persons, a certain declaration in writing made by the said Lords and Commons in the words following, viz. :

1. Whereas the late King James the Second, by the assistance of divers evil counsellors, judges and ministers employed by him, did endeavour to subvert and extirpate[2] the Protestant religion and the laws and liberties of this kingdom;

2. By assuming and exercising a power of dispensing with and suspending of laws and the execution of laws without consent of Parliament; By committing and prosecuting divers worthy prelates for humbly petitioning to be excused from concurring to the said assumed power;

3. By issuing and causing to be executed a commission under the great seal[3] for erecting a court called the Court of Commissioners for Ecclesiastical Causes;

4. By levying money for and to the use of the Crown by pretence of prerogative for other time and in other manner than the same was granted by Parliament;

5. By raising and keeping a standing army within this kingdom in time of peace without consent of Parliament, and quartering soldiers contrary to law;

6. By causing several good subjects being Protestants to be disarmed at the same time when papists were both armed and employed contrary to law;

7. By violating the freedom of election of members to serve in Parliament;

8. By prosecutions in the Court of King's Bench[4] for matters and causes cognizable only in Parliament, and by divers other arbitrary and illegal courses;

9. And whereas of late years partial corrupt and unqualified persons have been

returned and served on juries in trials, and particularly divers jurors in trials for high treason which were not freeholders;

10. And excessive bail hath been required of persons committed in criminal cases to elude the benefit of the laws made for the liberty of the subjects;

11. And excessive fines have been imposed;

12. And illegal and cruel punishments inflicted;

13. And several grants and promises made of fines and forfeitures before any conviction or judgment against the persons upon whom the same were to be levied;

14. All which are utterly and directly contrary to the known laws and statutes and freedom of this realm;

And whereas the said late King James the Second having abdicated the government and the throne being thereby vacant, his Highness the prince of Orange (whom it hath pleased Almighty God to make the glorious instrument of delivering this kingdom from popery and arbitrary power) did (by the advice of the Lords Spiritual and Temporal and divers principal persons of the Commons) cause letters to be written to the Lords Spiritual and Temporal being Protestants, and other letters to the several counties, cities, universities, boroughs and cinque ports, for the choosing of such persons to represent them as were of right to be sent to Parliament, to meet and sit at Westminster upon the two and twentieth day of January in this year one thousand six hundred eighty and eight [old style date], in order to such an establishment as that their religion, laws and liberties might not again be in danger of being subverted, upon which letters elections having been accordingly made;

And thereupon the said Lords Spiritual and Temporal and Commons, pursuant to their respective letters and elections, being now assembled in a full and free representative of this nation, taking into their most serious consideration the best means for attaining the ends aforesaid, do in the first place (as their ancestors in like case have usually done) for the vindicating and asserting their ancient rights and liberties declare:

1. That the pretended power of suspending the laws or the execution of laws by regal authority without consent of Parliament is illegal;

2. That the pretended power of dispensing with laws or the execution of laws by regal authority, as it hath been assumed and exercised of late, is illegal;

3. That the commission for erecting the late Court of Commissioners for Ecclesiastical Causes, and all other commissions and courts of like nature, are illegal and pernicious;

4. That levying money for or to the use of the Crown by pretence of prerogative, without grant of Parliament, for longer time, or in other manner than the same is or shall be granted, is illegal;

5. That it is the right of the subjects to petition the king, and all commitments and prosecutions for such petitioning are illegal;

6. That the raising or keeping a standing army within the kingdom in time of peace, unless it be with consent of Parliament, is against law;

7. That the subjects which are Protestants may have arms for their defence suitable to their conditions and as allowed by law;

8. That election of members of Parliament ought to be free;

9. That the freedom of speech and debates or proceedings in Parliament ought not to be impeached or questioned in any court or place out of Parliament;

10. That excessive bail ought not to be required, nor excessive fines imposed, nor cruel and unusual punishments inflicted;

11. That jurors ought to be duly impanelled and returned, and jurors which pass upon men in trials for high treason ought to be freeholders;

12. That all grants and promises of fines and forfeitures of particular persons before conviction are illegal and void;

13. And that for redress of all grievances, and for the amending, strengthening and preserving of the laws, Parliaments ought to be held frequently.

And they do claim, demand and insist upon all and singular the premises as their undoubted rights and liberties, and that no declarations, judgments, doings or proceedings to the prejudice of the people in any of the said premises ought in any wise to be drawn hereafter into consequence or example; to which demand of their rights they are particularly encouraged by the declaration of his Highness the prince of Orange as being the only means for obtaining a full redress and remedy therein.

Having therefore an entire confidence that his said Highness the prince of Orange will perfect the deliverance[5] so far advanced by him, and will still preserve them from the violation of their rights which they have here asserted, and from all other attempts upon their religion, rights and liberties, the said

Lords Spiritual and Temporal and Commons assembled at Westminster do resolve that William and Mary, prince and princess of Orange, be and be declared king and queen of England, France and Ireland and the dominions thereunto belonging, to hold the crown and royal dignity of the said kingdoms and dominions to them, the said prince and princess, during their lives and the life of the survivor to them, and that the sole and full exercise of the regal power be only in and executed by the said prince of Orange in the names of the said prince and princess during their joint lives, and after their deceases the said crown and royal dignity of the same kingdoms and dominions to be to the heirs of the body of the said princess, and for default of such issue to the Princess Anne of Denmark and the heirs of her body, and for default of such issue to the heirs of the body of the said prince of Orange. And the Lords Spiritual and Temporal and Commons do pray the said prince and princess to accept the same accordingly.

And that the oaths hereafter mentioned be taken by all persons of whom the oaths have allegiance and supremacy might be required by law, instead of them; and that the said oaths of allegiance and supremacy be abrogated.

"I, A.B., do sincerely promise and swear that I will be faithful and bear true allegiance to their Majesties King William and Queen Mary. So help me God."

"I, A. B., do swear that I do from my heart abhor, detest and abjure as impious and heretical this damnable doctrine and position, that princes excommunicated or deprived by the Pope or any authority of the see of Rome may be deposed or murdered by their subjects or any other whatsoever. And I do declare that no foreign prince, person, prelate, state or potentate hath or ought to have any jurisdiction, power, superiority, pre-eminence or authority, ecclesiastical or spiritual, within this realm. So help me God."

Upon which their said Majesties did accept the crown and royal dignity of the kingdoms of England, France and Ireland, and the dominions thereunto belonging, according to the resolution and desire of the said Lords and Commons contained in the said declaration.

And thereupon their Majesties were pleased that the said Lords Spiritual and Temporal and Commons, being the two Houses of Parliament, should continue to sit, and with their Majesties' royal concurrence[6] make effectual provision for the settlement of the religion, laws and liberties of this kingdom, so that the same for the future might not be in danger again of being subverted, to which the said Lords Spiritual and Temporal and Commons did agree, and proceed to act accordingly.

Now in pursuance of the premises the said Lords Spiritual and Temporal and Commons in Parliament assembled, for the ratifying, confirming and establishing the said declaration and the articles, clauses, matters and things therein contained by the force of law made in due form by authority of Parliament, do pray that it may be declared and enacted that all and singular the rights and liberties asserted and claimed in the said declaration are the true, ancient and indubitable[7] rights and liberties of the people of this kingdom, and so shall be esteemed, allowed, adjudged, deemed and taken to be; and that all and every the particulars aforesaid shall be firmly and strictly holden and observed as they are expressed in the said declaration, and all officers and ministers whatsoever shall serve their Majesties and their successors according to the same in all time to come.

And the said Lords Spiritual and Temporal and Commons, seriously considering how it hath pleased Almighty God in his marvellous providence and merciful goodness to this nation to provide and preserve their said Majesties' royal persons most happily to reign over us upon the throne of their ancestors, for which they render unto him from the bottom of their hearts their humblest thanks and praises, do truly, firmly, assuredly and in the sincerity of their hearts think, and do hereby recognize, acknowledge and declare, that King James the Second having abdicated the government, and their Majesties having accepted the crown and royal dignity as aforesaid, their said Majesties did become, were, are and of right ought to be by the laws of this realm our sovereign liege lord and lady, king and queen of England, France and Ireland and the dominions thereunto belonging, in and to whose princely persons the royal state, crown and dignity of the said realms with all honours, styles, titles, regalities, prerogatives, powers, jurisdictions and authorities to the same belonging and appertaining are most fully, rightfully and entirely invested and incorporated, united and annexed. And for preventing all questions and divisions in this realm by reason of any pretended titles to the crown, and for preserving a certainty in the succession thereof, in and upon which the unity, peace, tranquility and safety of this nation doth under God wholly consist and depend, the said Lords Spiritual and Temporal and Commons do beseech their Majesties that it may be enacted, established and declared, that the crown and regal government of the said kingdoms and dominions, with all and singular the premises thereunto belonging and appertaining, shall be and continue to their said Majesties and the survivor of them during their lives and the life of the survivor of them, and that the entire, perfect and full exercise of the regal power and government be only in and executed by his Majesty in the names of both their Majesties during their joint lives; and after their deceases the said crown and premises shall be and remain to the heirs of the body of her Majesty, and for default of such issue to her Royal Highness the Princess Anne of Denmark and the heirs of the body of his said Majesty; and thereunto the said Lords Spiritual and Temporal and Commons do in the name of all the people aforesaid most humbly and faithfully submit themselves, their heirs and posterities for ever, and do faithfully promise that they will stand to, maintain and defend their said Majesties, and also the limitation and succession of the crown herein specified and contained, to the utmost of their powers with their lives and estates against all persons whatsoever that shall attempt anything to the contrary.

And whereas it hath been found by experience that it is inconsistent with the safety and welfare of this Protestant kingdom to be governed by a popish prince, or by any king or queen marrying a papist, the said Lords Spiritual and Temporal and Commons do further pray that it may be enacted, that all and every person and persons that is, are or shall be reconciled to or shall hold communion with the see or Church of Rome, or shall profess the popish religion, or shall marry a papist, shall be excluded and be for ever incapable to inherit, possess or enjoy the crown and government of this realm and Ireland and the dominions thereunto belonging or any part of the same, or to have, use or exercise any regal power, authority or jurisdiction within the same; and in all and every such case or cases the people of these realms shall be and are hereby absolved of their allegiance; and the said crown and government shall from time to time descend to and be enjoyed by such person or persons being Protestants as should have inherited and enjoyed the same in case the said person or persons so reconciled, holding communion or professing or marrying as aforesaid were naturally dead; and that every king and queen of this realm who at any time hereafter shall come to and succeed in the imperial crown of this kingdom shall on the first day of the meeting of the first Parliament next after his or her coming to the crown, sitting in his or her throne in the House of Peers in the presence of the Lords and Commons therein assembled, or at his or her coronation before such person or persons who shall administer the coronation oath to him or her at the time of his or her taking the said oath (which shall first happen), make, subscribe and audibly repeat the declaration mentioned in the statute made in the thirtieth year of the reign of King Charles the Second entitled, *An Act for the more effectual preserving the king's person and government by disabling papists from sitting in either House of Parliament*. But if it shall happen that such king or queen upon his or her succession to the crown of this realm shall be under the age of twelve years, then every such king or queen shall make, subscribe and audibly repeat the same declaration at his or her coronation or the first day of the meeting of the first Parliament as aforesaid which shall first happen after such king or queen shall have attained the said age of twelve years.

All which their Majesties are contented and pleased shall be declared, enacted and established by authority of this present Parliament, and shall stand, remain and be the law of this realm for ever; and the same are by their said Majesties, by and with the advice and consent of the Lords Spiritual and Temporal and Commons in Parliament assembled and by the authority of the same, declared, enacted and established accordingly.

一、导读

1689年12月，英国议会通过了《公民权利与自由及王位继承权宣言法令》，简称《权利法案》，经威廉三世（William Ⅲ）和玛丽二世（Mary Ⅱ）共同签署后生效，成为正式的法律条文。《权利法案》是"光荣革命"的重要成果，被看作是英国历史上自《大宪章》以来最重要的法案之一。它将自古以来英国公认的权利和自由以法律的形式固定下来，以此限制国王的权力。《权利法案》的通过标志着英国君主立宪制的初步形成，是英国现代政治制度发展中里程碑式的宪政文件。

《权利法案》的内容分为三个部分：第一部分列举了"光荣革命"前国王詹姆斯二世的种种恶行；第二部分宣布关于权利和自由的13项条款；第三部分规定了王位继承顺序。其中第二部分是《权利法案》的核心，共13条，主要涉及国王和议会的权力。实际上，《权利法案》中所列举的议会权力和民众自由，在17世纪之前就已经作为宪法惯例在英国政治生活中长期存在，并得到历代君主的基本认可和尊重。凭借这些惯例，议会同国王一起构成英国政治的两个权力中心，虽然根据国内外形势变化的需要，权力在两者之间反复倾斜，其重心时而偏向议会，时而偏向国王，但大体上维持着一种平衡，即便是在王权最为强大的都铎王朝时期亦是如此。

不过，自17世纪初斯图亚特王朝入主英格兰后，议会的传统权力开始面临危机，詹姆斯一世和查理一世试图绕过议会，实行君主专制统治，查理一世甚至11年不召开议会，国王与议会冲突是导致英国内战的重要原因之一。1660年，斯图亚特王朝复辟之初，在恢复君主制的同时，议会及其传统权力和地位也得到恢复，在查理二世统治时期，议会和王权之间相互牵制，双方基本权力得到尊重，从某种意义上说，英国政治又回到了正常的发展轨道上。但随着1685年詹姆斯二世继位，国王专断独行，公开进行宗教迫害，议会和王权之间的平衡再次被打破，最终发生了1688年的"光荣革命"。鉴于英国政治传统屡遭破坏，议会于1689年通过《权利法案》，将作为惯例的传统权利和自由写入法律文件，使之得到巩固、强化。因此，《权利法案》最重要的意义并不是提出了一系列议会的权力与民众的自由，而是将这种早已存在的宪政传统以成文法的形式确立下来，以消除君主对议会权力的干扰和破坏。

《权利法案》公布后，国王的法律地位也有了明确的规定：君主必须受制于法律，英国的现代法治原则也由此通过成文法而规定下来。此后，英国议会于1694年通过了《三年法案》，规定每三年必须召开一次议会，每届议会最长任期不得超过三年，从法律上限制了国王随意召集、解散议会的权力；1701年通过的《王位继承法案》被看作是对《权利法案》的补充，从多方面限制了王权，如国王必须信奉国教、未经议会许可不得擅离英伦三岛、大法官任职终身等。这些法案进一步限制了君主权力，确立了英国“议会至上”原则。此外，议会又通过一系列“财政解决”方案，摧毁了国王的财政独立性，削弱了王权，扩大了议会的权力，使议会逐渐成为国家的最高权力机关。

二、注释

1. Selected from Carl Stephenson, Frederick George Marcham（eds.）, *Sources of English Constitutional History: A Selection of Documents from A. D. 600 to the Present*, Harper & Row, 1937.

2. extirpate，“清除”“消灭”的意思。

3. the great seal，“国玺”之意。

4. King's Bench，即“王座法庭”，1875 年司法改革前位于威斯敏斯特的三个中央法庭之一，另外两个是民诉法庭（Court of Common Pleas）和财税法庭（Court of Exchequer）。“王座法庭”享有普通法上的广泛刑事司法管辖权和部分民事管辖权。

5. deliverance，“解放”的意思。

6. concurrence，“同时”之意。

7. indubitable，“不容置疑”的意思。

三、问题探讨

1.《权利法案》从哪些方面限制了君主的权力？

2.《权利法案》在英国政治制度发展进程中的意义。

四、参考文献

1. 钱乘旦、许洁明：《英国通史》，上海社会科学院出版社 2002 年版。

2. 阎照祥：《英国政治制度史》，人民出版社 2012 年版。

3. 程汉大：《英国政治制度史》，中国社会科学出版社 1995 年版。

4. [英] 哈里·狄金森：《1688 年“光荣革命”的革命性问题》，王章辉译、尔玉校，《世界历史》1988 年第 6 期。

5. [英] G. M. 屈威廉：《英国革命：1688—1689》，宋晓东译，商务印书馆 2016 年版。

UNIT 11

DECLARATION OF THE RIGHTS OF MAN AND CITIZEN[1]

The representatives of the French people, constituted as a National Assembly, considering that the ignorance, forgetfulness, or disregard for the rights of man are the sole causes of public misfortunes and the corruption of governments, have resolved to set out, in a solemn declaration, the natural, inalienable[2] and sacred rights of man, so that this declaration, constantly present for all the members of the social body, may ceaselessly remind them of their rights and their duties; so that the acts of the legislative body and those of the executive body, being comparable with the goal of all political institutions, be the more respected for it; and so that the demands of citizens, based henceforth on simple and incontestable principles, may be always directed towards the maintenance of the Constitution and the happiness of all men.

Consequently, the National Assembly, in the presence and under the auspices of the Supreme Being, recognises and declares the following rights of man and of the citizen:

Article 1. Men are born and remain free and equal in rights. Social distinctions may only be based on common usefulness.

Article 2. The goal of every political association is the preservation of man's natural and imprescriptible[3] rights. These rights are liberty, property, security, and resistance to oppression.

Article 3. The principle of all sovereignty resides essentially in the nation. No body or individual may exercise authority that does not expressly emanate from it.

Article 4. Liberty consists in being able to do anything that is not harmful to others. Thus, the only limits to the exercise of the natural rights of each man are those that ensure the enjoyment of the same rights for other members of society.

Only the law may determine these limits.

Article 5. The law has the right only to forbid acts that are harmful to society. Anything that is not forbidden by the law may not be prevented, and no one may be constrained to do what it does not command.

Article 6. The law is the expression of the general will.[4] All citizen, or their representatives, have the right to work solemnly towards its formulation. It must be the same for all, whether it protects or punishes. All citizens, being equal in its eyes, are equally admissible to all public dignities, posts and employment, according to their abilities, and without any distinction other than that of their virtues and their talents.

Article 7. No man may be accused, arrested or detained, other than in those cases determined by the law, and according to the conventions it has prescribed. Those who solicit, expedite or execute arbitrary orders, or have arbitrary orders executed, must be punished; but any citizen who is summoned[5] or apprehended by virtue of the law, must obey immediately; he makes himself guilty through resistance.

Article 8. The law may only establish punishments that are strictly and clearly necessary, and a man may be punished only by virtue of a *law* that is established and promulgated[6] prior to the crime, and legally enforced.

Article 9. All man being presumed innocent until they have been declared guilty, if it is deemed indispensable to arrest a man, any society that is not necessary in the apprehension of his person must be severely repressed by the law.

Article 10. No man may be harassed for his opinions, even religious ones, as long as their manifestation does not trouble the public order established by the law.

Article 11. The free communication of thoughts and opinions is one of the most precious rights of man; thus any citizen may speak, write and print freely, on condition that he will have to answer for the abuse of this freedom in those cases set down by the law.

Article 12. Guaranteeing the rights of man and the citizen necessitates a public force: thus this force is therefore instituted for the benefit of all, and not for the individual use of those to whom it is entrusted.

Article 13. To maintain the public force, and for the administrative costs, a common tax is indispensable; it must be equally divided among all citizens, on the basis of their property.

Article 14. All citizens have the right to observe for themselves, or through their representatives, the need for public taxation, to consent to it freely, to scrutinise its use, and to determine the quota, the basis on which it is assessed, its payment and duration.

Article 15. Society has the right to request an account of his administration from any public agent.

Article 16. Any society in which the guarantee of rights is not ensured, nor the separation of powers established, has no constitution.

Article 17. Property being an inviolable and sacred right, no man may be deprived of it, unless in cases where public necessity, legally recorded, clearly demands it, and on condition of just and prior compensation. The National Assembly, wishing to establish the French Constitution on the principles it has just recognised and declared, irrevocable abolishes those institutions that wounded the liberty and equality of rights.

一、导读

1789 年 8 月 26 日，由制宪会议通过的《人权和公民权利宣言》（简称《人权宣言》），是法国大革命时期颁布的纲领性文件。它在启蒙思想家卢梭、孟德斯鸠等人提出的平等和自然权学说的基础上，宣布个人私有财产神圣不可侵犯，法律面前人人平等，为法国大革命提供了明确的指导思想和坚实的理论基础。1789 年《人权宣言》不仅是法国历史上的第一部人权宣言，也是人类历史上第一部正式的人权宣言，具有重要的历史意义。

首先，1789 年《人权宣言》是对理想中的人权的规范化。该宣言在序文中一针见血地指出："不知人权、忽视人权或轻蔑人权是公众不幸和政府腐败的唯一原因。"宣言第一条就宣称，"在权利方面，人生来是而且始终是自由平等的"；第二条则把自由、财产、安全和反抗压迫宣布为"人的自然的和不可动摇的权利"。1789 年《人权宣言》确切表达了大革命的宗旨，宣布"任何政治结合的目的都在于保存人的自然的和不可动摇的权利"，从而使基本人权原则成为宣言的核心内容。它不仅体现了对人的价值的理性思考，而且反映了反封建的战斗激情，极大地推动了法国大革命的发展。

其次，在国家权力与公民个人权利关系上，1789 年《人权宣言》强调"主权在民"的原则。宣言在第三条中指出，"国家权力来自人民，国家以至任何团体、个人行使国家主权时，其权力立足点是人民"。既然国家的权力是人民赋予的，权力的来源就不是神，从而反驳了王权、贵族特权代表们坚持的君权神授的理论，突出了"主权在民"。

再次，《人权宣言》强调法律是国家的根本，需要通过法律这一工具来保障人民的主权。宣言在第六条明确宣布"法律是公共意志的体现"，"法律面前，所有公民都是平等的"，这种平等包括"全国公民都有权亲自或经由其代表去参与法律的制定"，"法律对所有的人，无论是实施保护或处罚都是一样的"，所有公民"都能平等地按其能力担任一切官职，公共职位和职务，除德行或才能上的差别外，不得有其它差别"。《人权宣言》还体现了在法律面前人人平等的原则，有所谓"罪刑相适应"的条款，即不管是何人，"同样的犯罪处以同样的刑罚，不因人而有所差别"。这一原则的规定，在否定封建阶级的特权，以及争取政治上权利平等方面有着重大意义。

最后，在国家制度方面，1789 年《人权宣言》提出了"分权原则"。宣言第十六条指出："凡权利无保障和分权未确立的社会，就没有宪法。"这里的所谓"分权"就是指"三权分立"。"三权分立"是孟德斯鸠提出来的法国资产阶级国家制度的基本原则，按照孟德斯鸠的理论，立法权应掌握在议会手里，行政权属于世袭的国王，司法权则由选出的常任法官行使，这种分权原则在 1791 年《宪法》中得以体现。根据 1791 年《宪法》的规定，法国为君主立宪国家，立法权属于国民议会，它有制定法律、监督各部部长，以及控制财政、外交和宣战与媾和等大权，是法国最高权力机关；行政权属于国王及各部大臣，国王在登基时必须对宪法宣誓，国王的任何命令必须经各部附署签字才能执行等等，严格限制了国王的权力；司法权属于法院，法官由选举产生，并且是常任制。

1789 年《人权宣言》体现了天赋人权、人人平等的原则，从宪法角度否定了封建等级制度，使资产阶级提倡的“人权”口号不仅深入人心，而且制度化、法律化，以“人权平等”取代了公开的等级特权，以资产阶级的“法治”代替了“朕即国家”的封建专横。它继承和发扬了 17—18 世纪的启蒙思想，并以法律的形式固定下来，不仅对法国大革命，而且对世界其他地区资产阶级革命或改革都产生了广泛影响，推动了很多国家民主思想的发展。

二、注释

1. Selected from Philip G. Dwyer, Peter McPhee (eds.), *The French Revolution and Napoleon: A Sourcebook*, Routledge, 2002.
2. inalienable，“不可剥夺的”的意思。
3. imprescriptible，“不可侵犯的”的意思。
4. general will，文中可以理解为“公意”。
5. summoned，“传唤”“召集”的意思。
6. promulgated，“公布的”“发布的”的意思。

三、问题探讨

1. 1789 年《人权宣言》的颁布对法国大革命有何影响？
2. 结合节选材料，试比较 1689 年英国《权利法案》和 1789 年《人权宣言》。

四、参考文献

1. [法] 马迪厄：《法国革命史》，杨人楩译，商务印书馆 2011 年版。
2. [法] 达尼埃尔·莫尔内：《法国革命的思想起源（1715—1787）》，黄艳红译，上海三联书店 2011 年版。
3. [法] 托克维尔：《旧制度与大革命》，冯棠译，商务印书馆 2012 年版。
4. P. M. Jones, *The French Revolution* 1787 - 1804, Routledge, 2016.
5. William Doyle, *The Oxford History of the French Revolution*, Oxford University Press, 2018.

UNIT 12

FAREWELL ADDRESS[1]

George Washington

Friends and Fellow Citizens:

The period for a new election of a citizen to administer the Executive Government of the United States being not far distant, and the time actually arrived when your thoughts must be employed in designating the person who is to be clothed with that important trust, it appears to me proper, especially as it may conduce to a more distinct expression of the public voice, that I should now apprise you of the resolution I have formed to decline being considered among the number of those out of whom a choice is to be made.

I beg you at the same time to do me the justice to be assured that this resolution has not been taken without a strict regard to all the considerations appertaining to the relation which binds a dutiful citizen to his country; and that in withdrawing the tender of service, which silence in my Situation might imply, I am influenced by no diminution of zeal for your future interest, no deficiency of grateful respect for your past kindness, but am supported by a full conviction that the step is compatible with both.

The acceptance of and continuance hitherto in the office to which your suffrages have twice called me have been a uniform sacrifice of inclination to the opinion of duty and to a deference for what appeared to be your desire. I constantly hoped that it would have been much earlier in my power, consistently with motives which I was not at liberty to disregard, to return to that retirement from which I had been reluctantly drawn. The strength of my inclination to do this previous to the last election had even led to the preparation of an address to declare it to you; but mature reflection on the then perplexed and critical posture of our affairs with foreign nations and the unanimous advice of persons entitled to my confidence impelled me to abandon the idea. I rejoice that the state of your concerns, external as well as internal, no longer renders the pursuit of inclination incompatible with the sentiment of duty or propriety, and am persuaded, whatever partiality may be retained for my services, that in the present circumstances of our country you will not disapprove my determination to retire.

The impressions with which I first undertook the arduous trust were explained on the proper occasion. In the discharge of this trust I will only say that I have, with good intentions, contributed toward the organization and administration of the Government the best exertions of which a very fallible judgment was capable, Not unconscious in the outset of the inferiority of my qualifications, experience in my own eyes, perhaps still more in the eyes of others, has strengthened the motives to diffidence of myself; and every day the increasing weight of years admonishes me more and more that the shade of retirement is as necessary to me as it will be welcome. Satisfied that if any circumstances have given peculiar value to my services they were temporary, I have the consolation[2] to believe that, while choice and prudence invite me to quit the political scene, patriotism does not forbid it.

In looking forward to the moment which is intended to terminate the career of my political life my feelings do not permit me to suspend the deep acknowledgment of that debt of gratitude which I owe to my beloved country for the many honors it has conferred upon me; still more for the steadfast confidence with which it has supported me, and for the opportunities I have thence enjoyed of manifesting my inviolable attachment by services faithful and persevering, though in usefulness unequal to my zeal. If benefits have resulted to our country from these services, let it always be remembered to your praise and as an instructive example in our annals that under circumstances in which the passions, agitated in every direction, were liable to mislead; amidst appearances sometimes dubious; vicissitudes of fortune often discouraging; in situations in which not unfrequently want of success has countenanced the spirit of criticism, the constancy of your support was the essential prop of the efforts and a guaranty of the plans by which they were effected. Profoundly penetrated with this idea, I shall carry it with me to my grave as a strong incitement to unceasing vows that Heaven may continue to you the choicest tokens of its beneficence; that your union and brotherly affection may be perpetual; that the free Constitution which is the work of your hands may be sacredly maintained; that its administration in every department may be stamped with wisdom and virtue; that, in fine, the happiness of the people of these States, under the auspices of liberty, may be made complete by so careful a preservation and so prudent a use of this blessing as will acquire to them the glory of recommending it to the applause, the affection, and adoption of every nation which is yet a stranger to it.

Here, perhaps, I ought to stop. But a solicitude for your welfare which can not end but with my life, and the apprehension of danger natural to that solicitude[3], urge me on an occasion like the present to offer to your solemn contemplation and to recommend to your frequent review some sentiments which are the result of much reflection, of no inconsiderable observation, and which appear to me all important to the permanency of your felicity as a people. These will be offered to you with the more freedom as you can only see in them the disinterested warnings of a parting friend, who can possibly have no personal motive to bias his counsel. Nor can I forget as an encouragement to it your indulgent reception of my sentiments on a former and not dissimilar occasion.

Interwoven as is the love of liberty with every ligament of your hearts, no recommendation of mine is necessary to fortify or confirm the attachment.

The unity of government which constitutes you one people is also now dear to you. It is justly so, for it is a main pillar in the edifice of your real independence, the support of your tranquillity at home, your peace abroad, of your safety, of your prosperity, of that very liberty which you so highly prize. But as it is easy to foresee that from different causes and from different quarters much pains will be taken, many artifices employed, to weaken in your minds the conviction of this truth, as this is the point in your political fortress against which the batteries of internal and external enemies will be most constantly and actively (though often covertly and insidiously) directed, it is of infinite moment that you should properly estimate the immense value of your national union to your collective and individual happiness; that you should cherish a cordial, habitual, and immovable attachment to it; accustoming yourselves to think and speak of it as of the palladium of your political safety and prosperity; watching for its preservation with jealous anxiety; discountenancing whatever may suggest even a suspicion that it can in any event be abandoned, and indignantly frowning upon the first dawning of every attempt to alienate any portion of our country from the rest or to enfeeble the sacred ties which now link together the various parts.

For this you have every inducement of sympathy and interest. Citizens by birth or choice of a common country, that country has a right to concentrate your affections. The name of American, which belongs to you in your national capacity, must always exalt the just pride of patriotism more than any appellation derived from local discriminations. With slight shades of difference, you have the same religion, manners, habits, and political principles. You have in a common cause fought and triumphed together. The independence and liberty you possess are the work of joint councils and joint efforts, of common dangers, sufferings, and successes.

But these considerations, however powerfully they address themselves to your sensibility, are greatly outweighed by those which apply more immediately to your interest. Here every portion of our country finds the most commanding motives for carefully guarding and preserving the union of the whole.

The *North,* in an unrestrained intercourse with the *South,* protected by the equal laws of a common government, finds in the productions of the latter great additional resources of maritime and commercial enterprise and precious materials of manufacturing industry. The *South,* in the same intercourse, benefiting by the same agency of the *North,* sees its agriculture grow and its commerce expand. Turning partly into its own channels the seamen of the *North,* it finds its particular navigation invigorated; and while it contributes in different ways to nourish and increase the general mass of the national navigation, it looks forward to the protection of a maritime strength to which itself is unequally adapted. The *East,* in a like intercourse with the *West,* already finds, and in the progressive improvement of interior communications by land and water will more and more find, a valuable vent for the commodities which it brings from abroad or manufactures at home. The *West* derives from the *East* supplies requisite to its growth and comfort, and what is perhaps of still greater consequence, it must of necessity owe the *secure* enjoyment of indispensable *outlets* for its own productions to the weight, influence, and the future maritime strength of the Atlantic side of the Union, directed by an indissoluble community of interest as *one nation.* Any other tenure by which the *West* can hold this essential advantage, whether derived from its own separate strength or from an apostate and unnatural connection with any foreign power, must be intrinsically precarious.

While, then, every part of our country thus feels an immediate and particular interest in union, all the parts combined can not fail to find in the united mass of means and efforts greater strength, greater resource, proportionably greater security from external danger, a less frequent interruption of their peace by foreign nations, and what is of inestimable value, they must derive from union an exemption from those broils and wars between themselves which so frequently afflict neighboring countries not tied together by the same governments, which their own rivalships alone would be sufficient to produce, but which opposite foreign alliances, attachments, and intrigues would stimulate and imbitter. Hence, likewise, they will avoid the necessity of those overgrown military establishments which, under any form of government, are inauspicious to liberty, and which are to be regarded as particularly hostile to republican liberty. In this sense it is that your union ought to be considered as a main prop of your liberty, and that the love of the one ought to endear to you the preservation of the other.

These considerations speak a persuasive language to every reflecting and virtuous mind, and exhibit the continuance of the union as a primary object of patriotic desire. Is there a doubt whether a common government can embrace so large a sphere? Let experience solve it. To listen to mere speculation in such a case were criminal. We are authorized to hope that a proper organization of the whole, with the auxiliary agency of governments for the respective subdivisions, will afford a happy issue to the experiment. It is well worth a fair and full experiment. With such powerful and obvious motives to union affecting all parts of our country, while experience shall not have demonstrated its impracticability, there will always be reason to distrust the patriotism of those who in any quarter may endeavor to weaken its bands.

In contemplating[4] the causes which may disturb our union it occurs as matter of serious concern that any ground should have been furnished for characterizing parties by *geographical discriminations* — *Northern* and *Southern, Atlantic* and *Western* — *whence* designing men may endeavor to excite a belief that there is a real difference of local interests and views. One of the expedients of party to acquire influence within particular districts is to misrepresent the opinions and aims of other districts. You can not shield yourselves too much against the jealousies and heart-burnings which spring from these misrepresentations[5]; they tend to render alien to each other those who ought to be bound together by fraternal affection. The inhabitants of our Western country have lately had a useful lesson on this head. They have seen in the negotiation by the Executive and in the unanimous ratification by the Senate of the treaty with Spain, and in the universal satisfaction at that event throughout the United States, a decisive proof how unfounded were the suspicions propagated among them of a policy in the General Government and in the Atlantic States unfriendly to their interests in regard to the Mississippi. They have been witnesses to the formation of two treaties that with Great Britain and that with Spain — which secure to them everything they could desire in respect to our foreign relations toward confirming their prosperity. Will it not be their wisdom to rely for the preservation of these advantages on the union by which they were procured? Will they not henceforth be deaf to those advisers, if such there are, who would sever them from their brethren and connect them with aliens?

To the efficacy and permanency of your union a government for the whole is indispensable. No alliances, however strict, between the parts can be an adequate substitute. They must inevitably experience the infractions and interruptions which all alliances in all times have experienced. Sensible of this momentous truth, you have improved upon your first essay by the adoption of a Constitution of Government better calculated than your former for an intimate union and for the efficacious management of your common concerns. This Government, the offspring of our own choice, uninfluenced and unawed, adopted upon full investigation and mature deliberation, completely free in its principles, in the distribution of its powers, uniting security with energy, and containing within itself a provision for its own amendment, has a just claim to your confidence and your support. Respect for its authority, compliance with its laws, acquiescence in its measures, are duties enjoined by the fundamental maxims of true liberty. The basis of our political systems is the right of the people to make and to alter their constitutions of government. But the constitution which at any time exists till changed by an explicit and authentic act of the whole people is sacredly obligatory upon all. The very idea of the power and the right of the people to establish government presupposes the duty of every individual to obey the established government.

All obstructions to the execution of the laws, all combinations and associations, under whatever plausible character, with the real design to direct, control, counteract, or awe the regular deliberation and action of the constituted authorities, are destructive of this fundamental principle and of fatal tendency. They serve to organize faction; to give it an artificial and extraordinary force; to put in the place of the delegated will of the nation the will of a party, often a small but artful and enterprising minority of the community, and, according to the alternate triumphs of different parties, to snake the public administration the mirror of the ill-concerted and incongruous projects of faction rather than the organ of consistent and wholesome plans, digested by common counsels and modified by mutual interests.

However combinations or associations of the above description may now and then answer popular ends, they are likely in the course of time and things to become potent engines by which cunning, ambitious, and unprincipled men will be enabled to subvert the power of the people, and to usurp for themselves the reins of government, destroying. afterwards the very engines which have lifted them to unjust dominion.

Toward the preservation of your Government and the permanency of your present happy state, it is requisite not only that you steadily discountenance irregular oppositions to its acknowledged authority, but also that you resist with care the spirit of innovation upon its principles, however specious the pretexts. One method of assault may be to effect in the forms of the Constitution alterations which will impair the energy of the system, and thus to undermine what can not be directly overthrown. In all the changes to which you may be invited remember that time and habit are at least as necessary to fix the true character of governments as of other human institutions; that experience is the surest standard by which to test the real tendency of the existing constitution of a country; that facility in changes upon the credit of mere hypothesis and opinion exposes to perpetual change, from the endless variety of hypothesis and opinion; and remember especially that for the efficient management of your common interests in a country so extensive as ours a government of as much vigor as is consistent with the perfect security of liberty is indispensable. Liberty itself will find in such a government, with powers properly distributed and adjusted, its surest guardian. It is, indeed, little else than a name where the government is too feeble to withstand the enterprises of faction, to confine each member of the society within the limits prescribed by the laws, and to maintain all in the secure and tranquil enjoyment of the rights of person and property.

I have already intimated[6] to you the danger of parties in the State, with particular reference to the founding of them on geographical discriminations. Let me now take a more comprehensive view, and warn you in the most solemn manner against the baneful effects of the spirit of party generally.

This spirit, unfortunately, is inseparable from our nature, having its root in the strongest passions of the human mind. It exists under different shapes in all governments, more or less stifled, controlled, or repressed; but in those of the popular form it is seen in its greatest rankness and is truly their worst enemy.

The alternate domination of one faction over another, sharpened by the spirit of revenge natural to party dissension, which in different ages and countries has perpetrated the most horrid enormities, is itself a frightful despotism. But this leads at length to a more formal and permanent despotism. The disorders and miseries which result gradually incline the minds of men to seek security and repose in the absolute power of an individual, and sooner or later the chief of some prevailing faction, more able or more fortunate than his competitors, turns this disposition to the purposes of his own elevation on the ruins of public liberty.

Without looking forward to an extremity of this kind (which nevertheless ought not to be entirely out of sight), the common and continual mischiefs of the spirit of party are sufficient to make it the interest and duty of a wise people to discourage and restrain it.

It serves always to distract the public councils and enfeeble the public administration. It agitates the community with ill-rounded jealousies and false alarms; kindles the animosity of one part against another; foments occasionally riot and insurrection. It opens the door to foreign influence and corruption, which find a facilitated access to the government itself through the channels of party passion. Thus the policy and the will of one country are subjected to the policy and will of another.

There is an opinion that parties in free countries are useful checks upon the administration of the government, and serve to keep alive the spirit of liberty. This within certain limits is probably true; and in governments of a monarchical cast patriotism may look with indulgence, if not with favor, upon the spirit of party. But in those of the popular character, in governments purely elective, it is a spirit not to be encouraged. From their natural tendency it is certain there will always be enough of that spirit for every salutary purpose; and there being constant danger of excess, the effort ought to be by force of public opinion to mitigate and assuage it. A fire not to be quenched[7], it demands a uniform vigilance to prevent its bursting into a flame, lest, instead of warming, it should consume.

It is important, likewise, that the habits of thinking in a free country should inspire caution in those entrusted with its administration to confine themselves within their respective constitutional spheres, avoiding in the exercise of the powers of one department to encroach upon another. The spirit of encroachment[8] tends to consolidate the powers of all the departments in one, and thus to create, whatever the form of government, a real despotism. A just estimate of that love of power and proneness to abuse it which predominates in the human heart is sufficient to satisfy us of the truth of this position. The necessity of reciprocal checks in the exercise of political power, by dividing and distributing it into different depositories, and constituting each the guardian of the public weal against invasions by the others, has been evinced by experiments ancient and modern, some of them in our country and under our own eyes. To preserve them must be as necessary as to institute them. If in the opinion of the people the distribution or modification of the constitutional powers be in any particular wrong, let it be corrected by an amendment in the way which the Constitution designates. But let there be no change by usurpation; for though this in one instance may be the instrument of good, it is the customary weapon by which free governments are destroyed. The precedent must always greatly overbalance in permanent evil any partial or transient benefit which the use can at any time yield.

Of all the dispositions and habits which lead to political prosperity, religion and morality are indispensable supports. In vain would that man claim the tribute of patriotism who should labor to subvert these great pillars of human happiness — these firmest props of the duties of men and citizens. The mere politician, equally with the pious man, ought to respect and to cherish them. A volume could not trace all their connections with private and public felicity. Let it simply be asked, Where is the security for property, for reputation, for life, if the sense of religious obligation *desert* the oaths which are the instruments of investigation in courts of justice? And let us with caution indulge the supposition that morality can be maintained without religion. Whatever may be conceded to the influence of refined education on minds of peculiar structure, reason and experience both forbid us to expect that national morality can prevail in exclusion of religious principle.

It is substantially true that virtue or morality is a necessary spring of popular government. The rule indeed extends with more or less force to every species of free government. Who that is a sincere friend to it can look with indifference upon attempts to shake the foundation of the fabric? Promote, then, as an object of primary importance, institutions for the general diffusion of knowledge. In proportion as the structure of a government gives force to public opinion, it is essential that public opinion should be enlightened.

As a very important source of strength and security, cherish public credit. One method of preserving it is to use it as sparingly as possible, avoiding occasions of expense by cultivating peace, but remembering also that timely disbursements to prepare for danger frequently prevent much greater disbursements to repel it; avoiding likewise the accumulation of debt, not only by shunning occasions of expense, but by vigorous exertions in time of peace to discharge the debts which unavoidable wars have occasioned, not ungenerously throwing upon posterity the burthen which we ourselves ought to bear. The execution of these maxims belongs to your representatives; but it is necessary that public opinion should cooperate. To facilitate to them the performance of their duty it is essential that you should practically bear in mind that toward the payment of debts there must be revenue; that to have revenue there must be taxes; that no taxes can be devised which are not more or less inconvenient and unpleasant; that thee intrinsic embarrassment inseparable from the selection of the proper objects (which is always a choice of difficulties), ought to be a decisive motive for a candid construction of the conduct of the Government in making it, and for a spirit of acquiescence in the measures for obtaining revenue which the public exigencies may at any time dictate.

Observe good faith and justice toward all nations. Cultivate peace and harmony with all. Religion and morality enjoin this conduct. And can it be that good policy does not equally enjoin it? It will be worthy of a free, enlightened, and at no distant period a great nation to give to mankind the magnanimous and too novel example of a people always guided by an exalted justice and benevolence. Who can doubt that in the course of time and things the fruits of such a plan would richly repay any temporary advantages which might be lost by a steady adherence to it? Can it be that Providence has not connected the permanent felicity of a nation with its virtue? The experiment, at least, is recommended by every sentiment which ennobles human nature. Alas! is it rendered impossible by its vices?

In the execution of such a plan nothing is more essential than that permanent, inveterate antipathies against particular nations and passionate attachments for others should be excluded, and that in place of them just and amicable feelings toward all should be cultivated. The nation which indulges toward another an habitual hatred or an habitual fondness is in some degree a slave. It is a slave to its animosity or to its affection, either of which is sufficient to lead it astray from its duty and its interest. Antipathy in one nation against another disposes each more readily to offer insult and injury, to lay hold of slight causes of umbrage, and to be haughty and intractable when accidental or trifling occasions of dispute occur.

Hence frequent collisions, obstinate, envenomed, and bloody contests. The nation prompted by ill will and resentment sometimes impels to war the government contrary to the best calculations of policy. The government sometimes participates in the national propensity, and adopts through passion what reason would reject. At other times it makes the animosity of the nation subservient to projects of hostility, instigated by pride, ambition, and other sinister and pernicious motives. The peace often, sometimes perhaps the liberty, of nations has been the victim.

So, likewise, a passionate attachment of one nation for another produces a variety of evils. Sympathy for the favorite nation, facilitating the illusion of an imaginary common interest in cases where no real common interest exists, and infusing into one the enmities of the other, betrays the former into a participation in the quarrels and wars of the latter without adequate inducement or justification. It leads also to concessions to the favorite nation of privileges denied to others, which is apt doubly to injure the nation making the concessions by unnecessarily parting with what ought to have been retained, and by exciting jealousy, ill will, and a disposition to retaliate in the parties from whom equal privileges are withheld; and it gives to ambitions, corrupted, or deluded citizens (who devote themselves to the favorite nation) facility to betray or sacrifice the interests of their own country without odium, sometimes even with popularity, gilding with the appearances of a virtuous sense of obligation, a commendable deference for public opinion, or a laudable zeal for public good the base or foolish compliances of ambition, corruption, or infatuation.

As avenues to foreign influence in innumerable ways, such attachments are particularly alarming to the truly enlightened and independent patriot. How many opportunities do they afford to tamper with domestic factions, to practice the arts of seduction, to mislead public opinion, to influence or awe the public councils! Such an attachment of a small or weak toward a great and powerful nation dooms the former to be the satellite of the latter. Against the insidious wiles of foreign influence (I conjure you to believe me, fellow-citizens) the jealousy of a free people ought to be *constantly* awake, since history and experience prove that foreign influence is one of the most baneful foes of republican government. But that jealousy, to be useful, must be impartial, else it becomes the instrument of the very influence to be avoided, instead of a defense against it. Excessive partiality for one foreign nation and excessive dislike of another cause those whom they actuate to see danger only on one side, and serve to veil and even second the arts of influence on the other. Real patriots who may resist the intrigues of the favorite are liable to become suspected and odious, while its tools and dupes usurp the applause and confidence of the people to surrender their interests.

The great rule of conduct for us in regard to foreign nations is, in extending our commercial relations to have with them as little political connection as possible. So far as we have already formed engagements let them be fulfilled with perfect good faith. Here let us stop.

Europe has a set of primary interests which to us have none or a very remote relation. Hence she must be engaged in frequent controversies, the causes of which are essentially foreign to our concerns. Hence, therefore, it must be unwise in us to implicate ourselves by artificial ties in the ordinary vicissitudes of her politics or the ordinary combinations and collisions of her friendships or enmities.

Our detached and distant situation invites and enables us to pursue a different course. If we remain one people, under an efficient government, the period is not far off when we may defy material injury from external annoyance; when we may take such an attitude as will cause the neutrality we may at any time resolve upon to be scrupulously respected; when belligerent nations, under the impossibility of making acquisitions upon us, will not lightly hazard the giving us provocation; when we may choose peace or war, as our interest, guided by justice, shall counsel.

Why forego the advantages of so peculiar a situation? Why quit our own to stand upon foreign ground? Why, by interweaving our destiny with that of any part of Europe, entangle our peace and prosperity in the toils of European ambition, rivalship, interest, humor, or caprice?

It is our true policy to steer clear of permanent alliances with any portion of the foreign world, so far, I mean, as we are now at liberty to do it; for let me not be understood as capable of patronizing infidelity to existing engagements. I hold the maxim no less applicable to public than to private affairs that honesty is always. the best policy. I repeat, therefore, let those engagements be unwise to extend them.

Taking care always to keep ourselves by suitable establishments on a respectable defensive posture, we may safely trust to temporary alliances for extraordinary emergencies.

Harmony, liberal intercourse with all nations are recommended by policy, humanity, and interest. But even our commercial policy should hold an equal and impartial hand, neither seeking nor granting exclusive favors or preferences; consulting the natural course of things; diffusing and diversifying by gentle means the streams of commerce, but forcing nothing; establishing with powers so disposed, in order to give trade a stable course, to define the rights of our merchants, and to enable the Government to support them, conventional rules of intercourse, the best that present circumstances and mutual opinion will permit, but temporary and liable to be from time to time abandoned or varied as experience and circumstances shall dictate; constantly keeping in view that it is folly in one nation to look for disinterested favors from another; that it must pay with a portion of its independence for whatever it may accept under that character; that by such acceptance it may place itself in the condition of having given equivalents for nominal favors, and yet of being reproached with ingratitude for not giving more. There can be no greater error than to expect or calculate upon real favors from nation to nation. It is an illusion which experience must cure, which a just pride ought to discard.

In offering to you, my countrymen, these counsels of an old and affectionate friend I dare not hope they will make the strong and lasting impression I could wish — that they will control the usual current of the passions or prevent our nation from running the course which has hitherto marked the destiny of nations. But if I may even flatter myself that they may be productive of some partial benefit, some occasional good — that they may now and then recur to moderate the fury of party spirit, to warn against the mischiefs of foreign intrigue, to guard against the impostures of pretended patriotism — this hope will be a full recompense for the solicitude for your welfare by which they have been dictated.

How far in the discharge of my official duties I have been guided by the principles which have been delineated the public records and other evidences of my conduct must witness to you and to the world. To myself, the assurance of my own conscience is that I have at least believed myself to be guided by them.

In relation to the still subsisting war in Europe my proclamation of the 22d of April, 1793, is the index to my plan. Sanctioned[9] by your approving voice and by that of your representatives in both Houses of Congress, the spirit of that measure has continually governed me, uninfluenced by any attempts to deter or divert me from it.

After deliberate examination, with the aid of the best lights I could obtain, I was well satisfied that our country, under all the circumstances of the case, had a right to take, and was bound in duty and interest to take, a neutral position. Having taken it, I determined as far as should depend upon me to maintain it with moderation, perseverance, and firmness.

The considerations which respect the right to hold this conduct it is not necessary on this occasion to detail. I will only observe that, according to my understanding of the matter, that right, so far from being denied by any of the belligerent powers, has been virtually admitted by all.

The duty of holding a neutral conduct may be inferred, without anything more, from the obligation which justice and humanity impose on every nation, in cases in which it is free to act, to maintain inviolate the relations of peace and amity toward other nations.

The inducements of interest for observing that conduct will best be referred to your own reflections and experience. With me a predominant motive has been to endeavor to gain time to our country to settle and mature its yet recent institutions, and to progress without interruption to that degree of strength and consistency which is necessary to give it, humanly speaking, the command of its own fortunes.

Though in reviewing the incidents of my Administration I am unconscious of intentional error, I am nevertheless too sensible of my defects not to think it probable that I may have committed many errors. Whatever they may be, I fervently beseech the Almighty to avert or mitigate the evils to which they may tend. I shall also carry with me the hope that my country will never cease to view them with indulgence, and that, after forty-five years of my life dedicated to its service with an upright zeal, the faults of incompetent abilities will be consigned to oblivion, as myself must soon be to the mansions of rest.

Relying on its kindness in this as in other things, and actuated by that fervent love toward it which is so natural to a man who views in it the native soil of himself and his progenitors for several generations, I anticipate with pleasing expectation that retreat in which I promise myself to realize without alloy the sweet enjoyment of partaking in the midst of my fellow-citizens the benign influence of good laws under a free government — the ever-favorite object of my heart, and the happy reward, as I trust, of our mutual cares, labors, and dangers.

一、导读

乔治·华盛顿（1732—1799），美国独立战争时期的大陆军总司令，率领大陆军赢得了战争胜利。1787 年主持制宪会议，制定了美国宪法，并于 1789 年当选美国第一任总统。华盛顿在连续两任总统届满之后，谢绝了连任总统的提议，退隐田园。1796 年 9 月 17 日，华盛顿在宾夕法尼亚州的费城发表了告别演说。

费城的《美国广告者日报》刊登了华盛顿的《告别演说辞》。这是美国历史上第一份总统告别演说辞。华盛顿在《告别演说辞》的开篇表明自己的退隐决心之后，清楚地表达了他的政治思想和观点：

第一，华盛顿坚决拥护联邦制和政府的统一，因为“它是你们真正独立的主要支柱，也是保证国内安定、国外和平、繁荣以及你们所珍视的自由的基石”。因此，“如果有人企图使我国的一部分脱离其余部分，或削弱现在将各部分连在一起的神圣纽带，在其初现时就应该加以强烈指责”。

第二，华盛顿厌恶政党政治，反对党派之争是其政党政治观点的核心。他认为以地域差别为特征建立起来的党派，是扰乱联邦的重要原因，“它会干扰公众会议并削弱其行政管理能力；引起骚乱和暴动；为外国势力的影响和腐蚀打开方便之门，使之可轻易通过派系倾向的渠道深入到政府中来，从而导致一个国家的政策和意志受制于另一个国家”。在由选举产生的民主政府中，党派精神不应予以鼓励。

第三，华盛顿指出，“宗教和道德是实现政治昌明必不可少的支柱”，政治家应当同虔诚的人一样，尊重并珍惜宗教和道德。他在此处强调了宗教对维护资产阶级统治的重要作用，对此读者应坚持唯物史观，辩论地看待宗教在历史上所起的作用。同时，华盛顿强调“道德是民意所归的政府所必需的原动力”，这条准则可或多或少地适用于每一种类型的自由政府，政府应该促进建立“普及知识的机构”，提高人们的道德。

第四，华盛顿在他的告别演说中反映出美国孤立主义的外交原则。他强调，欧洲的纷争在实质上与美国毫不相干，美国卷入欧洲的政治是极不明智的；美国应当遵循的“最高行动准则”是在发展同外国的贸易关系时，尽可能避免政治上的联系，避免与任何外国订立永久性的同盟。华盛顿虽然没有明确提出“孤立主义”一词，但他将传统的孤立思想上升为国家的基本政策，为美国未来的外交政策制定奠定了基石。

第五，华盛顿以谦逊的态度表达了自己对国家的贡献，承认自己的缺点和错误，并恳请人民的原谅，同时希望自己和其他爱国者一样享受到国家给他们带来的荣耀。

华盛顿的告别演说在当时引起了非常大的反响，被各州报纸转载，感动了整个美国。这篇《告别演说辞》不仅体现了他的爱国情怀，也是他政治经验的总结，对当时和以后美国的政治与外交产生了重大影响。

二、注释

1. Selected from Lewis Copeland, Lawrence W. Lamm (eds.), *The World's Great Speeches*, Dover Publications Inc., 1973.

2. consolation，“安慰”之意。

3. solicitude，“焦虑”“担心”的意思。

4. contemplating，“考虑”“思考”的意思。

5. misrepresentation，意为“歪曲”“误传”。

6. intimated，“向……暗示”之意。

7. quench，“熄灭”“结束”的意思。

8. encroachment，“入侵”“侵犯”的意思。

9. sanctioned，“制裁”的意思。

三、问题探讨

1. 结合材料，概述美国早期政治制度的特点。

2. 华盛顿在告别演说中向美国人民提出了哪些忠告?

四、参考文献

1. 李剑鸣：《美国的奠基时代，1585—1775》，中国人民大学出版社 2011 年版。

2. 王玮、戴超武：《美国外交思想史》，人民出版社 2007 年版。

3. [美] 乔治·华盛顿：《华盛顿选集》，聂崇信等译，商务印书馆 2012 年版。

4. [美] 戈登·S. 伍德：《美利坚共和国的缔造，1776—1787》，朱妍兰译，译林出版社 2016 年版。

5. [美] 理查德·霍夫施塔特：《美国政治传统及其缔造者》，崔永禄、王忠和译，商务印书馆 2010 年版。

UNIT 13

THE FUTURE RESULTS OF BRITISH RULE IN INDIA[1]

Carl Marx

London, Friday, July 22, 1853

I propose in this letter to conclude my observations on India.

How came it that English supremacy was established in India? The paramount power of the Great Mogul[2] was broken by the Mogul Viceroys. The power of the Viceroys was broken by the Mahrattas[3]. The power of the Mahrattas was broken by the Afghans, and while all were struggling against all, the Briton rushed in and was enabled to subdue them all. A country not only divided between Mahommedan and Hindoo, but between tribe and tribe, between caste and caste; a society whose framework was based on a sort of equilibrium, resulting from a general repulsion and constitutional exclusiveness between all its members. Such a country and such a society, were they not the predestined prey of conquest? If we knew nothing of the past history of Hindostan, would there not be the one great and incontestable fact, that even at this moment India is held in English thraldom by an Indian army maintained at the cost of India? India, then, could not escape the fate of being conquered, and the whole of her past history, if it be anything, is the history of the successive conquests she has undergone. Indian society has no history at all, at least no known history. What we call its history, is but the history of the successive intruders who founded their empires on the passive basis of that unresisting and unchanging society. The question, therefore, is not whether the English had a right to conquer India, but whether we are to prefer India conquered by the Turk, by the Persian, by the Russian, to India conquered by the Briton.

England has to fulfill a double mission in India: one destructive, the other regenerating — the annihilation[4] of old Asiatic society, and the laying the material foundations of Western society in Asia.

Arabs, Turks, Tartars[5], Moguls, who had successively overrun India, soon became *Hindooized*, the barbarian conquerors being, by an eternal law of history, conquered themselves by the superior civilization of their subjects. The British were the first conquerors superior, and therefore, inaccessible to Hindoo civilization. They destroyed it by breaking up the native communities, by uprooting the native industry, and by levelling all that was great and elevated in the native society. The historic pages of their rule in India report hardly anything beyond that destruction. The work of regeneration hardly transpires through a heap of ruins. Nevertheless it has begun.

The political unity of India, more consolidated, and extending farther than it ever did under the Great Moguls, was the first condition of its regeneration. That unity, imposed by the British sword, will now be strengthened and perpetuated by the electric telegraph. The native army, organized and trained by the British drill-sergeant, was the *sine qua non*[6] of Indian self-emancipation, and of India ceasing to be the prey of the first foreign intruder. The free press, introduced for the first time into Asiatic society, and managed principally by the common offspring of Hindoos and Europeans, is a new and powerful agent of reconstruction. The Zemindari[7] and Ryotwar[8] themselves, abominable as they are, involve two distinct forms of private property in land — the great desideratum of Asiatic society. From the Indian natives, reluctantly and sparingly educated at Calcutta, under English superintendence, a fresh class is springing up, endowed with the requirements for government and imbued with European science. Steam has brought India into regular and rapid communication with Europe, has connected its chief ports with those of the whole south-eastern ocean, and has revindicated it from the isolated position which was the prime law of its stagnation. The day is not far distant when, by a combination of railways and steam-vessels, the distance between England and India, measured by time, will be shortened to eight days, and when that once fabulous country will thus be actually annexed to the Western world.

The ruling classes of Great Britain have had, till now, but an accidental, transitory and exceptional interest in the progress of India. The aristocracy wanted to conquer it, the moneyocracy[9] to plunder it, and the millocracy to undersell it. But now the tables are turned. The millocracy have discovered that the transformation of India into a reproductive country has become of vital importance to them, and that, to that end, it is necessary, above all, to gift her with means of irrigation and of internal communication. They intend now drawing a net of railroads over India. And they will do it. The results must be inappreciable.

It is notorious that the productive powers of India are paralysed by the utter want of means for conveying and exchanging its various produce. Nowhere, more than in India, do we meet with social destitution in the midst of natural plenty, for want of the means of exchange. It was proved before a Committee of the British House of Commons, which sat in 1848, that

"when grain was selling from 6/ to 8/ a quarter at Khandesh, it was sold at 64/ to 70/ at Poona, where the people were dying in the streets of famine, without the possibility of gaining supplies from Khandesh, because the clay-roads were impracticable."

The introduction of railroads may be easily made to subserve agricultural purposes by the formation of tanks, where ground is required for embankment, and by the conveyance of water along the different lines. Thus irrigation, the *sine qua non* of farming in the East, might be greatly extended, and the frequently recurring local famines, arising from the want of water, would be averted. The general importance of railways, viewed under this head, must become evident, when we remember that irrigated lands, even in the districts near Ghauts, pay three times as much in taxes, afford ten or twelve times as much employment, and yield twelve or fifteen times as much profit, as the same area without irrigation.

Railways will afford the means of diminishing the amount and the cost of the military establishments. Col. Warren, Town Major of the Fort St. William[10], stated before a Select Committee of the House of Commons:

"The practicability of receiving intelligence from distant parts of the country, in as many hours as at present it requires days and even weeks, and of sending instructions, with troops and stores, in the more brief period, are considerations which cannot be too highly estimated. Troops could be kept at more distant and healthier stations than at present, and much loss of life from sickness would by this means be spared. Stores could not to the same extent be required at the various dépôts, and the loss by decay, and the destruction incidental to the climate, would also be avoided. The number of troops might be diminished in direct proportion to their effectiveness."

We know that the municipal organization and the economical basis of the village communities has been broken up, but their worst feature, the dissolution of society into stereotype and disconnected atoms, has survived their vitality. The village isolation produced the absence of roads in India, and the absence of roads perpetuated the village isolation. On this plan a community existed with a given scale of low conveniences, almost without intercourse with other villages, without the desires and efforts indispensable to social advance. The British having broken up this self-sufficient *inertia* of the villages, railways will provide the new want of communication and intercourse. Besides,

"one of the effects of the railway system will be to bring into every village affected by it such knowledge of the contrivances and appliances of other countries, and such means of obtaining them, as will first put the hereditary and stipendiary village artisanship of India to full proof of its capabilities, and then supply its defects."

I know that the English millocracy intend to endow India with railways with the exclusive view of extracting at diminished expenses the cotton and other raw materials for their manufactures. But when you have once introduced machinery into the locomotion of a country, which possesses iron and coals, you are unable to withhold it from its fabrication. You cannot maintain a net of railways over an immense country without introducing all those industrial processes necessary to meet the immediate and current wants of railway locomotion, and out of which there must grow the application of machinery to those branches of industry not immediately connected with railways. The railway-system will therefore become, in India, truly the forerunner of modern industry. This is the more certain as the Hindoos are allowed by British authorities themselves to possess particular aptitude for accommodating themselves to entirely new labor, and acquiring the requisite knowledge of machinery. Ample proof of this fact is afforded by the capacities and expertness of the native engineers in the Calcutta mint, where they have been for years employed in working the steam machinery, by the natives attached to the several steam engines in the Burdwan coal districts, and by other instances. Mr. Campbell himself, greatly influenced as he is by the prejudices of the East India Company, is obliged to avow

"that the great mass of the Indian people possesses a great *industrial energy*, is well fitted to accumulate capital, and remarkable for a mathematical clearness of head, and talent for figures and exact sciences." "Their intellects," he says, "are excellent."

Modern industry, resulting from the railway system, will dissolve the hereditary divisions of labor, upon which rest the Indian castes, those decisive impediments to Indian progress and Indian power.

All the English bourgeoisie may be forced to do will neither emancipate nor materially mend the social condition of the mass of the people, depending not only on the development of the productive powers, but on their appropriation by the people. But what they will not fail to do is to lay down the material premises for both. Has the bourgeoisie ever done more? Has it ever effected a progress without dragging individuals and people through blood and dirt, through misery and degradation?

The Indians will not reap the fruits of the new elements of society scattered among them by the British bourgeoisie, till in Great Britain itself the now ruling classes shall have been supplanted by the industrial proletariat, or till the Hindoos themselves shall have grown strong enough to throw off the English yoke altogether. At all events, we may safely expect to see, at a more or less remote period, the regeneration of that great and interesting country, whose gentle natives are, to use the expression of Prince Soltykov, even in the most inferior classes, "*plus fins et plus adroits que les Italiens*," whose submission even is counterbalanced by a certain calm nobility, who, notwithstanding their natural langor, have astonished the British officers by their bravery, whose country has been the source of our languages, our religions, and who represent the type of the ancient German in the Jat[11], and the type of the ancient Greek in the Brahmin[12].

I cannot part with the subject of India without some concluding remarks.

The profound hypocrisy and inherent barbarism of bourgeois civilization lies unveiled before our eyes, turning from its home, where it assumes respectable forms, to the colonies, where it goes naked. They are the defenders of property, but did any revolutionary party ever originate agrarian revolutions like those in Bengal, in Madras, and in Bombay? Did they not, in India, to borrow an expression of that great robber, Lord Clive[13] himself, resort to atrocious extortion, when simple corruption could not keep pace with their rapacity? While they prated in Europe about the inviolable sanctity of the national debt, did they not confiscate in India the dividends of the rajahs[14], who had invested their private savings in the Company's own funds? While they combatted the French revolution under the pretext of defending "our holy religion," did they not forbid, at the same time, Christianity to be propagated in India, and did they not, in order to make money out of the pilgrims streaming to the temples of Orissa and Bengal, take up the trade in the murder and prostitution perpetrated in the temple of Juggernaut? These are the men of "Property, Order, Family, and Religion."

The devastating effects of English industry, when contemplated with regard to India, a country as vast as Europe, and containing 150 millions of acres, are palpable and confounding. But we must not forget that they are only the organic results of the whole system of production as it is now constituted. That production rests on the supreme rule of capital. The centralization of capital is essential to the existence of capital as an independent power. The destructive influence of that centralization upon the markets of the world does but reveal, in the most gigantic dimensions, the inherent organic laws of political economy now at work in every civilized town. The bourgeois period of history has to create the material basis of the new world — on the one hand universal intercourse founded upon the mutual dependency of mankind, and the means of that intercourse; on the other hand the development of the productive powers of man and the transformation of material production into a scientific domination of natural agencies. Bourgeois industry and commerce create these material conditions of a new world in the same way as geological revolutions have created the surface of the earth. When a great social revolution shall have mastered the results of the bourgeois epoch, the market of the world and the modern powers of production, and subjected them to the common control of the most advanced peoples, then only will human progress cease to resemble that hideous, pagan idol, who would not drink the nectar but from the skulls of the slain.

一、导读

马克思的《不列颠在印度统治的未来结果》一文，写于 1853 年 7 月 22 日，载于 1853 年 8 月 8 日《纽约每日论坛报》第 3840 号，是马克思关于殖民主义在印度统治的经典论述。马克思在文中写道："英国在印度要完成的双重使命：一个是破坏性的使命，即消灭旧的亚洲式的社会；另一个是建设性的使命，即在亚洲为西方式的社会奠定物质基础。"而"殖民主义双重使命"说的提出，对我们辩证地分析殖民主义在印度乃至在东方的殖民统治及其对东方国家社会历史的影响都具有十分重要的意义，是我们分析殖民主义历史地位的指导思想和理论基础。

马克思认为，由于英国摧毁了印度传统的农业和手工业，从而破坏了农村公社和种姓制度相结合的封建体制的经济基础，不但打破了印度社会停滞孤立的状态，而且为整个印度社会的发展提供了众多物质条件。因此，对古老的印度而言，被殖民统治具有深远的意义，即英国殖民者充当了推动印度社会发展的"不自觉的工具"。

马克思认为，印度作为"一无抵抗，二无变化"的社会注定要成为"征服者的战利品"，但与以往其他侵略者不同，英国作为比印度高级的文明，其殖民统治将有着改造和提升印度文明的深远意义。在之前发表的《不列颠在印度的殖民统治》一文中，马克思就指出英国先是摧毁了作为印度社会结构枢纽的纺织业，继而破坏作为基础社会结构的自给自足的传统公社，英国殖民者无疑已经抽掉了印度传统社会最重要的基石，在亚洲造成了一场前所未闻的、最大的，也是唯一的一次社会革命。

除了指出英国对印度传统的生产分工方式的破坏与重建外，马克思在《不列颠在印度统治的未来结果》一文中还着重分析了现代交通——铁路的建设给印度社会带来的深远意义。现代铁路将印度广袤的土地连接起来，大大降低了村庄与村庄之间交通往来的难度，因此将极大地破坏印度各村庄从前那种相互隔绝、呈原子状零星分布的状态，为社会内部的往来提供了无数便利。因而，铁路系统的建设在很大程度上促进了当地工业水平的提高，直接推动了印度工业化进程。

之后，随着对殖民主义和殖民地传统社会认识的不断加深，马克思对殖民主义的批判也愈发严厉，认为残酷的殖民统治破坏了非西方社会发展的正常条件。比如，1877 年马克思在给俄国女革命家维·伊·查苏利奇的回信中指出，"英国以野蛮手段消灭了印度的土地公有制……他们得到的结果不过是破坏了当地的农业，使荒年更加频繁，灾难更加严重，他们不是使当地人前进，而是使他们后退"。

二、注释

1. Selected from Karl Marx & Frederick Engels, *Collected Worked*, Vol. 12, International Publishers, 1979.

2. Great Mogul，即“大莫卧儿”，1526 年巴布尔在印度北部建立了伊斯兰教国家大莫卧儿帝国，“大莫卧儿”即是这个王朝的名称。

3. Mahrattas，即马拉提人，印度境内居住在德干高原西北部地区的一个部族。从 17 世纪中叶起，马拉提人就武装反对莫卧儿王朝的异族统治，他们沉重地打击了大莫卧儿帝国，并加速了它的崩溃。

4. annihilation，文中意思为“消灭”“灭绝”。

5. Tartars，即鞑靼人。

6. *sine qua non*，意为“必要条件”。

7. Zemindari，汉译“柴明达尔”。柴明达尔在莫卧儿帝国时代是指被征服的印度教徒中的封建领主。统治者通过作为中间人的柴明达尔向农民征收田赋的制度被称为柴明达尔制。

8. Ryotwar，汉译“莱特瓦尔制”。“莱特”即印度农民，以莱特为对象确定地权和应交田赋的数额，是英国殖民当局在印度实行的一种田赋制度。

9. moneyocracy，即“金融寡头”。

10. Fort St. William，指圣威廉堡，是加尔各答的一个英国城堡，建于 1696 年，为纪念当时英国国王奥伦治的威廉三世而命名。英国人在 1757 年征服孟加拉以后，把政府机关设在这个城堡里，城堡的名字被用来指“孟加拉管区政府”，后来就指“印度英政府”。

11. Jat，汉译“贾特”，是印度北部和巴基斯坦的传统农民社区群体，在 17 世纪曾多次举行起义，反对外来的莫卧儿封建主的统治。

12. Brahmin，汉译“婆罗门”，即印度古代的僧侣贵族，印度的第一种姓，世代以祭祀、诵经（吠陀经）、传教为业。

13. Lord Clive，即罗伯特·克莱武，英国殖民者，孟加拉省督（1758—1760、1765—1767）。早年参加东印度公司与迈索尔在印度的争霸斗争。1757 年“普拉西战役”后，建立了东印度公司对孟加拉的统治。

14. rajahs，汉译“拉贾”，印度王公的称号。

三、问题探讨

1. 英国在印度主要采取哪些殖民统治措施？

2. 英国的殖民统治为印度的社会发展带来了哪些影响？

四、参考文献

1. 罗荣渠：《现代化新论》，商务印书馆 2002 年版。

2. 林承节：《殖民统治时期的印度史》，北京大学出版社 2004 年版。

3. [美] 爱德华·萨义德：《东方学》，王宇根译，生活·读书·新知三联书店 2007 年版。

4. D. K. Fieldhouse, *Colonialism* 1870 - 1945: *An Introduction*, Palgrave Macmillan, 1981.

5. Karl. Marx, *"The British Rule in India"*, in *Karl Marx & Frederick Engels, Collected Worked*, Vol. 12, International Publishers, 1979.

UNIT 14

DECLARATION OF INDEPENDENCE[1]

Thomas Jefferson

The unanimous Declaration of the thirteen united States of America, when in the Course of human events, it becomes necessary for one people to dissolve the political bands which have connected them with another, and to assume among the powers of the earth, the separate and equal station to which the Laws of Nature and of Nature's God entitle them, a decent respect to the opinions of mankind requires that they should declare the causes which impel them to the separation.

We hold these truths to be self-evident, that all men are created equal, that they are endowed by their Creator with certain unalienable Rights, that among these are Life, Liberty and the pursuit of Happiness. — That to secure these rights, Governments are instituted among Men, deriving their just powers from the consent of the governed, — That whenever any Form of Government becomes destructive of these ends, it is the Right of the People to alter or to abolish it, and to institute new Government, laying its foundation on such principles and organizing its powers in such form, as to them shall seem most likely to effect their Safety and Happiness. Prudence, indeed, will dictate that Governments long established should not be changed for light and transient causes; and accordingly all experience hath shewn, that mankind are more disposed to suffer, while evils are sufferable, than to right themselves by abolishing the forms to which they are accustomed. But when a long train of abuses and usurpations, pursuing invariably the same Object evinces a design to reduce them under absolute Despotism, it is their right, it is their duty, to throw off such Government, and to provide new Guards for their future security. — Such has been the patient sufferance of these Colonies; and such is now the necessity which constrains them to alter their former Systems of Government.

The history of the present King of Great Britain[2] is a history of repeated injuries and usurpations, all having in direct object the establishment of an absolute Tyranny over these States. To prove this, let Facts be submitted to a candid world.

He has refused his Assent to Laws, the most wholesome and necessary for the public good.

He has forbidden his Governors to pass Laws of immediate and pressing importance, unless suspended in their operation till his Assent should be obtained; and when so suspended, he has utterly neglected to attend to them.

He has refused to pass other Laws for the accommodation of large districts of people, unless those people would relinquish the right of Representation in the Legislature, a right inestimable to them and formidable to tyrants only.

He has called together legislative bodies at places unusual, uncomfortable, and distant from the depository of their public Records, for the sole purpose of fatiguing them into compliance with his measures.

He has dissolved Representative Houses repeatedly, for opposing with manly firmness his invasions on the rights of the people.

He has refused for a long time, after such dissolutions, to cause others to be elected; whereby the Legislative powers, incapable of Annihilation, have returned to the People at large for their exercise; the State remaining in the mean time exposed to all the dangers of invasion from without, and convulsions within.

He has endeavoured to prevent the population of these States; for that purpose obstructing the Laws for Naturalization of Foreigners; refusing to pass others to encourage their migrations hither, and raising the conditions of new Appropriations of Lands.

He has obstructed the Administration of Justice, by refusing his Assent to Laws for establishing Judiciary powers.

He has made Judges dependent on his Will alone, for the tenure of their offices, and the amount and payment of their salaries.

He has erected a multitude of New Offices, and sent hither swarms of Officers to harrass our people, and eat out their substance.

He has kept among us, in times of peace, Standing Armies[3] without the Consent of our legislatures.

He has affected to render the Military independent of and superior to the Civil power.

He has combined with others to subject us to a jurisdiction foreign to our constitution, and unacknowledged by our laws; giving his Assent to their Acts of pretended Legislation:

For Quartering large bodies of armed troops among us:

For protecting them, by a mock Trial, from punishment for any Murders which they should commit on the Inhabitants of these States:

For cutting off our Trade with all parts of the world:

For imposing Taxes on us without our Consent:

For depriving us in many cases, of the benefits of Trial by Jury:

For transporting us beyond Seas to be tried for pretended offences:

For abolishing the free System of English Laws in a neighbouring Province, establishing therein an Arbitrary government, and enlarging its Boundaries so as to render it at once an example and fit instrument for introducing the same absolute rule into these Colonies:

For taking away our Charters, abolishing our most valuable Laws, and altering fundamentally the Forms of our Governments:

For suspending our own Legislatures, and declaring themselves invested with power to legislate for us in all cases whatsoever.

He has abdicated Government here, by declaring us out of his Protection and waging War against us.

He has plundered our seas, ravaged our Coasts, burnt our towns, and destroyed the lives of our people.

He is at this time transporting large Armies of foreign Mercenaries to compleat the works of death, desolation and tyranny, already begun with circumstances of Cruelty & Perfidy scarcely paralleled in the most barbarous ages, and totally unworthy the Head of a civilized nation.

He has constrained our fellow Citizens taken Captive on the high Seas to bear Arms against their Country, to become the executioners of their friends and Brethren, or to fall themselves by their Hands.

He has excited domestic insurrections amongst us, and has endeavoured to bring on the inhabitants of our frontiers, the merciless Indian Savages, whose known rule of warfare, is an undistinguished destruction of all ages, sexes, and conditions.

In every stage of these Oppressions We have Petitioned for Redress in the most humble terms: Our repeated Petitions have been answered only by repeated injury. A Prince whose character is thus marked by every act which may define a Tyrant, is unfit to be the ruler of a free people.

Nor have We been wanting in attentions to our Brittish brethren. We have warned them from time to time of attempts by their legislature to extend an unwarrantable jurisdiction over us. We have reminded them of the circumstances of our emigration and settlement here. We have appealed to their native justice and magnanimity, and we have conjured them by the ties of our common kindred to disavow these usurpations, which, would inevitably interrupt our connections and correspondence. They too have been deaf to the voice of justice and of consanguinity. We must, therefore, acquiesce in the necessity, which denounces our Separation, and hold them, as we hold the rest of mankind, Enemies in War, in Peace Friends.

We, therefore, the Representatives of the united States of America, in General Congress, Assembled, appealing to the Supreme Judge of the world for the rectitude of our intentions, do, in the Name, and by Authority of the good People of these Colonies, solemnly publish and declare, That these United Colonies are, and of Right ought to be Free and Independent States; that they are Absolved from all Allegiance to the British Crown, and that all political connection between them and the State of Great Britain, is and ought to be totally dissolved; and that as Free and Independent States, they have full Power to levy War, conclude Peace, contract Alliances, establish Commerce, and to do all other Acts and Things which Independent States may of right do. And for the support of this Declaration, with a firm reliance on the protection of divine Providence[4], we mutually pledge to each other our Lives, our Fortunes and our sacred Honor.

一、导读

《独立宣言》是美国独立战争期间，由托马斯·杰斐逊（Thomas Jefferson）起草、第二届大陆会议通过的一份有关美国建国的纲领性文件，于1776年7月4日发表。它声称北美13个殖民地从此脱离英国的统治，并郑重宣告美利坚合众国成立。7月4日因此成为美国的国庆日。

《独立宣言》最直接的资料来源是1776年6月分别由托马斯·杰斐逊起草的《弗吉尼亚宪法序言》和乔治·梅森（George Mason）起草的《弗吉尼亚权利宣言》。这两份文件中的理念和短语在《独立宣言》中都有呈现。此外，英国的《权利法案》（1689年）、苏格兰的《阿布罗斯宣言》（1320年）和荷兰的《誓绝法案》（1581年）也是杰斐逊起草宣言时的范本。《独立宣言》的政治哲学来源于17、18世纪欧洲启蒙思想家所宣扬的天赋人权、社会契约、三权分立等思想，特别是英国启蒙思想家约翰·洛克的“自然权利”和“社会契约”思想。

《独立宣言》由四部分组成：第一部分为前言，阐述了宣言的目的；第二部分阐述天赋人权和政治体制思想；第三部分历数时任英国国王乔治三世压迫北美殖民地人民的条条罪状；第四部分，也就是宣言的最后一部分，宣告美利坚独立。

1776年7月4日，大陆会议决议采用该宣言。宣言的手写初稿由会议主席约翰·汉考克（John Hancock）与秘书查尔斯·汤姆森（Charles Thomson）签署后，即送往数个街口外的约翰·当列普（John Dunlap）印刷厂印制，当晚即印出150～200份的印刷本，今称“当列普单面印刷版”（Dunlap Broadside）。其中的一份于7月6日送达乔治·华盛顿手中，他于7月9日对驻扎纽约的部队宣读。今天尚存的25份“当列普单面印刷版”为宣言现存的最古老版本，手写原稿已遗失。

1776年7月19日，大陆会议裁示，手抄誊录一份印刷版的宣言以供与会代表签署。这份抄本的原稿由提摩西·梅拉克（Timothy Matlack）在议会秘书的协助下，大字正体誊录而成。大部分与会代表于1776年8月2日，依据各人所代表的殖民州之地理位置，由北而南排序签署宣言。数名代表因未出席会议，于日后补行签署。其中有两名代表没有签署，由后来加入大陆会议的代表允获补签，最终共有56名代表签署本宣言。这份抄本的原稿现存放于华盛顿特区的美国国家档案馆。

《独立宣言》所包含的资产阶级民主原则成为美国人民争取人权、平等、民主的指南，也成为美国政治家治国的基本政治哲学。1848年，在美国第一届妇女大会——塞尼卡福尔斯会议上，美国妇女以此为蓝本，通过了《美国妇女独立宣言》，公开提出“人人生而平等”（all men and all women are created equal），为女性争取权利；正是秉承“人人平等”的理念，1862年，亚伯拉罕·林肯

(Abraham Lincoln) 总统签署了《解放黑奴宣言》，给予美国黑人部分法律上的平等权利，并且在“葛底斯堡演说”中，将《独立宣言》中“政府来自于人民，政府的正当权力是经被统治者同意所授予的”表述引申为“政府来自于人民、依靠人民，也是为了人民”（of the people，by the people，for the people）；1962 年，马丁·路德·金（Martin Luther King）在其著名演说《我有一个梦》（I Have a Dream）中，借助《独立宣言》大声疾呼，“我梦想有一天，这个国家会站立起来，真正实现其信条的真谛：‘我们认为这些真理是不言而喻的：人人生而平等’。”从而掀起了一场轰轰烈烈的民权运动。

在美国之外，《独立宣言》也产生了巨大影响，它激励了法国《人权和公民权宣言》的诞生；它还是 19 世纪上半叶欧洲、拉丁美洲、非洲（利比里亚）和大洋洲（新西兰）许多《独立宣言》的主要蓝本。美国《独立宣言》自发表以来，其中所体现的原则一直在全世界为人传诵，因此，它被马克思称为人类历史上第一部人权宣言。

二、注释

1. Selected from *The Constitution of the United States and the Declaration of Independence*, Racehorse, 2016.
2. the present King of Great Britain，指当时的英国国王乔治三世（George Ⅲ）。
3. Standing Armies，“常备军”之意。
4. Providence，“上帝”“神”之意。

三、问题探讨

1. 如何理解《独立宣言》阐述的资产阶级民主原则?
2. 试评价《独立宣言》列举的乔治三世的反民主原则和压迫北美人民的事实。

四、参考文献

1. 王荣堂：《对于北美“独立宣言”与法国“人权宣言”的理解与分析》，《历史教学》1959 年第 7 期。
2. 刘祚昌：《美国的独立与独立宣言》，《山东师大学报》1982 年第 5 期。
3. [英] 约翰·洛克：《政府论》，瞿菊农、叶启芳译，商务印书馆 2003 年版。
4. [美] 卡尔·贝克尔：《〈论独立宣言〉——政治思想史研究》，彭刚译，江苏教育出版社 2004 年版。
5. Daniells S. Allen, *Our Declaration: A Reading of the Declaration of Independence in Defense of Equality*, Liveright Publishing Corporation, 2014.

UNIT 15

THE CHIEF FEATURES OF THE INDUSTRIAL REVOLUTION[1]

Arnold Toynbee

The essence of the Industrial Revolution is the substitution of competition for the mediaeval regulations which had previously controlled the production and distribution of wealth. On this account it is not only one of the most important facts of English history, but Europe owes to it the growth of two great systems of thought — Economic Science, and its antithesis, Socialism. The development of Economic Science in England has four chief landmarks, each connected with the name of one of the four great English economists. The first is the publication of Adam Smith's *Wealth of Nations* in 1776, in which he investigated the causes of wealth and aimed at the substitution of industrial freedom for a system of restriction. The production of wealth, not the welfare of man, was what Adam Smith had primarily before his mind's eye; in his own words, "the great object of the Political Economy of every country is to increase the riches and power of that country." His great book appeared on the eve of the Industrial Revolution. A second stage in the growth of the science is marked by Malthus's *Essay on Population*[2], published in 1798, which may be considered the product of that revolution, then already in full swing. Adam Smith had concentrated all his attention on a large production; Malthus directed his inquiries, not to the causes of wealth but to the causes of poverty, and found them in his theory of population. A third stage is marked by Ricardo's *Principles of Political Economy and Taxation*[3], which appeared in 1817, and in which Ricardo sought to ascertain the laws of the distribution of wealth. Adam Smith had shown how wealth could be produced under a system of industrial freedom, Ricardo showed how wealth is distributed under such a system, a problem which could not have occurred to any one before his time. The fourth stage is marked by John Stuart Mill's *Principles of Political Economy*[4], published in 1848. Mill himself asserted that "the chief merit of his treatise" was the distinction drawn between the laws of production and those of distribution, and the problem he tried to solve was, how wealth *ought to be* distributed. A great advance was made by Mill's attempt to show what was and what was not inevitable under a system of free competition. In it we see the influence which the rival system of Socialism was already beginning to exercise upon the economists. The whole spirit of Mill's book is quite different from that of any economic works which had up to his time been written in England. Though a re-statement of Ricardo's system, it contained the admission that the distribution of wealth is the result of "particular social arrangements," and it recognised that competition alone is not a satisfactory basis of society.

Competition, heralded by Adam Smith, and taken for granted by Ricardo and Mill, is still the dominant idea of our time; though since the publication of the *Origin of Species*[5], we hear more of it under the name of the "struggle for existence." I wish here to notice the fallacies involved in the current arguments on this subject. In the first place it is assumed that all competition is a competition for existence. This is not true. There is a great difference between a struggle for mere existence and a struggle for a particular kind of existence. For instance, twelve men are struggling for employment in a trade where there is only room for eight; four are driven out of that trade, but they are not trampled out of existence. A good deal of competition merely decides what kind of work a man is to do; though of course when a man can only do one kind of work, it may easily become a struggle for bare life. It is next assumed that this struggle for existence is a law of nature, and that therefore all human interference with it is wrong. To that I answer that the whole meaning of civilisation is interference with this brute struggle. We intend to modify the violence of the fight, and to prevent the weak being trampled under foot.

Competition, no doubt, has its uses. Without competition no progress would be possible, for progress comes chiefly from without, it is external pressure which forces men to exert themselves. Socialists, however, maintain that this advantage is gained at the expense of an enormous waste of human life and labour, which might be avoided by regulation. But here we must distinguish between competition in production and competition in distribution, a difference recognised in modern legislation, which has widened the sphere of contract in the one direction, while it has narrowed it in the other. For the struggle of men to outvie one another in production is beneficial to the community; their struggle over the division of the joint produce is not. The stronger side will dictate its own terms; and as a matter of fact, in the early days of competition the capitalists used all their power to oppress the labourers, and drove down wages to starvation point. This kind of competition has to be checked; there is no historical instance of its having lasted long without being modified either by combination or legislation, or both. In England both remedies are in operation, the former through Trades-Unions[6], the latter through factory legislation. In the past other remedies were applied. It is this desire to prevent the evils of competition that affords the true explanation of the fixing of wages by Justices of the Peace[7], which seemed to Ricardo a remnant of the old system of tyranny in the interests of the strong. Competition, we have now learnt, is neither good nor evil in itself; it is a force which has to be studied and controlled; it may be compared to a stream whose strength and direction have to be observed, that embankments may be thrown up within which it may do its work harmlessly and beneficially. But at the period we are considering it came to be believed in as a gospel, and, the idea of necessity being superadded, economic laws deduced from the assumption of universal unrestricted competition were converted into practical precepts, from which it was regarded as little short of immoral to depart.

Coming to the facts of the Industrial Revolution, the first thing that strikes us is the far greater rapidity which marks the growth of population. Before 1751 the largest decennial increase, so far as we can calculate from our imperfect materials, was 3 per cent. For each of the next three decennial periods the increase was 6 per cent.; then between 1781 and 1791 it was 9 per cent.; between 1791 and 1801, 11 per cent.; between 1801 and 1811, 14 per cent.; between 1811 and 1821, 18 per cent. This is the highest figure ever reached in England, for since 1815 a vast emigration has been always tending to moderate it; between 1815 and 1880 over eight millions (including Irish) have left our shores. But for this our normal rate of increase would be 16 or 18 instead of 12 per cent. in every decade.

Next we notice the relative and positive decline in the agricultural population. In 1811 it constituted 35 per cent. of the whole population of Great Britain; in 1821, 33 per cent.; in 1831, 28 per cent. And at the same time its actual numbers have decreased. In 1831 there were 1,243,057 adult males employed in agriculture in Great Britain; in 1841 there were 1,207,989. In 1851 the whole number of persons engaged in agriculture in England was 2,084,153; in 1861 it was 2,010,454, and in 1871 it was 1,657,138. Contemporaneously with this change, the centre of density of population has shifted from the Midlands to the North; there are at the present day 458 persons to the square mile in the counties north of the Trent, as against 312 south of the Trent. And we have lastly to remark the change in the relative population of England and Ireland. Of the total population of the three kingdoms, Ireland had in 1821 32 per cent, in 1881 only 14.6 per cent.

An agrarian revolution plays as large part in the great industrial change of the end of the eighteenth century as does the revolution in manufacturing industries, to which attention is more usually directed. Our next inquiry must therefore be: What were the agricultural changes which led to this noticeable decrease in the rural population? The three most effective causes were: the destruction of the common-field system of cultivation; the enclosure, on a large scale, of common and waste lands; and the consolidation of small farms into large. We have already seen that while between 1710 and 1760 some 300,000 acres were enclosed, between 1760 and 1843 nearly 7,000,000 underwent the same process. Closely connected with the enclosure system was the substitution of large for small farms. In the first half of the century Laurence, though approving of consolidation from an economic point of view, had thought that the odium attaching to an evicting landlord would operate as a strong check upon it. But these scruples had now disappeared. Eden in 1795 notices how constantly the change was effected, often accompanied by the conversion of arable to pasture; and relates how in a certain Dorsetshire village he found two farms where twenty years ago there had been thirty. The process went on uninterruptedly into the present century. Cobbett[8], writing in 1826, says: "In the parish of Burghclere one single farmer holds, under Lord Carnarvon, as one farm, the lands that those now living remember to have formed fourteen farms, bringing up in a respectable way fourteen families." The consolidation of farms reduced the number of farmers, while the enclosures drove the labourers off the land, as it became impossible for them to exist without their rights of pasturage for sheep and geese on common lands.

Severely, however, as these changes bore upon the rural population, they wrought, without doubt, distinct improvement from an agricultural point of view. They meant the substitution of scientific for unscientific culture. "It has been found," says Laurence, "by long experience, that common or open fields are great hindrances to the public good, and to the honest improvement which every one might make of his own." Enclosures brought an extension of arable cultivation and the tillage of inferior soils; and in small farms of 40 to 100 acres, where the land was exhausted by repeated corn crops, the farm buildings of clay and mud walls and three-fourths of the estate often saturated with water, consolidation into farms of 100 to 500 acres meant rotation of crops, leases of nineteen years, and good farm buildings. The period was one of great agricultural advance; the breed of cattle was improved, rotation of crops was generally introduced, the steam-plough was invented, agricultural societies were instituted. In one respect alone the change was injurious. In consequence of the high prices of corn which prevailed during the French war, some of the finest permanent pastures were broken up. Still, in spite of this, it was said in 1813 that during the previous ten years agricultural produce had increased by one-fourth, and this was an increase upon a great increase in the preceding generation.

Passing to manufactures, we find here the all-prominent fact to be the substitution of the factory for the domestic system, the consequence of the mechanical discoveries of the time. Four great inventions altered the character of the cotton manufacture; the spinning-jenny, patented by Hargreaves in 1770; the water-frame, invented by Arkwright the year before; Crompton's mule introduced in 1779, and the self-acting mule, first invented by Kelly in 1792, but not brought into use till Roberts improved it in 1825. None of these by themselves would have revolutionised the industry. But in 1769 — the year in which Napoleon and Wellington were born — James Watt took out his patent for the steam-engine. Sixteen years later it was applied to the cotton manufacture. In 1785 Boulton and Watt made an engine for a cotton-mill at Papplewick in Notts, and in the same year Arkwright's patent expired. These two facts taken together mark the introduction of the factory system. But the most famous invention of all, and the most fatal to domestic industry, the power-loom, though also patented by Cartwright in 1785, did not come into use for several years, and till the power-loom was introduced the workman was hardly injured. At first, in fact, machinery raised the wages of spinners and weavers owing to the great prosperity it brought to the trade. In fifteen years the cotton trade trebled itself; from 1788 to 1803 has been called " its golden age"; for, before the power-loom but after the introduction of the mule and other mechanical improvements by which for the first time yarn sufficiently fine for muslin and a variety of other fabrics was spun, the demand became such that "old barns, cart-houses, out-buildings of all descriptions were repaired, windows broke through the old blank walls, and all fitted up for loom-shops; new weavers' cottages with loom-shops arose in every direction, every family bringing home weekly from 40 to 120 shillings per week." At a later date, the condition of the workman was very different. Meanwhile, the iron industry had been equally revolutionised by the invention of smelting by pit-coal brought into use between 1740 and 1750, and by the application in 1788 of the steam-engine to blast furnaces. In the eight years which followed this latter date, the amount of iron manufactured nearly doubled itself.

A further growth of the factory system took place independent of machinery, and owed its origin to the expansion of trade, an expansion which was itself due to the great advance made at this time in the means of communication. The canal system was being rapidly developed throughout the country. In 1777 the Grand Trunk canal, 96 miles in length, connecting the Trent and Mersey, was finished; Hull and Liverpool were connected by one canal while another connected them both with Bristol; and in 1792, the Grand Junction canal, 90 miles in length, made a waterway from London through Oxford to the chief midland towns. Some years afterwards, the roads were greatly improved under Telford and Macadam; between 1818 and 1829 more than a thousand additional miles of turnpike road were constructed; and the next year, 1830, saw the opening of the first railroad. These improved means of communication caused an extraordinary increase in commerce, and to secure a sufficient supply of goods it became the interest of the merchants to collect weavers around them in great numbers, to get looms together in a workshop, and to give out the warp themselves to the workpeople. To these latter this system meant a change from independence to dependence; at the beginning of the century the report of a committee asserts that the essential difference between the domestic and the factory system is, that in the latter the work is done "by persons who have no property in the goods they manufacture." Another direct consequence of this expansion of trade was the regular recurrence of periods of over-production and of depression, a phenomenon quite unknown under the old system, and due to this new form of production on a large scale for a distant market.

These altered conditions in the production of wealth necessarily involved an equal revolution in its distribution. In agriculture the prominent fact is an enormous rise in rents. Up to 1795, though they had risen in some places, in others they had been stationary since the Revolution. But between 1790 and 1833, according to Porter, they at least doubled. In Scotland, the rental of land, which in 1795 had amounted to £2,000,000, had risen in 1815 to £5,278,685. A farm in Essex, which before 1793 had been rented at 10s. an acre, was let in 1812 at 50s., though, six years after, this had fallen again to 35s. In Berks and Wilts, farms which in 1790 were let at 14s., were let in 1810 at 70s., and in 1820 at 50s. Much of this rise, doubtless, was due to money invested in improvements — the first Lord Leicester is said to have expended £400,000 on his property — but it was far more largely the effect of the enclosure system, of the consolidation of farms, and of the high price of corn during the French war. Whatever may have been its causes, however, it represented a great social revolution, a change in the balance of political power and in the relative position of classes. The farmers shared in the prosperity of the landlords; for many of them held their farms under beneficial leases, and made large profits by them. In consequence, their character completely changed; they ceased to work and live with their labourers, and became a distinct class. The high prices of the war time thoroughly demoralised them, for their wealth then increased so fast, that they were at a loss what to do with it. Cobbett has described the change in their habits, the new food and furniture, the luxury and drinking, which were the consequences of more money coming into their hands than they knew how to spend. Meanwhile, the effect of all these agrarian changes upon the condition of the labourer was an exactly opposite and most disastrous one. He felt all the burden of high prices, while his wages were steadily falling, and he had lost his common-rights. It is from this period, viz., the beginning of the present century, that the alienation between farmer and labourer may be dated.

Exactly analogous phenomena appeared in the manufacturing world. The new class of great capitalist employers made enormous fortunes, they took little or no part personally in the work of their factories, their hundreds of workmen were individually unknown to them; and as a consequence, the old relations between masters and men disappeared, and a "cash nexus" was substituted for the human tie. The workmen on their side resorted to combination, and Trades-Unions began a fight which looked as if it were between mortal enemies rather than joint producers. The misery which came upon large sections of the working people at this epoch was often, though not always, due to a fall in wages, for, as I said above, in some industries they rose. But they suffered likewise from the conditions of labour under the factory system, from the rise of prices, especially from the high price of bread before the repeal of the corn-laws[9], and from those sudden fluctuations of trade, which, ever since production has been on a large scale, have exposed them to recurrent periods of bitter distress. The effects of the Industrial Revolution prove that free competition may produce wealth without producing wellbeing. We all know the horrors that ensued in England before it was restrained by legislation and combination.

一、导读

阿诺德·汤因比（Arnold Toynbee），英国著名的社会改革家和经济史学家，其社会实践和学术著作对英国19世纪的改革运动产生了重大影响。20世纪上半叶，因写作《历史研究》而蜚声世界的阿诺德·约瑟夫·汤因比（Arnold Joseph Toynbee）则是他的侄儿。

汤因比早年在牛津大学的贝列尔学院接受高等教育，1878年成为该学院的讲师。汤因比积极参与大学之外的社会改革活动，特别关注伦敦的穷人。他被认为是英国第一位经济史学家，且最早开始将工业革命视为一件伟大的历史事件，并一直致力于传授学生经济史的研究方法。

1884年，汤因比的《18世纪英国工业革命讲座》出版，这是关于工业革命最早的专题研究著作。在这本书的带动之下，西方学者掀起了研究工业革命的热潮，而在此之前，历史学家主要从事的是政治和思想的研究。“十九世纪的历史学者主要关心的是世界的政治，立宪君主制、宗教信仰自由和个人自由的增长。随着世纪的转换，人们开始探求不同的问题，诸如他们居住其中的工业社会。”不过，这本书原是汤因比的授课讲稿。在他离世后，他的朋友、学生将自己在汤因比1880—1881年在牛津大学开设讲座过程中所做的笔记，以及汤因比自己在这个课题上所做的注解，集结后出版。

本文献选自《18世纪英国工业革命讲座》第8章，原书第8章标题是THE CHIEF FEATURES OF THE REVOLUTION，选文为了明确说明节选部分的主题，加上了INDUSTRIAL一词。

二、注释

1. Selected from Arnold Toynbee, *Lectures on the Industrial Revolution of the 18th Century in England*, Longmans, Green and Co., 1894.

2. *Essay on Population*，即《人口论》，马尔萨斯所著，1789年出版。在此书中，马尔萨斯认为人类社会的物质财富按照算术基数增长，人口则依据几何基数增长。因此，人口增长超过社会财富的增长速度，未来将导致严重的人口问题。

3. *Principles of Political Economy and Taxation*，即《政治经济学及赋税原理》，大卫·李嘉图所著。

4. *Principles of Political Economy*，即《政治经济学原理》，约翰·斯图亚特·密尔所著。

5. *Origin of Species*，即《物种起源》，达尔文所著。

6. Trades-Unions，“工会”之意。

7. Justices of the Peace，指英国治安法官。

8. William Cobbett (1763—1835)，威廉·科贝特，英国激进的农业家和多产记者。

9. the corn-laws，意为“谷物法”。

三、问题探讨

1. It is next assumed that this struggle for existence is a law of nature, and that therefore all human interference with it is wrong. To that I answer that the whole meaning of civilization is interference with this brute struggle. We intend to modify the violence of the fight, and to prevent the weak being trampled under foot. 结合这段话，谈谈你对作者文明观的理解。

2. 结合材料，分析手工工场与工厂的区别。

四、参考文献

1. 林举岱：《英国工业革命史》，上海人民出版社1979年版。

2.《马克思恩格斯文集》(第一卷)，人民出版社2009年版。

3. [法] 保尔·芒图：《十八世纪产业革命——英国近代大工业初期的概况》，陈希秦等译，商务印书馆1997年版。

4. T. S. Ashton, *The Industrial Revolution* 1760 - 1830, Oxford University Press, 1968.

5. Phyllis Deane, *The First Industrial Revolution*, Cambridge University Press, 1986,

UNIT 16

ANIMADVERSIONS ON SOME OF THE WRITERS WHO HAVE RENDERED WOMEN OBJECTS OF PITY, BORDERING ON CONTEMPT[1]

Mary Wollstonecraft

Section Ⅱ

Dr. Fordyce's sermons[2] have long made a part of a young woman's library; nay, girls at school are allowed to read them; but I should instantly dismiss them from my pupil's, if I wished to strengthen her understanding, by leading her to form sound principles on a broad basis; or, were I only anxious to cultivate her taste; though they must be allowed to contain many sensible observations.

Dr. Fordyce may have had a very laudable end in view; but these discourses are written in such an affected style, that were it only on that account, and had I nothing to object against his *mellifluous* precepts, I should not allow girls to peruse them, unless I designed to hunt every spark of nature out of their composition, melting every human quality into female meekness and artificial grace. I say artificial, for true grace arises from some kind of independence of mind.

Children, careless of pleasing, and only anxious to amuse themselves, are often very graceful; and the nobility who have mostly lived with inferiours, and always had the command of money, acquire a graceful ease of deportment, which should rather be termed habitual grace of body, than that superiour gracefulness which is truly the expression of the mind. This mental grace, not noticed by vulgar eyes, often flashes across a rough countenance, and irradiating every feature, shows simplicity and independence of mind. — It is then we read characters of immortality in the eye, and see the soul in every gesture, though when at rest, neither the face nor limbs may have much beauty to recommend them; or the behaviour, any thing peculiar to attract universal attention. The mass of mankind, however, look for more *tangible* beauty; yet simplicity is, in general, admired, when people do not consider what they admire; and can there be simplicity without sincerity? But, to have done with remarks that are in some measure desultory, though naturally excited by the subject —

In declamatory periods Dr. Fordyce spins out Rousseau's eloquence[3]; and in most sentimental rant, details his opinions respecting the female character, and the behaviour which woman ought to assume to render her lovely.

He shall speak for himself, for thus he makes Nature address man. 'Behold these smiling innocents, whom I have graced with my fairest gifts, and committed to your protection; behold them with love and respect; treat them with tenderness and honour. They are timid and want to be defended. They are frail; O do not take advantage of their weakness! Let their fears and blushes endear them. Let their confidence in you never be abused. — But is it possible, that any of you can be such barbarians, so supremely wicked, as to abuse it? Can you find in your hearts to despoil the gentle, trusting creatures of their treasure, or do any thing to strip them of their native robe of virtue? Curst be the impious hand that would dare to violate the unblemished form of Chastity! Thou wretch! thou ruffian! forbear; nor venture to provoke heaven's fiercest vengeance.' I know not any comment that can be made seriously on this curious passage, and I could produce many similar ones; and some, so very sentimental, that I have heard rational men use the word indecent, when they mentioned them with disgust.

Throughout there is a display of cold artificial feelings, and that parade of sensibility which boys and girls should be taught to despise as the sure mark of a little vain mind. Florid appeals are made to heaven, and to the *beauteous innocents*, the fairest images of heaven here below, whilst sober sense is left far behind. — This is not the language of the heart, nor will it ever reach it, though the ear may be tickled

I shall be told, perhaps, that the public have been pleased with these volumes. —True — and *Hervey's Meditations*[4] are still read, though he equally sinned against sense and taste.

I particularly object to the lover-like phrases of pumped up passion, which are every where interspersed. If women be ever allowed to walk without leading-strings, why must they be cajoled into virtue by artful flattery and sexual compliments? — Speak to them the language of truth and soberness, and away with the lullaby strains of condescending endearment! Let them be taught to respect themselves as rational creatures, and not led to have a passion for their own insipid persons. It moves my gall to hear a preacher descanting on dress and needle-work; and still more to hear him address the *British fair, the fairest of the fair*, as if they had only feelings.

Even recommending piety he uses the following argument. "Never, perhaps, does a fine woman strike more deeply, than when, composed into pious recollection, and possessed with the noblest considerations, she assumes, without knowing it, superior dignity and new graces; so that the beauties of holiness seem to radiate about her, and the by-standers are almost induced to fancy her already worshipping amongst her kindred angels!" Why are women to be thus bred up with a desire of conquest? The very word, used in this sense, gives me a sickly qualm! Do religion and virtue offer no stronger motives, no brighter reward? Must they always be debased by being made to consider the sex of their companions? Must they be taught always to be pleasing? And when levelling their small artillery at the heart of man, is it necessary to tell them that a little sense is sufficient to render their attention *incredibly soothing*? "As a small degree of knowledge entertains in a woman, so from a woman, though for a different reason, a small expression of kindness delights, particularly if she have beauty!" I should have supposed for the same reason.

Why are girls to be told that they resemble angels; but to sink them below women? Or, that a gentle innocent female is an object that comes nearer to the idea which we have formed of angels than any other. Yet they are told, at the same time, that they are only like angels when they are young and beautiful; consequently, it is their persons, not their virtues, that procure them this homage.

Idle empty words! What can such delusive flattery lead to, but vanity and folly? The lover, it is true, has a poetical licence to exalt his mistress; his reason is the bubble of his passion, and he does not utter a falsehood when he borrows the language of adoration. His imagination may raise the idol of his heart, unblamed, above humanity; and happy would it be for women, if they were only flattered by the men who loved them; I mean, who love the individual, not the sex; but should a grave preacher interlard his discourses with such fooleries?

In sermons or novels, however, voluptuousness is always true to its text. Men are allowed by moralists to cultivate, as Nature directs, different qualities, and assume the different characters, that the same passions, modified almost to infinity, give to each individual. A virtuous man may have a choleric or a sanguine constitution, be gay or grave, unreproved; be firm till he is almost overbearing, or, weakly submissive, have no will or opinion of his own; but all women are to be levelled, by meekness and docility, into one character of yielding softness and gentle compliance.

I will use the preacher's own words. "Let it be observed, that in your sex manly exercises are never graceful; that in them a tone and figure, as well as an air and deportment, of the masculine kind, are always forbidding; and that men of sensibility desire in every woman soft features, and a flowing voice, a form, not robust, and demeanour delicate and gentle."

Is not the following portrait — the portrait of a house slave? "I am astonished at the folly of many women, who are still reproaching their husbands for leaving them alone, for preferring this or that company to theirs, for treating them with this and the other mark of disregard or indifference; when, to speak the truth, they have themselves in a great measure to blame. Not that I would justify the men in any thing wrong on their part. But had you behaved to them with more *respectful observance,* and a more *equal tenderness; studying their humours, overlooking their mistakes, submitting to their opinions* in matters indifferent, passing by little instances of unevenness, caprice, or passion, giving *soft* answers to hasty words, complaining as seldom as possible, and making it your daily care to relieve their anxieties and prevent their wishes, to enliven the hour of dulness, and call up the ideas of felicity: had you pursued this conduct, I doubt not but you would have maintained and even increased their esteem, so far as to have secured every degree of influence that could conduce to their virtue, or your mutual satisfaction; and your house might at this day have been the abode of domestic bliss." Such a woman ought to be an angel — or she is an ass — for I discern not a trace of the human character, neither reason nor passion in this domestic drudge, whose being is absorbed in that of a tyrant's.

Still Dr. Fordyce must have very little acquaintance with the human heart, if he really supposed that such conduct would bring back wandering love, instead of exciting contempt. No, beauty, gentleness, etc. etc. may gain a heart; but esteem, the only lasting affection, can alone be obtained by virtue supported by reason. It is respect for the understanding that keeps alive tenderness for the person.

As these volumes are so frequently put into the hands of young people, I have taken more notice of them than, strictly speaking, they deserve; but as they have contributed to vitiate the taste, and enervate the understanding of many of my fellow-creatures, I could not pass them silently over.

Section Ⅲ

Such paternal solicitude pervades Dr. Gregory's Legacy to his Daughters[5], that I enter on the task of criticism with affectionate respect; but as this little volume has many attractions to recommend it to the notice of the most respectable part of my sex, I cannot silently pass over arguments that so speciously support opinions which, I think, have had the most baneful effect on the morals and manners of the female world.

His easy familiar style is particularly suited to the tenor of his advice, and the melancholy tenderness which his respect for the memory of a beloved wife, diffuses through the whole work, renders it very interesting; yet there is a degree of concise elegance conspicuous in many passages that disturbs this sympathy; and we pop on the author, when we only expected to meet the-father.

Besides, having two objects in view, he seldom adhered steadily to either; for wishing to make his daughters amiable, and fearing lest unhappiness should only be the consequence, of instilling sentiments that might draw them out of the track of common life without enabling them to act with consonant independence and dignity, he checks the natural flow of his thoughts, and neither advises one thing nor the other.

In the preface he tells them a mournful truth, "that they will hear, at least once in their lives, the genuine sentiments of a man who has no interest in deceiving them."

Hapless woman! what can be expected from thee when the beings on whom thou art said naturally to depend for reason and support, have all an interest in deceiving thee! This is the root of the evil that has shed a corroding mildew on all thy virtues; and blighting in the bud thy opening faculties, has rendered thee the weak thing thou art! It is this separate interest — this insidious state of warfare, that undermines morality, and divides mankind!

If love have made some women wretched — how many more has the cold unmeaning intercourse of gallantry rendered vain and useless! yet this heartless attention to the sex is reckoned so manly, so polite that, till society is very differently organized, I fear, this vestige of gothic manners will not be done away by a more reasonable and affectionate mode of conduct. Besides, to strip it of its imaginary dignity, I must observe, that in the most uncivilized European states this lip-service prevails in a very great degree, accompanied with extreme dissoluteness of morals. In Portugal, the country that I particularly allude to, it takes place of the most serious moral obligations; for a man is seldom assassinated when in the company of a woman. The savage hand of rapine is unnerved by this chivalrous spirit; and, if the stroke of vengeance cannot be stayed — the lady is entreated to pardon the rudeness and depart in peace, though sprinkled, perhaps, with her husband's or brother's blood.

I shall pass over his strictures on religion, because I mean to discuss that subject in a separate chapter.

The remarks relative to behaviour, though many of them very sensible, I entirely disapprove of, because it appears to me to be beginning, as it were, at the wrong end. A cultivated understanding, and an affectionate heart, will never want starched rules of decorum — something more substantial than seemliness will be the result; and, without understanding the behaviour here recommended, would be rank affectation. Decorum, indeed, is the one thing needful! — decorum is to supplant nature, and banish all simplicity and variety of character out of the female world. Yet what good end can all this superficial counsel produce? It is, however, much easier to point out this or that mode of behaviour, than to set the reason to work; but, when the mind has been stored with useful knowledge, and strengthened by being employed, the regulation of the behaviour may safely be left to its guidance.

Why, for instance, should the following caution be given when art of every kind must contaminate the mind; and why entangle the grand motives of action, which reason and religion equally combine to enforce, with pitiful worldly shifts and slight of hand tricks to gain the applause of gaping tasteless fools? "Be even cautious in displaying your good sense. It will be thought you assume a superiority over the rest of the company — But if you happen to have any learning, keep it a profound secret, especially from the men who generally look with a jealous and malignant eye on a woman of great parts, and a cultivated understanding." If men of real merit, as he afterwards observes, be superior to this meanness, where is the necessity that the behaviour of the whole sex should be modulated to please fools, or men, who having little claim to respect as individuals, choose to keep close in their phalanx. Men, indeed, who insist on their common superiority, having only this sexual superiority, are certainly very excusable.

There would be no end to rules for behaviour, if it be proper always to adopt the tone of the company; for thus, for ever varying the key, a *flat* would often pass for a *natural* note.

Surely it would have been wiser to have advised women to improve themselves till they rose above the fumes of vanity; and then to let the public opinion come round — for where are rules of accommodation to stop? The narrow path of truth and virtue inclines neither to the right nor left — it is a straightforward business, and they who are earnestly pursuing their road, may bound over many decorous prejudices, without leaving modesty behind. Make the heart clean, and give the head employment, and I will venture to predict that there will be nothing offensive in the behaviour.

The air of fashion, which many young people are so eager to attain, always strikes me like the studied attitudes of some modern pictures, copied with tasteless servility after the antiques; — the soul is left out, and none of the parts are tied together by what may properly be termed character. This varnish of fashion, which seldom sticks very close to sense, may dazzle the weak; but leave nature to itself, and it will seldom disgust the wise. Besides, when a woman has sufficient sense not to pretend to any thing which she does not understand in some degree, there is no need of determining to hide her talents under a bushel. Let things take their natural course, and all will be well.

It is this system of dissimulation, throughout the volume, that I despise. Women are always to *seem* to be this and that — yet virtue might apostrophize them, in the words of Hamlet — Seems! I know not seems! — Have that within that passeth show! —

Still the same tone occurs; for in another place, after recommending, without sufficiently discriminating delicacy, he adds, "The men will complain of your reserve. They will assure you that a franker behaviour would make you more amiable. But, trust me, they are not sincere when they tell you so. — I acknowledge that on some occasions it might render you more agreeable as companions, but it would make you less amiable as women: an important distinction, which many of your sex are not aware of."

This desire of being always women, is the very consciousness that degrades the sex. Excepting with a lover, I must repeat with emphasis, a former observation, — it would be well if they were only agreeable or rational companions. — But in this respect his advice is even inconsistent with a passage which I mean to quote with the most marked approbation.

"The sentiment, that a woman may allow all innocent freedoms, provided her virtue is secure, is both grossly indelicate and dangerous, and has proved fatal to many of your sex." With this opinion I perfectly coincide. A man, or a woman, of any feeling, must always wish to convince a beloved object that it is the caresses of the individual, not the sex, that are received and returned with pleasure; and, that the heart, rather than the senses, is moved. Without this natural delicacy, love becomes a selfish personal gratification that soon degrades the character.

I carry this sentiment still further. Affection, when love is out of the question, authorises many personal endearments, that naturally flowing from an innocent heart, give life to the behaviour; but the personal intercourse of appetite, gallantry, or vanity, is despicable. When a man squeezes the hand of a pretty woman, handing her to a carriage, whom he has never seen before, she will consider such an impertinent freedom in the light of an insult, if she have any true delicacy, instead of being flattered by this unmeaning homage to beauty. These are the privileges of friendship, or the momentary homage which the heart pays to virtue, when it flashes suddenly on the notice — mere animal spirits have no claim to the kindnesses of affection!

Wishing to feed the affections with what is now the food of vanity, I would fain persuade my sex to act from simpler principles. Let them merit love, and they will obtain it, though they may never be told that — "The power of a fine woman over the hearts of men, of men of the finest parts, is even beyond what she conceives."

I have already noticed the narrow cautions with respect to duplicity, female softness, delicacy of constitution; for these are the changes which he rings round without ceasing — in a more decorous manner, it is true, than Rousseau; but it all comes home to the same point, and whoever is at the trouble to analyze these sentiments, will find the first principles not quite so delicate as the superstructure.

The subject of amusements is treated in too cursory a manner; but with the same spirit.

When I treat of friendship, love, and marriage, it will be found that we materially differ in opinion; I shall not the forestall what I have to observe on these important subjects; but confine my remarks to the general tenor of them, to that cautious family prudence, to those confined views of partial unenlightened affection, which exclude pleasure and improvement, by vainly wishing to ward off sorrow and error — and by thus guarding the heart and mind, destroy also all their energy. — It is far better to be often deceived than never to trust; to be disappointed in love than never to love; to lose a husband's fondness than forfeit his esteem.

Happy would it be for the world, and for individuals, of course, if all this unavailing solicitude to attain worldly happiness, on a confined plan, were turned into an anxious desire to improve the understanding. — "Wisdom is the principal thing: *therefore* get wisdom; and with all thy gettings get understanding." — "How long, ye simple ones, will ye love simplicity, and hate knowledge?" Saith Wisdom to the daughters of men!

一、导读

玛丽·沃斯通克拉夫特（Mary Wollstonecraft）是18世纪英国著名的作家、哲学家和女权主义者。《为女权辩护：关于政治和道德问题的批评》（简称《女权辩护》）是沃斯通克拉夫特最知名的作品，被誉为"女权主义的基石"，成为各国女性研究者的必读经典。

在《女权辩护》一书中，沃斯通克拉夫特的一个中心论点是：女性应该受到理性教育，以给予她们为社会做贡献的机会。她认为，当一个社会缺乏受过教育的女性时，那么这个社会便会退化，这主要是因为年幼子女启蒙教师的这一社会角色大都由母亲担任。同时，她将女性未受教育的问题归因于男性，是詹姆斯·福代斯（James Fordyce）、约翰·格雷戈里（John Gregory）和卢梭（Rousseau）等男性作家们所写的一些讨论教育问题的书籍，架构了一套错误的教育体系。在《女权辩护》中，沃斯通克拉夫特对上述人等的教育理念以及当时的教育制度进行了无情的批判，认为这种教育使得女性处于一种"无知和奴隶式依附"状态，是造成女性卑下的社会地位的罪魁祸首。她主张女性的权利同男性的权利应该是平等的，呼吁给予女性同男性一样的教育权、工作权和政治权。沃斯通克拉夫特的这些见解在当时看来是前卫大胆、惊世骇俗的。

2005年，在英国著名作家梅尔文·布拉格评选出的12部影响世界的作品中，《女权辩护》《圣经》《物种起源》及莎士比亚戏剧等一同入选；2015年11月，《女权辩护》被评为"最具影响力的20本学术书"之一。这部著作在人类进程中所产生的重要影响由此可见一斑。本文献节选自《女权辩护》的第5章第2、3节。

二、注释

1. Selected from Mary Wollstonecraft, *A Vindication of the Rights of Woman: With Strictures on Political and Moral Subjects*, Forgotten Books, 2016.

2. James Fordyce，詹姆斯·福代斯（1720—1796），苏格兰长老会派牧师和诗人。他收集整理了自己的布道词和一些人生格言，于1766年出版了《女性箴言》，通常被称为《福代斯箴言》（*Fordyce's Sermons*）。

3. 卢梭在其教育小说《爱弥儿》中提到过一些有关女性从属于男性、女性教育与男性教育完全不同的观点。作者在第5章的第1节重点批驳了卢梭的观点。

4. *Hervey's Meditations*，即《赫维沉思录》。约翰·赫维（1696—1743），英国朝臣、政治作家和回忆录作家。1727—1737年，赫维为乔治二世的宫廷写了详尽而率直的回忆录。

5. Dr. Gregory's Legacy to his Daughters，即 *A Father's Legacy to his Daughters*，译为《格雷戈里博士赠言》。格雷戈里（Gregory，1724—1773），苏格兰医学家，写有许多医学著作。《格雷戈里博士赠言》1774 年出版后，成为当时一部畅销著作。

三、问题探讨

1. 本文作者是如何批驳《福代斯箴言》和《格雷戈里博士赠言》的？
2. 作者认为女性应该接受怎样的教育？

四、参考文献

1. 裔昭印等：《西方妇女史》，商务印书馆 2009 年版。

2. [法] 卢梭：《爱弥儿》，李平沤译，商务印书馆 2012 年版。

3. [法] 西蒙娜·德·波伏瓦：《第二性》，郑克鲁译，上海译文出版社 2011 年版。

4. [英] 约翰·斯图亚特·密尔：《论妇女的屈从地位》，汪溪译，商务印书馆 1995 年版。

5. Bonnie S. Anderson, Judith P. Zinsser, *A History of Their Own: Women in Europe from Prehistory to the Present*, Karper & Row Publishers, 1989.

UNIT 17

THE GREAT PLAGUE OF 1665[1]

Robert O. Bucholz & Joseph P. Ward

Sometime after Christmas, 1664, Dr. Nathaniel Hodges (1629 – 1688) "was called to a young man in a Fever, who after two days course of alexiterial medicines, had two Risings about the bigness of a Nytmeg broke out, one on each Thigh." The young man survived, but he was the first harbinger of London's last and most notorious outbreak of the plague. Plague was a constant worry in early modern London, but the winter of 1664/65 was one of the hardest in years, and it was thought that this would keep the scourge at bay. May and June 1665 were, however, unusually warm, and the parish clerks who compiled the Bills of Mortality[2] began to notice that they were recording more burials, and that most of those were from plague. For example, in the parish of St. Giles-in-the-Fields, the tallies rose as follows:

Week ending:	*Plague Deaths:*
May 30:	9
June 6:	31
June 13:	68
June 20:	101
June 27:	143

The statistical impulse is a modern one, but these figures are not entirely reliable. As Samuel Pepys[3] noted, the poor were underreported, and Dissenters[4] often lived outside the parish structure in a variety of ways. For example, Quakers would not toll a bell for the dead. Later, at the height of the epidemic, parish clerks tried to avoid mass panic by reporting plague deaths as being from "dropsy" or French pox[5], griping of the guts, "frighted," or lethargy. Thus, the clerk at St. Olave Hart Street admitted to Pepys that "there died nine this week though I have returned only six." In any case, the diarist knew that something was amiss by early June:

> This day, much against my Will, I did in Drury-lane see two or three houses marked with a red cross upon the doors, and "Lord have mercy upon us" writ there — which was a sad sight to me, being the first of that kind that to my remembrance I ever saw. It put me into an ill conception of myself and my smell, so that I was forced to buy some roll-tobacco to smell to and chaw — which took away the apprehension.

People who remembered the epidemics of 1636 and 1647 began to remove their families from London. What were they so afraid of?

It is generally agreed, although not without dissent, that from 1347 through the 1720s Europe was subjected to repeated visitations of the same disease. Although medieval Europeans called it "the Black Death" (not the "Black Plague" as careless students sometimes do), by the seventeenth century they referred to it simply as "the plague." There are two types of plague, bubonic and pneumonic, both caused by enterobacteria. Pneumonic plague, passed through the air, is the less common. Bubonic plague is contracted from the bite of a flea carried on the European black rat (*Rattus rattus*); the fleas carry *Yersinia pestis*, the bacteria responsible for the infection. Most contemporaries missed this connection completely, leading to a great many mistaken strategies to combat the disease, such as the setting of fires to purge the air of supposed plague "effluvia."

One of the most frightening aspects of the plague was its suddenness. If a person were breathed on or bitten, symptoms appeared in 3 to 7 days, but their onset could be abrupt. You could be fine one minute, dying the next, as happened to Samuel Pepys's coachman on June 17, 1665:

> It stroke me very deep this afternoon, going with a Hackny-coach from my Lord Treasurer's down Holborne — the coachman I found to drive easily and easily; at last stood still, and came down hardly able to stand; and told me that he was suddenly stroke very sick and almost blind, he could not see. So I light and went into another coach with a sad heart for the poor man and trouble for myself, lest he should have been stroke with the plague, being at that end of town that I took him up. But God have mercy upon us all.

Typically, the victim experienced fever, then diarrhea, headaches, swelling of the armpits and groin (infected lymph nodes), and finally rampaging internal bleeding. It was the resulting pooling of blood under the skin that produced the characteristic black blotches, or "buboes," that inspired the name *Black Death*. Once you were infected, your chances of dying were high: the death rate varied in London's past plague epidemics from 30% to 70%. This was partly because there was little that you could do: popular remedies were rosemary (sold for 8 shillings a handful in 1603), cakes of arsenic under the armpits, charms, amulets, and the maintaining of open fires to "burn" the plague out of the air as noted previously. Dr. Hodges, who stayed at his post throughout the epidemic, drank sack "to dissipate any Lodgment of the Infection." It worked: Hodges survived. Dr. William Boghurst (? 1631 – 1682), who also remained in London, recalled what little else a medical professional could do, the risk in doing it, and the poignancy of many last moments:

> I commonly drest forty soares in a day, held their pulse sweating in the bed half a quarter of an hour together to give judgment and informe myself in the various tricks of it. I lett one blood, gave glisters though but to a few, held them up in their bedds to keepe them from strangling and choking half an houre together, commonly suffered their breathing in my face severall tymes when they were dying, eate and dranke with them, especially those that had soares; sate downe by their bedd sides and upon their bedds discoursing with them an houre together if I had tyme, and stayd by them to see the manner of their death, and closed up their mouth and eyes (for they dyed with their mouth and eyes very much open and stareing); then if people had noe body to helpe them (for helpe was scarce at such tyme and place) I helpt to lay them forth out of the bedd and afterwards into the coffin, and last of all, accompanying them to the grave.

Somehow, despite such close attendance, Boghurst also survived. Contemporaries thought that survival guaranteed immunity, but sadly this had been disproved by London physicians in the sixteenth century.

Londoners were no strangers to plague. The first known plague epidemic in London was recorded by Bede for the year 664. The plague returned in 1258 and then most infamously in 1348/49, when perhaps 15,000 people died, of a total population of about 45,000. Medieval London was scourged again in 1361/62, 1368/69, 1405 – 07 (when 30,000 were said to have died), 1426, 1433/34, 1437, 1439, 1450, 1452, 1454, 1474, 1499/1500 (when 20,000 died), 1517 – 1521, 1531, and 1535. The worst early modern visitations are recorded (or, more likely, under-recorded) here:

	Year	*Deaths*	*Population*	*% of Population*
a.	1563	17,404	85,000	20.5
b.	1593	10,675	125,000	8.5
c.	1603	25,045	141,000	17.7
d.	1625	26,350	206,000	12.8

e. 1636	10,400	313,000	3.3
f. 1665	55,797	459,000	12.1

So, when was the Great Plague? In *absolute* terms, 1665 killed more people, a devastating 56,000 or more than 12% of London's population. If one includes the suburbs and outlying areas, the estimate rises to between 70,000 and 100,000. As a percentage of the city's population, however, 1348/49 was far worse, killing 33%. The years 1563, 1603, and 1625 were also bad: in each case London lost one-tenth to one-fifth of its people within a few short months. The worst months were in the summer: in contrast to modern urban dwellers, who tend to dread winter, early modern people hated summer because disease seemed to thrive in the warmer months. By July 1665, 1,000 were dying per week. The previous weekly record had been set in 1603, when 2,795 died in one week, but in the third week of September 1665, the Bills of Mortality report 8,297 dead, and the French ambassador thought the real figure was 14,000.

It is worth pausing to reflect on the fact that between 1563 and 1665, on average every 25 years or so, London saw about a tenth or more of its population simply wiped out. What was the impact of these successive disasters? Demographically and economically, plague epidemics had little *long-term* significance: London continued to grow through them; indeed, one wonders how the metropolis would have coped if these people had *not* died. In the *short term*, the loss was devastating at every level. That summer, Samuel Pepys faithfully recorded the rising death toll as well as his own personal losses: August 8 "...And poor Will that used to sell us ale at the Hall-door — his wife and three children dead, all I think in a day." By mid-August, the city streets were deserted, and London began to take on the atmosphere of a city abandoned, as in a postapocalyptic science fiction epic:

> But Lord, how sad a sight it is to see the streets empty of people, and very few upon the Change — jealous of every door that one sees shut up, lest it should be the plague — and about us, two shops in three, if not more, generally shut up.

Indeed, when plague hit, economic London ground to a halt (see Illustration 8.1): Shops closed, the Royal Exchange grew quiet, and long-distance trade became impossible: foreign merchant vessels were stopped or quarantined, and no one wanted anything that had passed through the city. Although contemporaries did not understand about the fleas, they knew that objects could carry disease. Thus, Pepys wondered what would happen to "the fashion after the plague is done as to periwigs, for nobody will dare to buy any haire for fear of the infection — that it had been cut off of the heads of people dead of the plague." London's entertainment industry also shut down, because people avoided taverns and theaters. On July 22, 1665 Pepys records, "I to Fox-hall, where to the Spring-garden[6], but I do not see one guest there — the town being so empty of anybody to come thither." The political world also came to a standstill during plague epidemics: both James Ⅰ and Charles Ⅰ postponed their coronations because of the 1603 and 1625 outbreaks, respectively. In 1665, Charles Ⅱ and his court fled London for parts west, abandoning the capital to the care of the City authorities. Pepys, a central government official, complained at the end of the year that "all goes to wrack as to public matters, they at this distance not thinking of it." Although this is what rich people did, Charles Ⅱ's flight in 1665 was viewed by many as ignominious.

In contrast and in keeping with tradition, Lord Mayor Sir John Lawrence (d. 1692) and the Court of Aldermen stayed at their posts to frame the civic response to the plague. The City had issued its first Book of Plague Orders in 1583. This and subsequent measures were a mixture of the practical and what we now know to be fanciful. For example, directives to stop foreign vessels from entering the Thames, close schools, and restrict begging and attendance at inns, taverns, coffeehouses, and funerals made sense by limiting exposure to, and propagation of, the disease. But orders to expel vagrants and clear the streets of dogs and cats must have made things worse: the former would have tended to spread the disease to the countryside; the latter eliminated the one major predator for the rats carrying the fleas that infected the people. Each dog or cat destroyed was worth a tuppence reward: a day's wage for a laborer. The result was more corpses, often left in the streets to rot. The restriction on alehouse attendance, combined with a ban on ballad singers and hawkers, was ostensibly to prevent gatherings of people in close quarters and on the streets, but this was also a convenient way for the authorities to stick it to a counter-culture that they hated. Finally, the City started its first pest house or plague hospital in St. Giles Cripplegate in 1594; subsequently it added new pest houses beyond the walls in Marylebone, Soho, and Stepney, to which the homeless were ordered. In 1665, these and the other municipal hospitals were soon overwhelmed: it was said that medical personnel could not walk around the rickety pallet beds on which victims lay; they had to walk *on* them.

In any case, the real war against the plague was fought in the parishes. From the late sixteenth century, City authorities required parish clerks to examine the Bills of Mortality for any uptick in plague deaths. From 1581, each parish was to nominate "two discreet matrons" as paid searchers to inquire in neighborhoods as to who was sick. Any house in which plague was reported was marked with a red cross and quarantined for 40 days. These measures were controversial: first, they violated the Christian duty to care for the sick. Second, the confinement of healthy and infected members of a household together was a virtual death sentence. No wonder that one physician reported seeing the confined "crying and roaring at their windows." To enforce the quarantine, guards with sharpened halberds were positioned at front doors.

As this implies, because local government normally relied on ordinary citizens who were now dead, dying, or afraid of their own neighbors, order and community, paternalism and neighborliness threatened to break down at the parish level. Masters turned out apprentices, pastors abandoned their flocks, doctors their patients, and parish authorities might pay to remove the infected beyond the bounds. Some ratepayers refused to pay the special plague rate; fortunately, in 1625 and 1665 supplementary collections were taken up throughout England. In theory, the parish brought food to the quarantined and left it, but in reality families suffered in terrible isolation or worse. For example, when in 1603 one of the servants of the physician and astrologer Simon Forman (1552 - 1611) became infected, his whole family was shut up. Instead of sympathy from their fellow parishioners, they received abuse: "They would say to me that it was better that I and my household should starve and die than any of them should be put in danger." Some victims refused to stay put and die: for example, in 1630 a distraught widow escaped quarantine and marched into Westminster Abbey, bewailing her fate. By late summer 1665, people began to attack their guards, throw themselves from upper-story windows, or run into the streets naked and delirious, foaming at the mouth. One contemporary hinted at the psychological, governmental, and social fallout:

> Death is now become so familiar and the people so insensible of danger, that they look upon such as provide for the public safety as tyrants and oppressors; whilst neither the richer sort will

be brought to contribute, nor the meaner to submit, though to their own apparent good and preservation.

London's responsibility to its inhabitants did not end with death. The City hired servants abandoned by their masters to drive the notorious "dead carts". There was perhaps no more melancholy sight in the diseased metropolis than the stacks of bodies being trundled through otherwise empty streets, grass growing through cobblestones, dead animals littering the roadway. The stench of rot, mingled with the soot and smoke from the perpetually burning "purging" fires, must have made London seem like the antechamber to hell. The carts carried the dead out to mass graves or "plague pits" just beyond the City walls. Because of the sheer volume of corpses, bodies were stacked nearly up to the surface, then covered over with a few inches of dirt and quicklime by shifts of gravediggers who worked around the clock, drinking profusely to get through their work. By late summer, the cart drivers and gravediggers themselves began to be infected: "Some died at the reins of their carts which, stacked with corpses, moved on aimlessly at the whim of the horses." As Pepys noted on August 22, 1665, even this last City service began to be neglected:

I went away and walked to Greenwich, in my way seeing a coffin with a dead body therein, dead of the plague, lying in an open close belonging to Coome farme, which was carried out last night and the parish hath not appointed anybody to bury it — but only set a watch there day and night, that nobody should go thither or come thence, which is a most cruel thing — this disease making us more cruel to one another then we are [to] dogs.

Still, some Londoners continued to attend the funerals of loved ones in violation of the City Plague Orders.

The greatest impact of London's plague epidemics may have been psychological. Perhaps the first reaction to the plague was alarm at the news of death, still distant: "30 [April 1665] ... Great fears of the Sickenesse here in the City, it being said that two or three houses are already shut up. God preserve us all." Then came the dreadful first encounter with the red-crossed doors and uncertainty about your own health, hence Pepys's worry about his "smell," quoted earlier. Soon you would be affected by the deaths of your neighbors, as Pepys was by that of "poor Will ... his wife and three children." In 1665, Samuel Pepys experienced two more psychological effects of the plague, a sense of isolation as the city became a ghost town, as well as widespread obsession with the fundamental fact of relentless death:

> But Lord, how empty the streets are, and melancholy, so many poor sick people in the streets, full of sores, and so many sad stories overheard as I walk, everybody talking of this dead, and that man sick, and so many in this place, and so many in that. And they tell me that in Westminster there is never a physitian, and but one apothecary left, all being dead — but that there are great hopes of a great decrease this week. God send it.

Of course, he was an eyewitness to much grief as well: "But in the street did overtake and almost run upon two women, crying and carrying a man's Coffin between them: I suppose the husband of one of them, which methinks is a sad thing." Dr. Thomas Lodge (1558 – 1625), writing at the time of the 1603 epidemic, worried about the utter despair and isolation of patients in pest houses.

Some reactions might strike us as perverse but are all too familiar from modern disasters. For example, wild rumors flew of people infecting each other deliberately, "And in spite to well people, would breathe in the faces (out of their windows) of well people going by." Others fell into a fatalistic despair of eat, drink, and be merry, or busied themselves by looting abandoned shops or waylaying passersby. Some became disoriented: "But now, how few people I see, and those walking like people that had taken leave of the world." Perhaps finally came resignation:

> Thence to the office; and after writing letters, home to draw over anew my Will, which I had bound myself by oath to despatch by tomorrow night, the town growing so unhealthy that a man cannot depend upon living two days to an end.

Sixty years later, Daniel Defoe[7], who was a small boy during the 1665 epidemic, captured all of these reactions in one of the greatest psychological novels in the English language, *Journal of the Plague Year* (1722).

None of this is to imply that all Londoners suffered equally. In 1563 the City was still fairly compact, and it was the center parishes that had the highest rates of mortality. But as London expanded, it was the out parishes that did worse in 1665, especially to the south and northeast. Why? These were the areas where newcomers and the poor settled; as a result, they were already overcrowded and unhealthy. Those who lived in the better areas might not have been present to fall ill, because the rich could, as we saw in the case of the court, get away. But as the summer epidemic raged on, country towns began to lock their gates against London refugees; some were met by thrown stones and manure. The best survival rates were among the 10,000 Londoners who moved to boats on the river. Among those who did not take to the roads or river, Boghurst and Hodges; the Duke of Albemarle, delegated by the king to watch things while he was gone; Lord Mayor Lawrence and his fellow aldermen; and Pepys himself stayed at their posts and in their various ways kept the city running.

London did not get a reprieve until late autumn 1665: casualties fell by half in the last week of September, and to 900 by the last week of November. Plague deaths continued into the spring of 1666, and the stench remained in the city for weeks. Still, Londoners began to drift back and reclaim their boarded-up properties. The city sprang again to life with remarkable quickness. Writing in January 1666, Samuel Pepys found it

> ... a delightful thing ... to see the town so full of people again, as now it is, and shops begin to open, though in many places, seven or eight together, and more, all shut; but yet the town is full compared with what is used to be — I mean the City-end, for Covent Gu[a]rden and Westminster are yet very empty of people, no Court nor gentry being there.

The court finally returned on February 1 to the peal church bells. With it came the elite and a revival of business for local merchants.

The 1665/66 visitation was the last major plague epidemic in London's history. There was to be one more significant scare in 1720—1722, when an outbreak in Marseille threw the metropolis into a panic. The plague regulations were debated again, and Defoe wrote the *Journal of the Plague Year* as part of that debate. The quarantine of French trade worked, however, and London's Dreadful Visitation did not return. Why not? Contemporaries thought that the fire of 1666 "burned it out," but this is nonsense. Later, historians argued that the brown rat (*Rattus norvegicus*) drove out the black rat (*Rattus rattus*), but this did not happen until the eighteenth century. It is possible that the rats themselves acquired immunity. In any case, the Commercial Revolution of the late seventeenth and early eighteenth centuries should have left London wide open to a relapse, yet the plague did not return.

Still, London's *anni horribili* continued[8].

一、导读

1550—1750 年，伦敦发展成为欧洲最大的城市。它支配了不列颠群岛的经济、政治、社会和文化生活，同时也是世界上最具生机与活力的经济和文化中心之一。《伦敦：1550—1750 的社会文化史》（*London: A Social and Cultural History*, 1550 - 1750）就是一部描述伦敦逐渐崛起为现代大都市的这一关键时期的城市史专著。这本书吸收了近年来城市史方面最好的著作成果，引用了当时伦敦人和旅游者的描述，以及以伦敦为特写的文学作品来追踪伦敦的崛起，并揭示它怎样扮演现代化先驱的角色、它的居民如何应对其发展过程中所面临的问题等。该书是西方城市史的代表作，具有重要的史料价值。

这部书的作者是罗伯特·O. 布霍尔茨（Robert O. Bucholz）和约瑟夫·P. 沃德（Joseph P. Ward）。布霍尔茨是芝加哥洛约拉大学的历史学教授，他还是《近代早期英格兰叙事史：1485—1714 年》（*Early-Modern England* 1485 - 1714: *a Narrative History*）和《英国历史上的信息来源和辩议：1485—1714》（*Sources and Debates in English History* 1485 - 1714）的作者〔与牛顿·基（Newton Key）合著〕，以及《中世纪和近代早期英格兰的女王和权力》（*Queens and Power in Medieval and Early Modern England*）的编者〔与卡萝尔·莱文（Carol Levin）合编〕。沃德是密西西比大学历史系主任，代表作是《大都市社团：近代早期伦敦的行会，认同和改变》（*Metropolitan Communities: Trade Guilds, Identity, and Change in Early Modern London*），另外编撰或与他人合编了其他几部学术著作。

中世纪和近代早期，伦敦连续不断地遭遇黑死病的袭击，每一次黑死病的来临都造成伦敦城人口的大量死亡。1665 年，伦敦遭遇了历史上死亡人数最多的一次黑死病，大约有 5.6 万人（如果把郊区和边远区域包括在内，这一数字估计会上涨到 7 万～10 万）在这次瘟疫中丧失了生命。1665—1666 年的鼠疫也是伦敦历史上最后一次严重的流行鼠疫，在这以后，虽然 1720—1722 年曾经发生过一次瘟疫恐慌，但是鼠疫却再也没有踏上伦敦的土地。

本文献节选自《伦敦：1550—1750 年社会文化史》第 8 章的前半部分，主要记述了 1665—1666 年伦敦的大瘟疫。

二、注释

1. Selected from Robert O. Bucholz, Joseph P. Ward, *London: A Social and Cultural History*, 1550 - 1750, Cambridge University Press, 2012.

2. Bills of Mortality，指死亡周报表。

3. Samuel Pepys，塞缪尔·佩皮斯（1633—1703），17世纪英国作家和政治家，曾任海军大臣。从1660年1月1日—1669年5月31日，佩皮斯用日记的形式记述了当时伦敦发生的事情，这些日记后来成为研究伦敦历史的重要史料。

4. Dissenters，意为“持异议者”，也可译为“不信奉国教者”。这里特指英国的清教徒。

5. French pox，意为“法国疱疹”，指代性病。英国人将性病来源归因于法国。

6. Fox-hall 和 the Spring-garden 是当时伦敦城内的娱乐场所。

7. Daniel Defoe，丹尼尔·笛福（1660—1731），英国启蒙时期现实主义小说的奠基人，被誉为“欧洲小说之父”，代表作有《鲁滨孙漂流记》《摩尔·弗兰德斯》等。1722年，他出版了心理小说《灾年记事》（*Journal of the Plague Year*，也有的汉译为《瘟疫年纪事》《伦敦大瘟疫亲历记》等）。在这本书中，笛福记载了1665年的伦敦大瘟疫，他把这场鼠疫的发生、传播引起的恐慌以及伦敦的死亡数字、伦敦人的逃疫情况等写得栩栩如生，读后使人有身临其境之感。

8. 指1666年伦敦大火。

三、问题探讨

1. 鼠疫带给人们的心理恐慌表现在哪些方面？

2. 17世纪的英国人认为鼠疫是如何发生的，他们如何应对？抗击鼠疫的斗争怎样促使伦敦城走向现代？

四、参考文献

1. 谢谦：《鼠疫困扰下的伦敦——近代早期城市生活管窥》，《历史教学问题》1998年第1期。

2. 邹翔：《鼠疫与伦敦城市公共卫生（1518—1667）》，人民出版社2015年版。

3. [英] 丹尼尔·笛福：《伦敦大瘟疫亲历记》，谢萍译，内蒙古人民出版社2003年版。

4. [英] 彼得·阿克罗伊德：《伦敦传》，翁海贞译，译林出版社2016年版。

5. A. L. Abeier, Roger Finlay, *The Making of the Metropolis: London, 1500-1700*, Longman Group Limited, 1986.

UNIT 18

PEACE WITHOUT VICTORY[1]

Woodrow Wilson

Gentlemen of the Senate:

On the 18th of December last I addressed an identic note to the governments of the nations now at war requesting them to state, more definitely than they had yet been stated by either group of belligerents, the terms upon which they would deem it possible to make peace. I spoke on behalf of humanity and of the rights of all neutral nations like our own, many of whose most vital interests the war puts in constant jeopardy. The Central Powers[2] united in a reply which stated merely that they were ready to meet their antagonists in conference to discuss terms of peace. The Entente Powers[3] have replied much more definitely and have stated, in general terms, indeed, but with sufficient definiteness to imply details, the arrangements, guarantees, and acts of reparation which they deem to be the indispensable conditions of a satisfactory settlement. We are that much nearer a definite discussion of the peace which shall end the present war. We are that much nearer the definite discussion of the international concert which must thereafter hold the world at peace. In every discussion of peace that must end this war, it is taken for granted that the peace must be followed by some definite concert of power which will make it virtually impossible that any such catastrophe should ever overwhelm us again. Every lover of mankind, every sane and thoughtful man must take that for granted.

I have sought this opportunity to address you because I thought that I owed it to you, as the council associated with me in the final determination of our international obligations, to disclose to you without reserve the thought and purpose that have been taking form in my mind in regard to the duty of our Government in the days to come when it will be necessary to lay afresh and upon a new plan the foundations of peace among the nations.

It is inconceivable that the people of the United States should play no part in that great enterprise. To take part in such a service will be the opportunity for which they have sought to prepare themselves by the very principles and purposes of their polity and the approved practices of their Government ever since the days when they set up a new nation in the high and honourable hope that it might in all that it was and did show mankind the way to liberty. They cannot in honour withhold the service to which they are now about to be challenged. They do not wish to withhold it. But they owe it to themselves and to the other nations of the world to state the conditions under which they will feel free to render it.

That service is nothing less than this, to add their authority and their power to the authority and force of other nations to guarantee peace and justice throughout the world. Such a settlement cannot now be long postponed. It is right that before it comes this Government should frankly formulate the conditions upon which it would feel justified in asking our people to approve its formal and solemn adherence to a League for Peace[4]. I am here to attempt to state those conditions.

The present war must first be ended; but we owe it to candour and to a just regard for the opinion of mankind to say that, so far as our participation in guarantees of future peace is concerned, it makes a great deal of difference in what way and upon what terms it is ended. The treaties and agreements which bring it to an end must embody terms which will create a peace that is worth guaranteeing and preserving, a peace that will win the approval of mankind, not merely a peace that will serve the several interests and immediate aims of the nations engaged. We shall have no voice in determining whether they shall be made lasting or not by the guarantees of a universal covenant; and our judgment upon what is fundamental and essential as a condition precedent to permanency should be spoken now, not afterwards when it may be too late.

No covenant of co-operative peace that does not include the peoples of the New World[5] can suffice to keep the future safe against war; and yet there is only one sort of peace that the peoples of America could join in guaranteeing. The elements of that peace must be elements that engage the confidence and satisfy the principles of the American governments, elements consistent with their political faith and with the practical convictions which the peoples of America have once for all embraced and undertaken to defend.

I do not mean to say that any American government would throw any obstacle in the way of any terms of peace the governments now at war might agree upon or seek to upset them when made, whatever they might be. I only take it for granted that mere terms of peace between the belligerents will not satisfy even the belligerents themselves. Mere agreements may not make peace secure. It will be absolutely necessary that a force be created as a guarantor of the permanency of the settlement so much greater than the force of any nation now engaged or any alliance hitherto formed or projected that no nation, no probable combination of nations could face or withstand it. If the peace presently to be made is to endure, it must be a peace made secure by the organized major force of mankind.

The terms of the immediate peace agreed upon will determine whether it is a peace for which such a guarantee can be secured. The question upon which the whole future peace and policy of the world depends is this: Is the present war a struggle for a just and secure peace, or only for a new balance of power? If it be only a struggle for a new balance of power, who will guarantee, who can guarantee, the stable equilibrium of the new arrangement? Only a tranquil Europe can be a stable Europe. There must be, not a balance of power, but a community of power; not organized rivalries, but an organized common peace.

Fortunately we have received very explicit assurances on this point. The statesmen of both of the groups of nations now arrayed against one another have said, in terms that could not be misinterpreted, that it was no part of the purpose they had in mind to crush their antagonists. But the implications of these assurances may not be equally clear to all, may not be the same on both sides of the water. I think it will be serviceable if I attempt to set forth what we understand them to be.

They imply, first of all, that it must be a peace without victory. It is not pleasant to say this. I beg that I may be permitted to put my own interpretation upon it and that it may be understood that no other interpretation was in my thought. I am seeking only to face realities and to face them without soft concealments. Victory would mean peace forced upon the loser, a victor's terms imposed upon the vanquished. It would be accepted in humiliation, under duress, at an intolerable sacrifice, and would leave a sting, a resentment, a bitter memory upon which terms of peace would rest, not permanently, but only as upon quicksand. Only a peace between equals can last. Only a peace the very principle of which is equality and a common participation in a common benefit.

The right state of mind, the right feeling between nations, is as necessary for a lasting peace as is the just settlement of vexed questions of territory or of racial and national allegiance.

The equality of nations upon which peace must be founded if it is to last must be an equality of rights; the guarantees exchanged must neither recognize nor imply a difference between big nations and small, between those that are powerful and those that are weak. Right must be based upon the common strength, not upon the individual strength, of the nations upon whose concert peace will depend. Equality of territory or of resources there of course cannot be; nor any sort of equality not gained in the ordinary peaceful and legitimate development of the peoples themselves. But no one asks or expects anything more than an equality of rights. Mankind is looking now for freedom of life, not for equipoises[6] of power.

And there is a deeper thing involved than even equality of right among organized nations. No peace can last, or ought to last, which does not recognize and accept the principle that governments derive all their just powers from the consent of the governed, and that no right anywhere exists to hand peoples about from sovereignty to sovereignty as if they were property. I take it for granted, for instance, if I may venture upon a single example, that statesmen everywhere are agreed that there should be a united, independent, and autonomous Poland, and that henceforth inviolable security of life, of worship, and of industrial and social development should be guaranteed to all peoples who have lived hitherto under the power of governments devoted to a faith and purpose hostile to their own.

I speak of this, not because of any desire to exalt an abstract political principle which has always been held very dear by those who have sought to build up liberty in America, but for the same reason that I have spoken of the other conditions of peace which seem to me clearly indispensable, because I wish frankly to uncover realities. Any peace which does not recognize and accept this principle will inevitably be upset. It will not rest upon the affections or the convictions of mankind. The ferment of spirit of whole populations will fight subtly and constantly against it, and all the world will sympathize. The world can be at peace only if its life is stable, and there can be no stability where the will is in rebellion, where there is not tranquillity of spirit and a sense of justice, of freedom, and of right.

So far as practicable, moreover, every great people now struggling towards a full development of its resources and of its powers should be assured a direct outlet to the great highways of the sea. Where this cannot be done by the cession of territory, it can no doubt be done by the neutralization of direct rights of way under the general guarantee which will assure the peace itself. With a right comity of arrangement no nation need be shut away from free access to the open paths of the world's commerce.

And the paths of the sea must alike in law and in fact be free. The freedom of the seas is the *sine qua non* of peace, equality, and co-operation. No doubt a somewhat radical reconsideration of many of the rules of international practice hitherto thought to be established may be necessary in order to make the seas indeed free and common in practically all circumstances for the use of mankind, but the motive for such changes is convincing and compelling. There can be no trust or intimacy between the peoples of the world without them. The free, constant, unthreatened intercourse of nations is an essential part of the process of peace and of development. It need not be difficult either to define or to secure the freedom of the seas if the governments of the world sincerely desire to come to an agreement concerning it.

It is a problem closely connected with the limitation of naval armaments and the co-operation of the navies of the world in keeping the seas at once free and safe. And the question of limiting naval armaments opens the wider and perhaps more difficult question of the limitation of armies and of all programmes of military preparation. Difficult and delicate as these questions are, they must be faced with the utmost candour and decided in a spirit of real accommodation if peace is to come with healing it its wings, and come to stay. Peace cannot be had without concession and sacrifice. There can be no sense of safety and equality among the nations if great preponderating armaments are henceforth to continue here and there to be built up and maintained. The statesmen of the world must plan for peace and nations must adjust and accommodate their policy to it as they have planned for war and made ready for pitiless contest and rivalry. The question of armaments, whether on land or sea, is the most immediately and intensely practical question connected with the future fortunes of nations and of mankind.

I have spoken upon these great matters without reserve and with the utmost explicitness because it has seemed to me to be necessary if the world's yearning desire for peace was anywhere to find free voice and utterance. Perhaps I am the only person in high authority amongst all the peoples of the world who is at liberty to speak and hold nothing back. I am speaking as an individual, and yet I am speaking also, of course, as the responsible head of a great government, and I feel confident that I have said what the people of the United States would wish me to say. May I not add that I hope and believe that I am in effect speaking for liberals and friends of humanity in every nation and of every programme of liberty? I would fain[7] believe that I am speaking for the silent mass of mankind everywhere who have as yet had no place or opportunity to speak their real hearts out concerning the death and ruin they see to have come already upon the persons and the homes they hold most dear.

And in holding out the expectation that the people and Government of the United States will join the other civilized nations of the world in guaranteeing the permanence of peace upon such terms as I have named I speak with the greater boldness and confidence because it is clear to every man who can think that there is in this promise no breach in either our traditions or our policy as a nation, but a fulfilment, rather, of all that we have professed or striven for.

I am proposing, as it were, that the nations should with one accord adopt the doctrine of President Monroe[8] as the doctrine of the world: That no nation should seek to extend its policy over any other nation or people, but that every people should be left free to determine its own polity, its own way of development, unhindered, unthreatened, unafraid, the little along with the great and powerful.

I am proposing that all nations henceforth avoid entangling alliances which would draw them into competitions of power, catch them in a net of intrigue and selfish rivalry, and disturb their own affairs with influences intruded from without. There is no entangling alliance in a concert of power. When all unite to act in the same sense and with the same purpose all act in the common interest and are free to live their own lives under a common protection.

I am proposing government by the consent of the governed; that freedom of the seas which in international conference after conference representatives of the United States have urged with the eloquence of those who are the convinced disciples of liberty; and that moderation of armaments which makes of armies and navies a power for order merely, not an instrument of aggression or of selfish violence.

These are American principles, American policies. We could stand for no others. And they are also the principles and policies of forward looking men and women everywhere, of every modern nation, of every enlightened community. They are the principles of mankind and must prevail.

一、导读

伍德罗·威尔逊（Woodrow Wilson），1856 年出生于美国弗吉尼亚州的斯汤顿市一个长老会牧师家庭。1875 年进入普林斯顿大学，4 年后进入弗吉尼亚大学专攻法律。1882—1883 年，他当过律师，但业绩并不理想，便转而从事教育事业。1885—1902 年，威尔逊先后在宾夕法尼亚州的布林莫尔学院、康涅狄格州的韦斯利安大学和普林斯顿大学任教。1902 年，威尔逊当选普林斯顿大学校长，因倡导教育改革而成为著名的教育界领袖。

但是，由于威尔逊的教育改革计划在推行中受到重重阻碍，1910 年，他辞去校长职务，转而进入政界。同年，在《哈泼斯周刊》编辑乔治·哈维的推荐下，新泽西州民主党党魁詹姆斯·史密斯提名威尔逊为州长候选人，并在州长竞选中胜出。鉴于日益高涨的要求改革的选民情绪与政治氛围，威尔逊在任职州长期间，大力推行改革。1912 年，他以民主党总统候选人身份在全国总统大选中胜出，并在 1913 年初入主白宫。

威尔逊从政期间，适值他领导的州和全国的进步运动都处于完成阶段，而且此时在野 20 年的民主党领袖也想有所作为，以及民主党在国会两院中是多数党，这些有利条件为他成为美国历史上最为杰出且成就斐然的领导人之一铺平了道路。

作为著述等身的教授型总统，威尔逊将政治学中的新理念贯穿于现代政治实践中，将总统一职改造成为政党领导的工具与指导立法的手段。他认为，美国需要改革政治制度，以便建立更负责任的政府，进而主张加强和扩大总统的权力。他赞成效仿英国首相在议会依赖政党纪律的这套做法，确信在美国一个强有力的总统也可以将政党纪律施加于国会。他为了争取改革立法的通过，亲自到国会发表演说；如果必要，他甚至敢于越过国会，直接诉诸选民与公众舆论。他扩展了西奥多·罗斯福总统运用新闻媒介引导社会舆论的手法，成为第一位举行总统新闻发布会的总统。同时，他赞成运用总统的权力推动进步立法。

在总统的首个任期里，他在关税、银行、工业等领域的立法改革中均取得了很大的成功。不过，1914 年第一次世界大战的爆发将人们的注意力日益从国内问题转向国际领域。1916 年，威尔逊以“他使我们免于战争”的竞选口号，再度当选总统。之后，由于德国采取的“无限制潜艇战”以及“齐默尔曼电报事件”的发生，最终促使美国放弃中立政策，于 1917 年 4 月对德宣战，正式参加第一次世界大战。

本文献选自詹姆斯·D. 理查德逊（James D. Richardson）编辑的《美国总统咨文与文件汇编，1789 年至 1922 年》第 17 卷，文中部分内容参照刘易斯·科普兰（Lewis Copeland）和劳伦斯·W. 拉姆编辑的《世界上的伟大演说》进行校对。该文献是 1917 年 1 月 21 日威尔逊在美国参议院发表的演讲，中心是美国要以中立国的身份调停一战，媾和的基本原则是没有胜利者的和平。然而，他的和平希望落空，该演说发表仅 2 个多月后，美国对德宣战。

二、注释

1. Selected from James D. Richardson(ed.), *A Compilation of the Messages and Papers of the Presidents,* 1789 - 1922, Vol. 17, Bureau of National Literature, Inc., 1922.

2. the Central Powers，指一战中的“同盟国”，主要由德国、奥匈帝国、奥斯曼土耳其帝国和保加利亚等国家组成；由于它们都处在东面的沙俄与西面的法国、英国之间，故称“the Central”。

3. the Entente Powers，指一战中的“协约国”，主要由英、法、俄等国家组成。

4. a League for Peace，即“和平联盟”，后来国联的建立受此思想影响。

5. the New World，指美洲，尤指美国。

6. equipoises，即“均势”。

7. fain，意为“欣然地”。

8. the doctrine of President Monroe，即“门罗主义”。

三、问题探讨

1. 美国总统威尔逊和平主张的基本精神有哪些？

2. 巴黎和会上，威尔逊的哪些主张得以实现？产生了什么样的影响？

四、参考文献

1. 赵辉兵：《美国总统与进步运动》，《哈尔滨工业大学学报》（社会科学版）2009 年第 1 期。

2. 赵辉兵：《美国进步主义政治思潮与实践研究》，中国社会科学出版社 2013 年版。

3. [美] 詹姆斯·多尔蒂、[美] 小罗伯特·普法尔茨格拉夫 ：《争论中的国际关系理论》，阎学通等译，世界知识出版社 2002 年版。

4. James D. Richardson (ed.), *A Compilation of the Messages and Papers of the Presidents,* 1789 - 1922, Vol. 17, Bureau of National Literature, Inc., 1922.

5. Lewis Copeland, Lawrence W. Lamm (eds.), *The World's Great Speeches*, Dover Publications Inc., 1973.

UNIT 19

NON-COOPERATION[1]

Mohandas K. Gandhi

What is this non-cooperation, about which you have heard much, and why do we want to offer this non-cooperation? I wish to go for the time being into the way. There are two things before this country: the first and the foremost is the Khilafat[2] question. On this the heart of the Mussalmans of India has become lascerated[3]. British pledges given after the greatest deliberation by the Prime Minister of England in the name of the English nation, have been dragged into the mire. The promises given to Moslem India on the strength of which, the consideration that was expected by the British nation was exacted, have been broken, and the great religion of Islam has been placed in danger. The Mussalmans hold — and I venture to think they rightly hold — that, so long as British promises remain unfulfilled, so long is it impossible for them to tender whole-hearted fealty and loyalty to the British connection; and if it is to be a choice for a devout Mussalman between loyalty to the British connection and loyalty to his Code and Prophet, he will not require a second to make his choice, — and he has declared his choice. The Mussalmans say frankly, openly, and honourably to the whole world that if the British Ministers and the British nation do not fulfil the pledges given to them and do not wish to regard with respect the sentiments of the 70 millions of the inhabitants of India who profess the faith of Islam, it will be impossible for them to retain Islamic loyalty. It is a question, then, for the rest of the Indian population to consider whether they want to perform a neighbourly duty by their Mussalman countrymen, and if they do, they have an opportunity of a life time which will not occur for another hundred years, to show their good-will, fellowship and friendship and to prove what they have been saying for all these long years that the Mussalman is the brother of the Hindu. If the Hindu regards that before the connection with the

British nation comes his natural connection with his Moslem brother, then I say to you that if you find that the Moslem claim is just, that it is based upon real sentiment, and that its back ground is this great religious feeling, you cannot do otherwise than help the Mussalman through and through, so long as their cause remains just, and the means for attaining the end remains equally just, honourable and free from harm to India. These are the plain conditions which the Indian Mussalmans have accepted; and it was when they saw that they could accept the proffered aid of the Hindus, that they could always justify the cause and the means before the whole world, that they decided to accept the proffered hand of fellowship. It is then for the Hindus and Mohammedans to offer a united front to the whole of the Christian powers of Europe and tell them that weak as India is, India has still got the capacity of preserving her self-respect, she still knows how to die for her religion and for her self-respect.

That is the Khilafat in a nut-shell; but you have also got the Punjab[4]. The Punjab has wounded the heart of India as no other question has for the past century. I do not exclude from my calculation the Mutiny of 1857[5]. Whatever hardships India had to suffer during the Mutiny, the insult that was attempted to be offered to her during the passage of the Rowlatt[6] legislation and that which was offered after its passage were unparalleled in Indian history. It is because you want justice from the British nation in connection with the Punjab atrocities you have to devise ways and means as to how you can get this justice. The House of Commons, the House of Lords, Mr. Montagu[7], the Viceroy[8] of India, every one of them know what the feeling of India is on this Khilafat question and on that of the Punjab; the debates in both the Houses of Parliament, the action of Mr. Montagu and that of the Viceroy have demonstrated to you completely that they are not willing to give the justice which is India's due and which she demands. I suggest that our leaders have got to find a way out of this great difficulty and unless we have made ourselves even with the British rulers in India and unless we have gained a measure of self-respect at the hands of the British rulers in India, no connection, and no friendly intercourse is possible between them and ourselves. I, therefore, venture to suggest this beautiful and unanswerable method of non-cooperation.

I have been told that non-cooperation is unconstitutional. I venture to deny that it is unconstitutional. On the contrary, I hold that non-cooperation is a just and religious doctrine; it is the inherent right of every human being and it is perfectly constitutional. A great lover of the British Empire has said that under the British constitution even a successful rebellion is perfectly constitutional and he quotes historical instances, which I cannot deny, in support of his claim. I do not claim any constitutionality for a rebellion successful or otherwise, so long as that rebellion means in the ordinary sense of the term, what it does mean, namely, wresting justice by violent means. On the contrary, I have said it repeatedly to my countrymen that violence, whatever end it may serve in Europe, will never serve us in India.

My brother and friend Shaukat Ali[9] believes in methods of violence; and if it was in his power to draw the sword against the British Empire, I know that he has got the courage of a man and he has got also the wisdom to see that he should offer that battle to the British Empire. But because he recognises as a true soldier that means of violence are not open to India, he sides with me accepting my humble assistance and pledges his word that so long as I am with him and so long as he believes in the doctrine, so long will he not harbour even the idea of violence against any single Englishman or any single man on earth. I am here to tell you that he has been as true as his word and has kept it religiously. I am here to bear witness that he has been following out this plan of non-violent Non-cooperation to the very letter and I am asking India to follow this non-violent non-cooperation. I tell you that there is not a better soldier living in our ranks in British India than Shaukat Ali. When the time for the drawing of the sword comes, if it ever comes, you will find him drawing that sword and you will find me retiring to the jungles of Hindustan. As soon as India accepts the doctrine of the sword, my life as an Indian is finished. It is because I believe in a mission special to India and it is because I believe that the ancients of India after centuries of experience have found out that the true thing for any human being on earth is not justice based on violence but justice based on sacrifice of self, justice based on Yagna and Kurbani[10], — I cling to that doctrine and I shall cling to it for ever, — it is for that reason I tell you that whilst my friend believes also in the doctrine of violence and has adopted the doctrine of non-violence as a weapon of the weak, I believe in the doctrine of non-violence as a weapon of the strongest. I believe that a man is the strongest soldier for daring to die unarmed with his breast bare before the enemy. So much for the non-violent part of non-cooperation. I therefore, venture to suggest to my learned countrymen that so long as the doctrine of non-cooperation remains non-violent, so long there is nothing unconstitutional in that doctrine.

I ask further, is it unconstitutional for me to say to the British Government "I refuse to serve you?" Is it unconstitutional for our worthy Chairman to return with every respect all the titles that he has ever held from the Government? Is it unconstitutional for any parent to withdraw his children from a Government or aided school? Is it unconstitutional for a lawyer to say "I shall no longer support the arm of the law so long as that arm of law is used not to raise me but to debase me"? Is it unconstitutional for a civil servant or for a judge to say, "I refuse to serve a Government which does not wish to respect the wishes of the whole people?" I ask, is it unconstitutional for a policeman or for a soldier to tender his resignation when he knows that he is called to serve a Government which traduces[11] his own countrymen? Is it unconstitutional for me to go to the "krishan"[12], to the agriculturist, and say to him "it is not wise for you to pay any taxes, if these taxes are used by the Government not to raise you but to weaken you?" I hold and I venture to submit, that there is nothing unconstitutional in it. What is more, I have done every one of these things in my life and nobody has questioned the constitutional character of it. I was in Kaira[13] working in the midst of 7 lakhs[14] of agriculturists. They had all suspended the payment of taxes and the whole of India was at one with me. Nobody considered that it was unconstitutional. I submit that in the whole plan of non-cooperation, there is nothing unconstitutional. But I do venture to suggest that it will be highly unconstitutional in the midst of this unconstitutional Government, — in the midst of a nation which has built up its magnificent constitution, — for the people of India to become weak and to crawl on their belly — it will be highly unconstitutional for the people of India to pocket every insult that is offered to them; it is highly unconstitutional for the 70 millions of Mohammedans of India to submit to a violent wrong done to their religion; it is highly unconstitutional for the whole of India to sit still and cooperate with an unjust Government which has trodden under its feet the honour of the Punjab. I say to my countrymen so long as you have a sense of honour and so long as you wish to remain the descendants and defenders of the noble traditions that have been handed to you for generations after generations, it is unconstitutional for you not to non-cooperate and unconstitutional for you to cooperate with a Government which has become so unjust as our Government has become. I am not anti-English; I am not anti-British; I am not anti any Government; but I am anti-untruth — anti-humbug[15] and anti-injustice. So long as the Government spells injustice, it may regard me as its enemy, implacable enemy. I had hoped at the Congress at Amritsar — I am speaking God's truth before you — when I pleaded on bended knees before some of you for cooperation with the Government. I had full hope that the British ministers who are wise, as a rule, would placate the Mussalman sentiment that they would do full justice in the matter of the Punjab atrocities; and therefore, I said: — let us return good-will to the hand of fellowship that has been extended to us, which I then believed was extended to us through the Royal Proclamation. It was on that account that I pleaded for cooperation. But to-day that faith having gone and obliterated by the acts of the British ministers, I am here to plead not for futile obstruction in the Legislative council but for real substantial non-cooperation which would paralyse the mightiest Government on earth. That is what I stand for to-day. Until we have wrung justice, and until we have wrung our self-respect from unwilling hands and from unwilling pens there can be no cooperation. Our Shastras say and I say so with the greatest deference to all the greatest religious preceptors of India but without fear of contradiction, that our Shastras teach us that there shall be no cooperation between injustice and justice, between an unjust man and a justice-loving man, between truth and untruth. Cooperation is a duty only so long as Government protects your honour, and non-cooperation is an equal duty when the Government instead of protecting robs you of your honour. That is the doctrine of non-cooperation.

ATTACHED

NATIONALISM IN INDIA[16]

Rabindranath Tagore

Our real problem in India is not political. It is social. This is a condition not only prevailing in India, but among all nations. I do not believe in an exclusive political interest. Politics in the West have dominated Western ideals, and we in India are trying to imitate you. We have to remember that in Europe, where peoples had their racial unity from the beginning, and where natural resources were insufficient for the inhabitants, the civilization has naturally taken the character of political and commercial aggressiveness. For on the one hand they had no internal complications, and on the other they had to deal with neighbours who were strong and rapacious. To have perfect combination among themselves and a watchful attitude of animosity against others was taken as the solution of their problems. In former days they organized and plundered, in the present age the same spirit continues — and they organize and exploit the whole world.

...The whole world is becoming one country through scientific facility. And the moment is arriving when you also must find a basis of unity which is not political. If India can offer to the world her solution, it will be a contribution to humanity. There is only one history — the history of man. All national histories are merely chapters in the larger one. ...

The most important fact of the present age is that all the different races of men have come close together. And again we are confronted with two alternatives. The problem is whether the different groups of peoples shall go on fighting with one another or find out some true basis of reconciliation and mutual help; whether it will be interminable competition or cooperation. ...

Americais destined to justify Western civilization to the East. Europe has lost faith in humanity, and has become distrustful and sickly. America, on the other hand, is not pessimistic or blasé. ...

India has never had a real sense of nationalism. Even though from childhood I had been taught that idolatry of the Nation is almost better than reverence for God and humanity, I believe I have outgrown that teaching, and it is my conviction that my countrymen will truly gain their India by fighting against the education which teaches them that a country is greater than the ideals of humanity.

The educated Indian at present is trying to absorb some lessons from history contrary to the lessons of our ancestors. The East, in fact, is attempting to take unto itself a history which is not the outcome of its own living. Japan, for example, thinks she is getting powerful through adopting Western methods, but, after she has exhausted her inheritance, only the borrowed weapons of civilization will remain to her. She will not have developed herself from within.

Europe has her past. Europe's strength therefore lies in her history. We, in

India, must make up our minds that we cannot borrow other people's history, and that if we stifle our own, we are committing suicide. When you borrow things that do not belong to your life, they only serve to crush your life.

And therefore I believe that it does India no good to compete with Western civilization in its own field. But we shall be more than compensated if, in spite of the insults heaped upon us, we follow our own destiny.

We must know for certain that there is a future before us and that future is waiting for those who are rich in moral ideals and not in mere things. And it is the privilege of man to work for fruits that are beyond his immediate reach, and to adjust his life not in slavish conformity to the examples of some present success or even to his own prudent past, limited in its aspiration, but to an infinite future bearing in its heart the ideals of our highest expectations.

We must, however, know that it is providential that the West has come to India. Yet, some one must show the East to the West, and convince the West that the East has her contribution to make to the history of civilization. India is no beggar of the West. And yet even though the West may think she is, I am not for thrusting off Western civilization and becoming segregated in our independence. Let us have a deep association. If Providence wants England to be the channel of that communication, of that deeper association, I am willing to accept it with all humility. I have great faith in human nature, and I think the West will find its true mission. I speak bitterly of Western civilization when I am conscious that it is betraying its trust and thwarting its own purpose. The West must not make herself a curse to the world by using her power for her own selfish needs, but by teaching the ignorant and helping the weak, by saving herself from the worst danger that the strong is liable to incur by making the feeble acquire power enough to resist her intrusion. And also she must not make her materialism to be the final thing, but must realize that she is doing a service in freeing the spiritual being from the tyranny of matter.

I am not against one nation in particular, but against the general idea of all nations. What is the Nation?

It is the aspect of a whole people as an organized power. This organization incessantly keeps up the insistence of the population on becoming strong and efficient. But this strenuous effort after strength and efficiency drains man's energy from his higher nature where he is self-sacrificing and creative. For thereby man's power of sacrifice is diverted from his ultimate object, which is moral, to the maintenance of this organization, which is mechanical. Yet in this he feels all the satisfaction of moral exaltation and therefore becomes supremely dangerous to humanity. He feels relieved of the urging of his conscience when he can transfer his responsibility to this machine which is the creation of his intellect and not of his complete moral personality. By this device the people which loves freedom perpetuates slavery in a large portion of the world with the comfortable feeling of pride of having done its duty; men who are naturally just can be cruelly unjust both in their act and their thought, accompanied by a feeling that they are helping the world to receive its deserts; men who are honest can blindly go on robbing others of their human rights for self-aggrandizement, all the while abusing the deprived for not deserving better treatment. We have seen in our everyday life even small organizations of business and profession produce callousness of feeling in men who are not naturally bad, and we can well imagine what a moral havoc it is causing in a world where whole peoples are furiously organizing themselves for gaining wealth and power.

Nationalism is a great menace. It is the particular thing which for years has been at the bottom of India's troubles. And inasmuch as we have been ruled and dominated by a nation that is strictly political in its attitude, we have tried to develop within ourselves, despite our inheritance from the past, a belief in our eventual political destiny.

It was my conviction that what India most needed was constructive work coming from within herself. In this work we must take all risks and go on doing the duties which by right are ours, though in the teeth of persecution; winning moral victory at every step, by our failure and suffering. We must show those who are over us that we have in ourselves the strength of moral power, the power to suffer for truth.

一、导读

莫罕达斯·卡拉姆昌德·甘地（Mohandas Karamchand Gandhi），被世人尊称为“圣雄甘地”（Mahatma Gandhi），是印度民族解放运动的领导人、印度国大党领袖、20 世纪非暴力主义倡导者。

甘地出生在印度西海岸一个小土邦的中等家庭，其家族属于吠舍种姓。甘地的母亲是一位虔诚的印度教信徒，对他早年影响很大。1888 年，甘地赴英国就读伦敦大学，1891 年获律师资格后回国。1893 年，甘地应邀赴南非处理债务纠纷。在南非期间，他多次运用非暴力方式进行反种族歧视的斗争。1915 年，甘地回国后周游各地，了解民众疾苦，并创立了非暴力抵抗学院。1916 年，他反对不可接触者制度，主张经济自主，呼吁印度教徒与穆斯林团结。1918 年，甘地成功组织了艾哈迈达巴德纺织工人罢工和凯达县农民抗税运动。第一次世界大战结束不久，为了抗议政府通过的剥夺人民民主的《罗拉特法》，甘地在孟买成立了非暴力抵抗大会，并发动非暴力抵抗运动。1919 年 4 月 13 日，旁遮普发生了英国军警屠杀集会群众的阿姆利则惨案，孟买等地群众为抗议英国当局暴行，举行暴动，捣毁警局，各地纷纷宣布实施戒严法。甘地认为，群众行动有违非暴力原则，他亲赴艾哈迈达巴德宣布停止非暴力抵抗运动。为此，甘地通过报刊宣传非暴力抵抗的原理。1919 年底，英国当局以“孟塔古-蔡姆斯福德改革方案”为蓝本推出了《印度政府法》，而这与印度民族主义者与民族资产阶级的预期落差很大，他们意识到英国政府无意让他们很快实现真正的自治。这时，印度的穆斯林则对英国在处置土耳其问题上的食言十分不满。当初他们支持英国作战时，要求英国战胜土耳其后要为其保留伊斯兰教圣地和阿拉伯属地，并维护哈里发的地位，但英国政府并没有打算兑现这一承诺。因此，这就加剧了印度社会各阶层对英国政府的不满。而在印度民众需要国大党和穆斯林联盟做出回应之时，他们却拿不出有力的对策。甘地主义以及甘地领导的非暴力不合作运动正是在这样的历史时刻应运而生的。

此篇演讲节选自 1920 年 8 月 12 日甘地对 5 万多名追随者所发表的演说。他发表演说之际，正是全印度第一次非暴力不合作运动拉开序幕之时。俄国十月革命的胜利、亚洲其他被压迫民族争取自由的斗争、威尔逊倡导的民族自决原则等国际因素都刺激并推动了印度争取自治乃至独立的斗争。这篇演说可以视为甘地的“主要解决方案”。那么，甘地的非暴力原则到底是什么呢？他在《甘地自传》中总结道：“我的人生经验让我确信，真理是这个世界上唯一的神灵。如果这些篇章中哪一页没有向读者揭示实现真理的唯一途径就是‘非暴力’这个道理，我的写作就是失败的。读者朋友们应该明白，即使在这方面我的努力没有见到成效，但过错在于我的方式而不在于‘非暴力’的原则。尽管我诚挚地竭尽所能地追求着非暴力主义，毕竟还有没达到尽善尽美的程度。所以我真的很难形容自己于瞬间捕捉到的真理，它的光辉之强烈，实在超过我们日常亲眼所见的太阳的光辉的百万倍，而我抓到的不过只是最微弱的一线光明而已。”而“要与无所不在的真理面对面，人们必须爱护这世界所有的生物，一如爱护人们自己。一个有此志向的人就不能对万事万物都等闲视之，这就是我为了追求真理而投身于政治的原因”。对此，印度文学家泰戈尔（Rabindranath Tagore）1916 年在美国写就的《印度的民族主义》一文中提出的看法与甘地的思考有着异曲同工之妙（该篇文章附于本书节选的甘地演说辞之后）。

二、注释

1. Selected from Lewis Copeland, Lawrence W. Lamm (eds.), *The World's Great Speeches*, Dover Publications Inc., 1973.

2. Khilafat，汉译“基拉法特”，指 1919—1922 年印度穆斯林发起的泛伊斯兰政治抗议运动，要求英国政府不要废除奥斯曼土耳其帝国的哈里发，抗议一战后《色佛尔条约》所强加于奥斯曼帝国与哈里发的丧权辱国的相关条款。

3. lascerated，即 lacerated，意“四分五裂的”。

4. Punjab，即“旁遮普”。

5. the Mutiny of 1857，指 1857 年兵变，即 1857 年印度民族大起义。

6. Rowlatt，西德尼·罗拉特（Sidney Rowlatt），英国律师、法官，是罗拉特委员会主席，负责起草了《罗拉特法案》。

7. Montagu，埃德温·塞缪尔·孟塔古（Edwin Samuel Montagu），英国政治家，时任印度事务大臣，协助制定了 1919 年的印度政府法案。

8. the Viceroy，“总督”的意思。

9. Shaukat Ali，肖卡特·阿里（1873—1939），基拉法特运动的领袖之一。

10. Yagna and Kurbani，即 Yajna and Qurbani，指“献祭”“自我牺牲”。

11. traduce，意为“中伤”“诽谤”。

12. krishan，即农民。

13. Kaira，指“凯达县”。

14. lakh，印度货币单位“拉克”。

15. anti-humbug，意为“反欺骗”。

16. Selected from Rabindranath Tagore, *Nationalism*, The Macmillan Company, 1917.

三、问题探讨

1. 如何理解甘地主义?
2. 泰戈尔的民族思想是什么?它与甘地主义有何异同?

四、参考文献

1. 林承节:《印度史》,人民出版社 2004 年版。

2. [印] 罗宾德罗纳特·泰戈尔:《民族主义》,谭仁侠译,商务印书馆 1986 年版。

3. [印] 莫罕达斯·卡拉姆昌德·甘地:《甘地自传》,钟杰译,北京联合出版公司 2014 年版。

4. Rabindranath Tagore, *Nationalism*, The Macmillan Company, 1917.

5. Lewis Copeland, Lawrence W. Lamm (eds.), *The World's Great Speeches*, Dover Publications Inc., 1973.

UNIT 20

"WHY THEY JOIN THE KLAN"[1]

For the student of social phenomena there is rich food for reflection in the fact that all the adverse criticism to which the Ku Klux Klan[2] has been subjected has not apparently hampered the growth of the organization even in the slightest degree. Indeed, it seems as though rapidity of growth and bitterness of criticism must have some direct relationship. In part, this is the result of the natural human trait of sympathy for the "under dog," and especially when he is the object of attacks by the press. In part, it is due to a failure by most critics of the hooded order to make due allowance for the forces which have brought it into being.

No matter how much you may, as we do, deplore the fact, the Klan today has no fewer than 2,500,000 members, and perhaps as many as 4,000,000; the national headquarters alone have assets of about $ 1,000,000; it virtually dominates the politics of Texas[3], Oklahoma[4], Arkansas[5] and Indiana[6]; and is very strong in Ohio[7], Oregon[8], Maine[9], Connecticut[10], New Jersey[11] and a dozen other states. It has sent Earle B. Mayfield[12] to the United States Senate from Texas, and has kept out of the same body Albert J. Beveridge of Indiana. It has gone into national politics with all its might, and to stay; it fully intends that there shall be a Klan candidate for President next year, and that he shall win. Under the circumstances, it is perhaps about time that we should lay aside mere abuse long enough to make an attempt to understand this phenomenon, and the factors in American life which have brought it into being.

It is absurd to suppose that the Ku Klux Klan is composed exclusively of the community's dregs, mere hoodlums who welcome the opportunity it affords for participation in sadistic orgies with the whip. In the South this element appears to be at least an active minority in the organization everywhere, and a majority in many localities; but there are also, both in the South and North (and particularly the latter) hundreds of thousands of Klansmen who are solid, respectable citizens, kind and loving husbands of and fathers, conscientious members of their churches. The worst crime to be assessed against these individuals is ignorance, and the bigotry which ignorance produces.

It should be noted that the Klan, as it enters any new community, begins with the leading citizens, and works down. After the first novelty has worn off, it is frequently the case that the rougher and more lawless members get control and set the tone. Though only a small fraction of the members, as a rule, actually participate in crimes of violence, it is by this group and its deeds that the organization as a whole is judged.

The Klan, like every other proselyting[13] organization, adapts itself to each community it enters. In the South, it uses the Negro as a stalking horse[14]. In California it is anti-Japanese. Along the Atlantic seaboard, where anti-Semitism[15] is found, it attacks the Jew; and in the northern part of the Middle West the Catholic church[16] is its foe. It is worth noting that the worst outrages of the Klan have been reported from communities where similar outrages had taken places at fairly frequent intervals for years before the Klan had this recent rebirth. While mob psychology certainly plays its part in lowering the standards of an erstwhile decent individual, it is safe to assume that a man who has been sober and upright all his life will still retain some measure of sobriety and uprightness even after he has gone through the childish nonsense of signing his name in blood to the Klansman's oath of fealty[17].

The members of the order, then, taking them by and large, are not vicious, but misled. Their very zeal for the maintenance of American institutions which they believe are endangered, has caused them to embrace a philosophy absolutely opposed to the democratic principle. Probably the war, which has become so universal a scapegoat must also be blamed for the mental attitude which makes prospective members of the Klan. The war produced in many millions of Americans a profound disillusionment and destruction of existing beliefs. The principles of security and justice which were supposed to rule the civilized world were suddenly found to be far less substantial than has been supposed. Moreover, persons with a private axe to grind[18] both then and later spread strange stories about those in authority. President Wilson, for example, was alleged to be controlled by the Jews — "look at Brandeis[19] and Baruch[20]," or by the Catholics — "look at Tumulty[21]". The "Bolshevist menace" has also been exploited for all it is worth by the numerous individuals and societies which have made a living by selling hysteria; and out in the country districts sober and worthy, if none too intelligent, citizens have had no means of discovering how exaggerated these alarmists statements really were. Finally, prohibition has done its part. The law has been evaded so generally and flagrantly that it is small wonder the average citizen, especially in the small towns, has believed the persuasive Ku Klux salesman who has told him that the government at Washington has lost all authority, and that the people must take into their own hands the task of preserving law and order, just as they had to do throughout the entire West in pioneer days.

It may or may not be true that the Ku Klux Klan will fall of its own weight; but even if it does the conditions which made it possible will not disappear and as long as they continue the danger of a recrudescence of Klannishness, perhaps on an even greater scale, will be constantly present. In the long run, the only answer to the Ku Klux Klan is to offer the people convincing proof that some of the supposed evils against which it is directed are non-existent, and that the rest are being attacked through proper and adequate channels. There is only one sovereign remedy for this disease, and it is education — both to raise the general intellectual level of the community, and to puncture the specific superstitions as to the malevolent designs of any one religious or racial group.

There is undoubtedly much truth in the charge that newspapers are afraid to discuss with any frankness the affairs of the Catholic church. So are educators, public speakers, and most of all, politicians. It is the existence of such taboos that makes it possible for the Klan to work underground and gain widespread adherence for its fantastic stories — such as the report, for instance, that the birth of every male child in a Catholic family is celebrated by burying a gun and ammunition underneath the church, in preparation for The Day when the government is to be overthrown on behalf of the Pope. Similar taboos exist in lesser degree in regard to the position of the Jew and the Negro in the community. There is little hope for improvement in the present situation until all of them are broken, and a healthy atmosphere of free discussion is substituted.

Above all, we need historical education as to what American ideals really are, and as to how and why these ideals are violated by the creed of the "little Americans." Until we are willing to make a genuine effort of this sort, we must be prepared to see either a continuance of the Klan itself or at best, a continued fertility of the soil from which it has sprung, with the likelihood that the whole phenomenon may be repeated at almost any time.

一、导读

《新共和》(*The New Republic*) 创刊于 1914 年美国进步主义运动如火如荼展开之时。该刊物的宗旨是为了迎接 20 世纪的种种新挑战，力图在人道的进步主义与思想上的科学主义之间寻求平衡，但后来逐渐摒弃了科学主义的理念。

该刊物是在多萝西·佩恩·惠特尼 (Dorothy Payne Whitney) 及其丈夫威拉德·斯特雷特 (Willard Straight) 的资助下，由进步主义政论家赫伯特·克罗利 (Herbert Croly)、沃尔特·李普曼 (Walter Lippmann) 和沃尔特·韦尔 (Walter Weyl) 联合创办的。十月革命前，该刊物的政治立场是自由主义和进步主义；十月革命后到 1947 年前，该刊物对苏联和斯大林的看法持积极的正面态度。20 世纪 50 年代，刊物主旨回归美国主流的自由主义，既批判苏联的对外政策，又反对麦卡锡主义；60 年代，刊物反对越战，批评"新左派"；80—90 年代，该刊物吸收了"第三条道路"的新自由主义以及保守主义理念。

本篇文献《为什么他们加入"三 K 党"》选自《新共和》，收录于小阿瑟·施莱辛格主编的《美国政党史》(第 3 卷)。20 世纪 20 年代，美国社会基本上实现了由农业社会向工业社会的转型，或者说完成了第一波的现代化，其国内经历了近 30 年的社会政治改革运动，史称进步运动或进步主义运动。但是，随着一战的爆发、美国的参战，以及俄国革命的爆发，美国国内的进步主义运动趋于衰落，转而复归传统的自由主义思想。这一时期在政治上，种族的、文化的民族主义思想杂陈交织在一起，左翼运动和工人运动受到打压，右翼力量主导着美国的主流政治。"三 K 党"即是其中一支颇具影响力的组织。

本篇文献主要针对的问题是：尽管"三 K 党"饱受批评，何以其成员有增无减？何以看似批评的猛烈度表面上对"三 K 党"产生了一定的直接影响，实际上"三 K 党"却依然"风雨不动安如山"？作者认为，究其原因，"三 K 党"的存在是由于有着各种容许其存在的土壤以及地方上一些民众的支持。例如：在南方，黑人就是欲加之罪的替罪羊；在加州，则是反对日本人；在大西洋沿岸，则是反犹主义；在上中西部地区，则是反对天主教。这些极端分子打着"维护美国制度"的爱国旗号，却是在误导民众，破坏了美国的民主原则。因此，要解决这一顽疾关键在于教育，以改变民众的无知或被误导的状态。

二、注释

1. Selected from Arthur M. Schlesinger Jr., *History of U. S. Political Parties*, Vol. 3, Chelsea House Publishers, 1980.

2. Ku Klux Klan，即"三 K 党"，亦通常可用"the KKK"或"the Klan"

表示，是一个美国白人至上的种族主义组织。

3. Texas，得克萨斯州。

4. Oklahoma，俄克拉荷马州。

5. Arkansas，阿肯色州。

6. Indiana，印第安纳州。

7. Ohio，俄亥俄州。

8. Oregon，俄勒冈州。

9. Maine，缅因州。

10. Connecticut，康涅狄格州。

11. New Jersey，新泽西州。

12. Earle B. Mayfield，厄尔·布拉福德·梅菲尔德（1881—1964），美国律师，来自得克萨斯州的民主党政客，州与联邦参议员。

13. proselyting，意为“传教的”“劝诱改宗的”。

14. stalking horse，意为“障眼法”。

15. anti-Semitism，意为“反犹主义”。

16. Catholic church，即“天主教会”。

17. fealty，意为“效忠”。

18. private axe to grind，意为“别有用心”。

19. Brandeis，路易斯·布兰代斯（Louis Brandeis，1856—1941），美国律师，美国最高法院大法官，威尔逊总统的顾问，出生于犹太移民家庭。

20. Baruch，伯纳德·巴鲁克（Bernard Baruch，1870—1965），美国金融家、股票投资家、慈善家、政治家，威尔逊总统和富兰克林·罗斯福总统的顾问。

21. Tumulty，约瑟夫·帕特里克·乔·塔马尔蒂（Joseph Patrick “Joe” Tumulty，1879—1954），威尔逊总统顾问，美国爱尔兰裔天主教政治界领袖之一。

三、问题探讨

1. 20 世纪 20 年代的美国面临着怎样的社会政治问题？
2. 这篇文章认为解决当时美国种族主义问题的办法是什么？

四、参考文献

1. [美] 埃里克·方纳：《美国历史：理想与现实》（下册），王希译，商务印书馆 2017 年版。

2. [美] 艾伦·布林克利：《美国史》，邵旭东等译，海南出版社 2009 年版。

UNIT 21

DEMOCRATIC PLATFORM OF 1936[1]

We hold this truth to be self-evident — that the test of a representative government is its ability to promote the safety and happiness of the people.

We hold this truth to be self-evident — that 12 years of Republican leadership left our Nation sorely stricken in body, mind, and spirit; and that three years of Democratic leadership have put it back on the road to restored health and prosperity.

We hold this truth to be self-evident — that 12 years of Republican surrender to the dictatorship of a privileged few have been supplanted[2] by a Democratic leadership which has returned the people themselves to the places of authority, and has revived in them new faith and restored the hope which they had almost lost.

We hold this truth to be self-evident — that this three-year recovery in all the basic values of life and the reestablishment of the American way of living has been brought about by humanizing the policies of the Federal Government as they affect the personal, financial, industrial, and agricultural well-being of the American people.

We hold this truth to be self-evident — that government in a modern civilization has certain inescapable obligations to its citizens, among which are:

(1) Protection of the family and the home.

(2) Establishment of a democracy of opportunity for all the people.

(3) Aid to those overtaken by disaster.

These obligations, neglected through 12 years of the old leadership, have once more been recognized by American Government. Under the new leadership they will never be neglected.

For the Protection of the Family and the Home

(1) We have begun and shall continue the successful drive to rid our land of kidnappers[3] and bandits[4]. We shall continue to use the powers of government to end the activities of the malefactors[5] of great wealth who defraud and exploit the people.

Savings and Investment

(2) We have safeguarded the thrift of our citizens by restraining those who would gamble with other peoples savings, by requiring truth in the sale of securities; by putting the brakes upon the use of credit for speculation; by outlawing the manipulation of prices in stock and commodity markets; by curbing the overweening[6] power and unholy practices of utility holding companies[7]; by insuring fifty million bank accounts.

Old Age and Social Security

(3) We have built foundations for the security of those who are faced with the hazards of unemployment and old age; for the orphaned, the crippled, and the blind. On the foundation of the Social Security Act we are determined to erect a structure of economic security for all our people, making sure that this benefit shall keep step with the ever-increasing capacity of America to provide a high standard of living for all its citizens.

Consumer

(4) We will act to secure to the consumer fair value, honest sales and a decreased spread between the price he pays and the price the producer receives.

Rural Electrification

(5) This administration has fostered power rate yardsticks[8] in the Tennessee Valley[9] and in several other parts of the Nation. As a result, electricity has been made available to the people at a lower rate. We will continue to promote plans for rural electrification and for cheap power by means of the yardstick method.

Housing

(6) We maintain that our people are entitled to decent, adequate housing at a price which they can afford. In the last three years, the Federal Government, having saved more than two million homes from foreclosure[10], has taken the first

steps in our history to provide decent housing for people of meagre[11] incomes. We believe every encouragement should be given to the building of new homes by private enterprise; and that the Government should steadily extend its housing program toward the goal of adequate housing for those forced through economic necessities to live in unhealthy and slum conditions.

Veterans

(7) We shall continue just treatment of our war veterans and their dependents.

For the Establishment of a Democracy of Opportunity

Agriculture

We have taken the farmers off the road to ruin.

We have kept our pledge to agriculture to use all available means to raise farm income toward its pre-war purchasing power. The farmer is no longer suffering from 15-cent corn, 3-cent hogs, $2^{1/2}$-cent beef at the farm, 5-cent wool, 30-cent wheat, 5-cent cotton, and 3-cent sugar.

By Federal legislation, we have reduced the farmer's indebtedness and doubled his net income. In cooperation with the States and through the farmers' own committees, we are restoring the fertility of his land and checking the erosion of his soil. We are bringing electricity and good roads to his home.

We will continue to improve the soil conservation and domestic allotment program with payments to farmers.

We will continue a fair-minded administration of agricultural laws, quick to recognize and meet new problems and conditions. We recognize the gravity of the evils of farm tenancy, and we pledge the full cooperation of the Government in the refinancing of farm indebtedness at the lowest possible rates of interest and over a long term of years.

We favor the production of all the market will absorb, both at home and abroad, plus a reserve supply sufficient to insure fair prices to consumers; we favor judicious commodity loans on seasonal surpluses; and we favor assistance within Federal authority to enable farmers to adjust and balance production with demand, at a fair profit to the farmers.

We favor encouragement of sound, practical farm co-operatives.

By the purchase and retirement of ten million acres of sub-marginal land, and assistance to those attempting to eke out[12] an existence upon it, we have made a good beginning toward proper land use and rural rehabilitation[13].

The farmer has been returned to the road to freedom and prosperity. We will keep him on that road.

Labor

We have given the army of America's industrial workers something more substantial than the Republicans' dinner pail[14] full of promises. We have increased the worker's pay and shortened his hours; we have undertaken to put an end to the sweated labor of his wife and children; we have written into the law of the land his right to collective bargaining and self-organization free from the interference of employers; we have provided Federal machinery for the peaceful settlement of labor disputes.

We will continue to protect the worker and we will guard his rights, both as wage-earner and consumer, in the production and consumption of all commodities, including coal and water power and other natural resource products.

The worker has been returned to the road to freedom and prosperity. We will keep him on that road.

Business

We have taken the American business man out of the red. We have saved his bank and given it a sounder foundation; we have extended credit; we have lowered interest rates; we have undertaken to free him from the ravages[15] of cutthroat[16] competition.

The American business man has been returned to the road to freedom and prosperity. We will keep him on that road.

Youth

We have aided youth to stay in school; given them constructive occupation; opened the door to opportunity which 12 years of Republican neglect had closed.

Our youth have been returned to the road to freedom and prosperity. We will keep them on that road.

Monopoly and Concentration of Economic Power

Monopolies and the concentration of economic power, the creation of Republican rule and privilege, continue to be the master of the producer, the exploiter of the consumer, and the enemy of the independent operator. This is a problem challenging the unceasing effort of untrammeled[17] public officials in every branch of the Government. We pledge vigorously and fearlessly to enforce the criminal and civil provisions of the existing anti-trust laws, and to the extent that their effectiveness has been weakened by new corporate devices or judicial construction, we propose by law to restore their efficacy[18] in stamping out monopolistic practices and the concentration of economic power.

Aid to Those Overtaken By Disaster

We have aided and will continue to aid those who have been visited by widespread drought and floods, and have adopted a Nation-wide flood-control policy.

Unemployment

We believe that unemployment is a national problem, and that it is an inescapable obligation of our Government to meet it in a national way. Due to our stimulation of private business, more than five million people have been reemployed; and we shall continue to maintain that the first objective of a program of economic security is maximum employment in private industry at adequate wages. Where business fails to supply such employment, we believe that work at prevailing wages should be provided in cooperation with State and local governments on useful public projects, to the end that the national wealth may be increased, the skill and energy of the worker may be utilized, his morale[19] maintained, and the unemployed assured the opportunity to earn the necessities of life.

The Constitution

The Republican platform proposes to meet many pressing national problems solely by action of the separate States. We know that drought, dust storms, floods, minimum wages, maximum hours, child labor, and working conditions in industry, monopolistic and unfair business practices cannot be adequately handled exclusively by 48 separate State legislatures, 48 separate State administrations, and 48 separate State courts. Transactions and activities which inevitably overflow State boundaries call for both State and Federal treatment.

We have sought and will continue to seek to meet these problems through legislation within the Constitution.

If these problems cannot be effectively solved by legislation within the Constitution, we shall seek such clarifying amendment as will assure to the legislatures of the several States and to the Congress of the United States, each within its proper jurisdiction, the power to enact those laws which the State and

Federal legislatures, within their respective spheres, shall find necessary, in order adequately to regulate commerce, protect public health and safety and safeguard economic security. Thus we propose to maintain the letter and spirit of the Constitution.

The Merit System in Government

For the protection of government itself and promotion of its efficiency, we pledge the immediate extension of the merit system through the classified civil service — which was first established and fostered under Democratic auspices — to all non-policy-making positions in the Federal service.

We shall subject to the civil service law all continuing positions which, because of the emergency, have been exempt from its operation.

Civil Liberties

We shall continue to guard the freedom of speech, press, radio, religion and assembly which our Constitution guarantees; with equal rights to all and special privileges to none.

Government Finance

The Administration has stopped deflation, restored values and enabled business to go ahead with confidence.

When national income shrinks, government income is imperilled[20]. In reviving national income, we have fortified[21] government finance. We have raised the public credit to a position of unsurpassed security. The interest rate on Government bonds has been reduced to the lowest point in twenty-eight years. The same Government bonds which in 1932 sold under 83 are now selling over 104.

We approve the objective of a permanently sound currency so stabilized as to prevent the former wide fluctuations in value which injured in turn producers, debtors, and property owners on the one hand, and wage-earners and creditors on the other, a currency which will permit full utilization of the country's resources.

We assert that today we have the soundest currency in the world.

We are determined to reduce the expenses of government. We are being aided therein by the recession in unemployment. As the requirements of relief decline and national income advances, an increasing percentage of Federal expenditures can and will be met from current revenues, secured from taxes levied in accordance with ability to pay. Our retrenchment[22], tax and recovery programs thus reflect our firm determination to achieve a balanced budget and the reduction of the national debt at the earliest possible moment.

Foreign Policy

In our relationship with other nations, this Government will continue to extend the policy of the Good Neighbor[23]. We reaffirm our opposition to war as an instrument of national policy, and declare that disputes between nations should be settled by peaceful means. We shall continue to observe a true neutrality in the disputes of others; to be prepared, resolutely to resist aggression against ourselves; to work for peace and to take the profits out of war; to guard against being drawn, by political commitments, international banking or private trading, into any war which may develop anywhere.

We shall continue to foster the increase in our foreign trade which has been achieved by this administration; to seek by mutual agreement the lowering of those tariff barriers, quotas and embargoes which have been raised against our exports of agricultural and industrial products; but continue as in the past to give adequate protection to our farmers and manufacturers against unfair competition or the dumping on our shores of commodities and goods produced abroad by cheap labor or subsidized by foreign governments.

The Issue

The issue in this election is plain. The American people are called upon to choose between a Republican administration that has and would again regiment them in the service of privileged groups and a Democratic administration dedicated to the establishment of equal economic opportunity for all our people.

We have faith in the destiny of our nation. We are sufficiently endowed with natural resources and with productive capacity to provide for all a quality of life that meets the standards of real Americanism.

Dedicated to a government of liberal American principles, we are determined to oppose equally, the despotism of Communism and the menace of concealed Fascism.

We hold this final truth to be self-evident — that the interests, the security and the happiness of the people of the United States of America can be perpetuated[24] only under democratic government as conceived by the founders of our nation.

一、导读

美国的民主党，一般认为是当今世界上历史最为悠久的资产阶级政党之一，始于18世纪90年代由托马斯·杰斐逊和詹姆斯·麦迪逊创建的民主共和党(Democratic-Republican Party)，专门反对由亚历山大·汉密尔顿领导的执政党，即一般所说的联邦党。民主共和党与联邦党构成了“第一代政党体系”（First Party System，1792—1824)。当时，联邦党提倡建立一个强大的中央政府、从宽解释宪法以及一个由精英统治的政府；民主共和党则强调州权、从严解释宪法以及一个民主的权力有限的政府，或曰小政府。

1800年，民主共和党在总统和国会选举中同时获胜，杰斐逊当选美国第三任总统，史称“1800年革命”，标志着共和主义的兴起。而联邦党的重要领袖汉密尔顿因决斗而死，该党在内外交困下基本上解体了，从此开始了民主共和党一党独大的时期。但无外忧，则往往生内患，在约翰·昆西·亚当斯任总统期间，民主共和党一分为二：亨利·克莱等人从民主共和党中分离出来，自称国民共和党人，亚当斯、丹尼尔·韦伯斯特等是主要成员，在1834年左右，该党为辉格党吸收；1828年，安德鲁·杰克逊、威廉·克劳福德、卡尔霍恩等人组成了民主党。史称“第二代政党体系”（1828—1854)。

随着美国南北方矛盾的加剧，辉格党对此无力应对，由此在1854年创建了以反奴隶制为核心的大联盟，强调“言论自由、土地自由、劳动自由、人身自由”，由此形成了与民主党相对的“第三代政党体系”（1854—19世纪90年代)。

工业化的发展急剧地改造了美国的社会，美国选民的基础发生了重大变化，民主党的政纲与意识形态也发生了很大的改变，乃至翻转。民主党将平民党人拉了进来，由此形成了“第四代政党体系”（1896—1932)。这一时期，民主党从其施政举措来看，尽管十分不情愿，但渐趋有了从限权政府向大政府或民主转向的趋向；而共和党很大程度上接过了此前民主党的说辞。这是一个重要的悖论，其核心仍然离不开权力或政府更多地掌握在哪个政党的手中的问题。共和党越来越像是一个上层或精英的政党，而民主党则似乎是更多地代表了下层或民众的政党。

1929—1933年的经济大危机，造成了美国“第五代政党体系”（1933年至现在）的到来。

本篇文献《1936年民主党党纲》节选自小阿瑟·施莱辛格主编的《美国政党史》(第3卷)。在阅读的过程中，我们要着重关注开篇的5句“We hold this truth”，解读这种修辞背后的意蕴；同时也要注意结尾处，缘何再次祭出“We hold this final truth” 的字眼。

二、注释

1. Selected from Arthur M. Schlesinger Jr., *History of U. S. Political Parties*, Vol. 3, Chelsea House Publishers, 1980.

2. supplant，“取代”之意。

3. kidnappers，“绑架者”之意。

4. bandits，“强盗”之意。

5. malefactor，“为非作歹者”之意。

6. overweening，意为“自负的”。

7. holding company，“股份公司”之意。

8. yardstick，“准绳”“举措”之意。

9. Tennessee Valley，田纳西河流域。

10. foreclosure，指“法院拍卖房屋”“丧失抵押品赎回权”。

11. meagre，意为“贫乏的”。

12. eke out，意为“凑合”“勉强维持”。

13. rehabilitation，“恢复”之意。

14. dinner pail，“餐盒”之意。

15. ravages，“蹂躏”“肆虐”之意。

16. cutthroat，意为“你死我活的”。

17. untrammeled，意为“不受制约的”。

18. efficacy，“效力”之意。

19. morale，“士气”之意。

20. imperilled，意为“处于危险之中”。

21. fortified，“加强”之意。

22. retrenchment，意为“紧缩”“削减”。

23. the policy of the Good Neighbor，即“睦邻政策”。

24. perpetuated，意为“使……永恒”。

三、问题探讨

1.《1936 年民主党党纲》出台的历史背景是什么？

2. 美国民主党党纲的主要内容是什么，其开篇与结尾说明了什么问题？

四、参考文献

1. [美] 埃里克·方纳:《给我自由! 一部美国的历史》,王希译,商务印书馆 2010 年版。

2. [美] 加里·纳什等:《美国人民:创建一个国家和一种社会》,刘德斌等译,北京大学出版社 2008 年版。

UNIT 22

CIVIL RIGHTS ACT[1]

To enforce the constitutional right to vote, to confer jurisdiction upon the district courts of the United States[2] to provide injunctive relief against discrimination in public accommodations, to authorize the Attorney General[3] to institute suits to protect constitutional rights in public facilities and public education, to extend the Commission on Civil Rights, to prevent discrimination in federally assisted programs, to establish a Commission on Equal Employment Opportunity[4], and for other purposes.

Be it enacted by the Senate and House of Representatives of the United States of America in Congress assembled, That this Act may be cited as the "Civil Rights Act of 1964".

Tittle I: Voting Rights

SEC.101.

...

"(2) No person acting under color of law shall:

"(A) in determining whether any individual is qualified under State law or laws to vote in any Federal election, apply any standard, practice, or procedure different from the standards, practices, or procedures applied under such law or laws to other individuals within the same county, parish, or similar political subdivision who have been found by State officials to be qualified to vote;

"(B) deny the right of any individual to vote in any Federal election because of an error or omission on any record or paper relating to any application, registration, or other act requisite to voting, if such error or omission is not material in determining whether such individual is qualified under State law to vote in such election; or

"(C) employ any literacy test as a qualification for voting in any Federal election unless (i) such test is administered to each individual and is conducted wholly in writing, and (ii) a certified copy of the test and of the answers given by the individual is furnished to him within twenty-five days of the submission of his request made within the period of time during which records and papers are required to be retained and preserved pursuant to title Ⅲ of the Civil Rights Act of 1960 (42 U. S. C. 1974 – 74e; 74 Stat. 88): Provided, however, That the Attorney General may enter into agreements with appropriate State or local authorities that preparation, conduct, and maintenance of such tests in accordance with the provisions of applicable State or local law, including such special provisions as are necessary in the preparation, conduct, and maintenance of such tests for persons who are blind or otherwise physically handicapped, meet the purposes of this subparagraph and constitute compliance therewith.

...

Title Ⅱ: Injunctive Relief against Discrimination in Places of Public Accommodation

SEC. 201.

(a) All persons shall be entitled to the full and equal enjoyment of the goods, services, facilities, privileges, advantages, and accommodations of any place of public accommodation, as defined in this section, without discrimination or segregation on the ground of race, color, religion, or national origin.

(b) Each of the following establishments which serves the public is a place of public accommodation within the meaning of this title if its operations affect commerce, or if discrimination or segregation by it is supported by State action:

(1) any inn, hotel, motel, or other establishment which provides lodging to transient guests, other than an establishment located within a building which contains not more than five rooms for rent or hire and which is actually occupied by the proprietor of such establishment as his residence;

(2) any restaurant, cafeteria, lunchroom, lunch counter, soda fountain, other facility principally engaged in selling food for consumption on the premises, including but not limited to, any such facility located on the premises of any retail establishment; or any gasoline station;

(3) any motion picture house, theater, concert hall, sports arena, stadium or other place of exhibition or entertainment; and

(4) any establishment (A)(i) which is physically located within the premises of any establishment otherwise covered by this subsection, or (ii) within the premises of which is physically located any such covered establishment, and (B) which holds itself out as serving patrons of such covered establishment.

...

SEC.202.

All persons shall be entitled to be free, at any establishment or place, from discrimination or segregation of any kind on the ground of race, color, religion, or national origin, if such discrimination or segregation is or purports to be required by any law, statute, ordinance, regulation, rule, or order of a State or any agency or political subdivision thereof.

SEC.203.

No person shall (a) withhold, deny, or attempt to withhold or deny, or deprive or attempt to deprive, any person of any right or privilege secured by section 201 or 202, or (b) intimidate, threaten, or coerce, or attempt to intimidate, threaten, or coerce any person with the purpose of interfering with any right or privilege secured by section201 or 202, or (c) punish or attempt to punish any person for exercising or attempting to exercise any right or privilege secured by section 201 or 202.

SEC.204.

(a) Whenever any person has engaged or there are reasonable grounds to believe that any person is about to engage in any act or practice prohibited by section 203, a civil action for preventive relief, including an application for a permanent or temporary injunction, restraining order, or other order, may be instituted by the person aggrieved and, upon timely application, the court may, in its discretion, permit the Attorney General to intervene in such civil action if he certifies that the case is of general public importance. Upon application by the complainant, and in such circumstances as the court may deem just, the court may appoint an attorney for such complainant, and may authorize the commencement of the civil action without the payment of fees, costs, or security.

(b) In any action commenced pursuant to this title, the court, in its discretion, may allow the prevailing party, other than the United States, a reasonable attorney's fee as part of the costs, and the United States shall be liable for costs the same as a private person.

(c) In the case of an alleged act or practice prohibited by this title which occurs in a State, or political subdivision of a State, which has a State or local law prohibiting such act or practice and establishing or authorizing a State or local authority to grant or seek relief from such practice or to institute criminal proceedings with respect thereto upon receiving notice thereof, no civil action may be brought under subsection (a) before the expiration of thirty days after written notice of such alleged act or practice has been given to the appropriate State or local authority by registered mail or in person, provided that the court may stay proceedings in such civil action pending the termination of State or local enforcement proceedings.

...

Title Ⅳ: Desegregation of Public Education Definitions

SEC. 401.

As used in this title:

(a) "Commissioner" means the Commissioner of Education.

(b) "Desegregation" means the assignment of students to public schools and within such schools without regard to their race, color, religion, sex or national origin, but "desegregation" shall not mean the assignment of students to public schools in order to overcome racial imbalance.

(c) "Public school" means any elementary or secondary educational institution, and "public college" means any institution of higher education or any technical or vocational school above the secondary school level, provided that such public school or public college is operated by a State, subdivision of a State, or governmental agency within a State, or operated wholly or predominantly from or through the use of governmental funds or property, or funds or property derived from a governmental source.

(d) "School board" means any agency or agencies which administer a system of one or more public schools and any other agency which is responsible for the assignment of students to or within such system.

Survey and Report of Educational Opportunities

SEC. 402.

The Commissioner shall conduct a survey and make a report to the President and the Congress, within two years of the enactment of this title, concerning the lack of availability of equal educational opportunities for individuals by reason of race, color, religion, or national origin in public educational institutions at all levels in the United States, its territories and possessions, and the District of Columbia.

Technical Assistance

SEC.403.

The Commissioner is authorized, upon the application of any school board, State, municipality, school district, or other governmental unit legally responsible for operating a public school or schools, to render technical assistance to such applicant in the preparation, adoption, and implementation of plans for the desegregation of public schools. Such technical assistance may, among other activities, include making available to such agencies information regarding effective methods of coping with special educational problems occasioned by desegregation, and making available to such agencies personnel of the Office of Education or other persons specially equipped to advise and assist them in coping with such problems.

Training Institutes

SEC.404.

The Commissioner is authorized to arrange, through grants or contracts, with institutions of higher education for the operation of short-term or regular session institutes for special training designed to improve the ability of teachers, supervisors, counselors, and other elementary or secondary school personnel to deal effectively with special educational problems occasioned by desegregation. Individuals who attend such an institute on a full-time basis may be paid stipends for the period of their attendance at such institute in amounts specified by the Commissioner in regulations, including allowances for travel to attend such institute.

Grants

SEC.405.

(a) The Commissioner is authorized, upon application of a school board, to make grants to such board to pay, in whole or in part, the cost of:

(1) giving to teachers and other school personnel inservice training in dealing with problems incident to desegregation, and

(2) employing specialists to advise in problems incident to desegregation.

(b) In determining whether to make a grant, and in fixing the amount thereof and the terms and conditions on which it will be made, the Commissioner shall take into consideration the amount available for grants under this section and the other applications which are pending before him; the financial condition of the applicant and the other resources available to it; the nature, extent, and gravity of its problems incident to desegregation; and such other factors as he finds relevant.

Payments

SEC.406.

Payments pursuant to a grant or contract under this title may be made (after necessary adjustments on account of previously made overpayments or underpayments) in advance or by way of reimbursement, and in such installments, as the Commissioner may determine.

Suits by the Attorney general

...

SEC.408.

In any action or proceeding under this title the United States shall be liable for costs the same as a private person.

SEC.409.

Nothing in this title shall affect adversely the right of any person to sue for or obtain relief in any court against discrimination in public education.

SEC.410.

Nothing in this title shall prohibit classification and assignment for reasons other than race, color, religion, or national origin.

Title Ⅵ: Nondiscrimination in Federally Assisted Programs

SEC. 601.

No person in the United States shall, on the ground of race, color, or national origin, be excluded from participation in, be denied the benefits of, or be subjected to discrimination under any program or activity receiving Federal financial assistance.

SEC. 602.

Each Federal department and agency which is empowered to extend Federal financial assistance to any program or activity, by way of grant, loan, or contract other than a contract of insurance or guaranty, is authorized and directed to effectuate the provisions of section 601 with respect to such program or activity by issuing rules, regulations, or orders of general applicability which shall be consistent with achievement of the objectives of the statute authorizing the financial assistance in connection with which the action is taken. No such rule, regulation, or order shall become effective unless and until approved by the President. Compliance with any requirement adopted pursuant to this section may be effected (1) by the termination of or refusal to grant or to continue assistance under such program or activity to any recipient as to whom there has been an express finding on the record, after opportunity for hearing, of a failure to comply with such requirement, but such termination or refusal shall be limited to the particular political entity, or part thereof, or other recipient as to whom such a finding has been made and, shall be limited in its effect to the particular program, or part thereof, in which such non-compliance has been so found, or (2) by any other means authorized by law: Provided, however, That no such action shall be taken until the department or agency concerned has advised the appropriate person or persons of the failure to comply with the requirement and has determined that compliance cannot be secured by voluntary means. In the case of any action terminating, or refusing to grant or continue, assistance because of failure to comply with a requirement imposed pursuant to this section, the head of the federal department or agency shall file with the committees of the House and Senate having legislative jurisdiction over the program or activity involved a full written report of the circumstances and the grounds for such action. No such action shall become effective until thirty days have elapsed after the filing of such report.

SEC. 603.

Any department or agency action taken pursuant to section 602 shall be subject to such judicial review as may otherwise be provided by law for similar action taken by such department or agency on other grounds. In the case of action, not otherwise subject to judicial review, terminating or refusing to grant or to continue financial assistance upon a finding of failure to comply with any requirement imposed pursuant to section 602, any person aggrieved (including any State or political subdivision thereof and any agency of either) may obtain judicial review of such action in accordance with section 10 of the Administrative Procedure Act, and such action shall not be deemed committed to unreviewable agency discretion within the meaning of that section.

SEC. 604.

Nothing contained in this title shall be construed to authorize action under this title by any department or agency with respect to any employment practice of any employer, employment agency, or labor organization except where a primary objective of the Federal financial assistance is to provide employment.

SEC. 605.

Nothing in this title shall add to or detract from any existing authority with respect to any program or activity under which Federal financial assistance is extended by way of a contract of insurance or guaranty.

...

Equal Employment Opportunity Commission

SEC. 705. [42 U.S.C.2000e—4]

(a) There is hereby created a Commission to be known as the Equal Employment Opportunity Commission, which shall be composed of five members, not more than three of whom shall be members of the same political party. Members of the Commission shall be appointed by the President by and with the advice and consent of the Senate for a term of five years. Any individual chosen to fill a vacancy shall be appointed only for the unexpired term of the member whom he shall succeed, and all members of the Commission shall continue to serve until their successors are appointed and qualified, except that no such member of the Commission shall continue to serve (1) for more than sixty days when the Congress is in session unless a nomination to fill such vacancy shall have been submitted to the Senate, or (2) after the adjournment sine die of the session of the Senate in which such nomination was submitted. The President shall designate one member to serve as Chairman of the Commission, and one member to serve as Vice Chairman. The Chairman shall be responsible on behalf of the Commission for the administrative operations of the Commission, and, except as provided in subsection (b), shall appoint, in accordance with the provisions of title 5, United States Code, governing appointments in the competitive service, such officers, agents, attorneys, administrative law judges, and employees as he deems necessary to assist it in the performance of its functions and to fix their compensation in accordance with the provisions of chapter 51 and subchapter Ⅲ of chapter 53 of title 5, United States Code, relating to classification and General Schedule pay rates: Provided, That assignment, removal, and compensation of administrative law judges shall be in accordance with sections 3105, 3344, 5362, and 7521 of title 5, United States Code.

(b) (1) There shall be a General Counsel of the Commission appointed by the President, by and with the advice and consent of the Senate, for a term of four years. The General Counsel shall have responsibility for the conduct of litigation as provided in sections 706 and 707 of this title. The General Counsel shall have such other duties as the Commission may prescribe or as may be provided by law and shall concur with the Chairman of the Commission on the appointment and supervision of regional attorneys. The General Counsel of the Commission on the effective date of this Act shall continue in such position and perform the functions specified in the subsection until a successor is appointed and qualified. (2) Attorneys appointed under this section may, at the direction of the Commission, appear for and represent the Commission in any case in court, provided that the Attorney General shall conduct all litigation to which the Commission is a party in the Supreme Court[5] pursuant to the title.

(c) A vacancy in the Commission shall not impair the right of the remaining members to exercise all the powers of the Commission and three members thereof shall constitute a quorum.

(d) The Commission shall have an official seal which shall be judicially noticed.

(e) The Commission shall at the close of each fiscal year report to the Congress and to the President concerning the action it has taken and the moneys it has disbursed. It shall make such further reports on the cause of and means of eliminating discrimination and such recommendations for further legislation as may appear desirable.

(f) The principal office of the Commission shall be in or near the District of Columbia, but it may meet or exercise any or all its powers at any other place. The Commission may establish such regional or State offices as it deems necessary to accomplish the purpose of this title.

(g) The Commission shall have power —

(1) to cooperate with, and, with their consent, utilize regional, State, local, and other agencies, both public and private, and individuals;

(2) to pay to witnesses whose depositions are taken or who are summoned before the Commission or any of its agents the same witness and mileage fees as are paid to witnesses in the courts of the United States;

(3) to furnish to persons subject to this title such technical assistance as they may request to further their compliance with this title or an order issued thereunder;

(4) upon the request of (i) any employer, whose employees or some of them, or (ii) any labor organization, whose members or some of them, refuse or threaten to refuse to cooperate in effectuating the provisions of this title, to assist in such effec-tuation by conciliation or such other remedial action as is provided by this title;

(5) to make such technical studies as are appropriate to effectuate the purposes and policies of this title and to make the results of such studies available to the public;

(6) to intervene in a civil action brought under section 706 by an aggrieved party against a respondent other than a government, governmental agency or political subdivision.

(h) (1) The Commission shall, in any of its educational or promotional activities, cooperate with other departments and agencies in the performance of such educational and promotional activities.

(2) In exercising its powers under this title, the Commission shall carry out educational and outreach activities (including dissemination of information in languages other than English) targeted to —

(A) individuals who historically have been victims of employment discrimination and have not been equitably served by the Commission; and

(B) individuals on whose behalf the Commission has authority to enforce any other law prohibiting employment discrimination, concerning rights and obligations under this title or such law, as the case may be.

(i) All officers, agents, attorneys, and employees of the Commission shall be subject to the provisions of section 9 of the Act of August 2, 1939, as amended (the Hatch Act), notwithstanding any exemption contained in such section.

(j) (1) The Commission shall establish a Technical Assistance Training Institute, through which the Commission shall provide technical assistance and training regarding the laws and regulations enforced by the Commission.

(2) An employer or other entity covered under this title shall not be excused from compliance with the requirements of this title because of any failure to receive technical assistance under this subsection.

(3) There are authorized to be appropriated to carry out this subsection such sums as may be necessary for fiscal year 1992.

一、导读

在美国历史上，黑人长期遭受种族歧视与种族迫害。从北美殖民地时期开始，被贩卖到美洲的黑人就深受白人种族主义者的残酷剥削和压迫。1776 年，北美 13 个英属殖民地宣布独立，并于 1787 年颁布联邦宪法，却仍保留了黑人奴隶制。南北战争之后，美国国会以宪法修正案的形式宣布废除黑人奴隶制，从而赋予了黑人法律上的平等地位，但现实生活中种族歧视现象仍然普遍存在，联邦宪法甚至允许种族隔离成为一种堂而皇之的社会制度。

20 世纪五六十年代，受广大亚非拉国家争取民族民主解放斗争胜利的鼓舞，美国黑人的自由民权意识不断增强，并最终引发了一系列大规模的黑人民权运动。黑人民权分子反对种族歧视和种族压迫，要求真正地享有平等的政治、经济和社会权利。1955 年 12 月，在亚拉巴马州的蒙哥马利市，黑人以全面罢乘来反对公交车上的种族隔离制度，标志着民权运动的开始。经过一年的抗争，1956 年，美国最高法院最终判决公共汽车上的种族隔离制违反宪法。受联邦最高法院判决的鼓舞，各类黑人民权组织不断成立并发展壮大，其中影响较大的有“全国有色人种协进会”“全国城市联盟”和“争取种族平等大会”等。这些民权组织的成立与发展壮大，有力地推动了美国民权运动的发展。

1963 年 4 月，亚拉巴马州的伯明翰市爆发了以取消公共设施中的种族隔离为目标的群众示威游行。8 月，又爆发了美国历史上规模最大的公众抗议示威活动，25 万黑人和白人聚集首都，举行进军华盛顿的活动，要求政府减少失业、提高最低工资标准、禁止就业歧视。在林肯纪念馆前，民权运动领袖马丁·路德·金发表了振奋人心的著名演说《我有一个梦想》，再次吹响了向种族隔离制度发起冲锋的号角，使民权运动达到顶峰。在全国黑人民权运动愈演愈烈的形势下，美国国会最终通过了 1964 年《公民权利法》、1965 年《选举权法案》和 1968 年《开放住宅法案》，正式以立法的形式结束了美国黑人在投票选举和各种公共设施方面所遭受的种族歧视、隔离等不公正待遇。

本篇文献为美国 1964 年《公民权利法》的部分节选内容。该法案围绕投票权、公共设施、公共教育、就业等社会各个方面拟定了一系列旨在保护黑人平等权利的措施。1964 年《公民权利法》是美国在 20 世纪 60 年代颁布最早、内容最全面、影响最深远的一部民权法案，在美国民权立法的历史上具有里程碑式的意义。

二、注释

1. 本文选自美国众议院立法委员会办公室网站https：//legcounsel. house. gov/

Comps/Civil%20Rights%20Act%20Of%201964.pdf。

2. the district courts of the United States，美国联邦地方法院。

3. the Attorney General，美国联邦司法部长。

4. Commission on Equal Employment Opportunity，就业机会平等委员会。

5. the Supreme Court，美国联邦最高法院。

三、问题探讨

1. 结合材料评述美国 1964 年《公民权利法》的主要内容。

2. 阐述美国 1964 年《公民权利法》颁布的历史意义和影响。

四、参考文献

1. 刘绪贻、杨生茂：《战后美国史：1945—2000》，人民出版社 2002 年版。

2. 王希：《原则与妥协：美国宪法的精神与实践》（增订版），北京大学出版社 2014 年版。

3. 于展：《非暴力直接运动与美国民权运动》，社会科学文献出版社 2015 年版。

4. 谢国荣：《美国民权运动史新探》，商务印书馆 2016 年版。

5. Heather E. Schwartz，*The Civil Rights Act of 1964：A Primary Source Exploration of the Landmark Legislation*，Capstone Press，2014.

UNIT 23

PEACE TREATY BETWEEN ISRAEL AND EGYPT[1]

The Government of the Arab Republic of Egypt and the Government of the State of Israel;

Preamble

Convinced of the urgent necessity of the establishment of a just, comprehensive and lasting peace in the Middle East in accordance with Security Council Resolutions 242 and 338;

Reaffirming their adherence to the "Framework for Peace in the Middle East Agreed at Camp David," dated September 17, 1978;

Noting that the aforementioned Framework as appropriate is intended to constitute a basis for peace not only between Egypt and Israel but also between Israel and each of its other Arab neighbors which is prepared to negotiate peace with it on this basis;

Desiring to bring to an end the state of war between them and to establish a peace in which every state in the area can live in security;

Convinced that the conclusion of a Treaty of Peace between Egypt and Israel is an important step in the search for comprehensive peace in the area and for the attainment of settlement of the Arab-Israeli conflict in all its aspects;

Inviting the other Arab parties to this dispute to join the peace process with Israel guided by and based on the principles of the aforementioned Framework;

Desiring as well to develop friendly relations and cooperation between themselves in accordance with the United Nations Charter and the principles of international law governing international relations in times of peace;

Agree to the following provisions in the free exercise of their sovereignty, in order to implement the "Framework for the Conclusion of a Peace Treaty Between Egypt and Israel";

Article Ⅰ

1. The state of war between the Parties will be terminated and peace will be established between them upon the exchange of instruments of ratification of this Treaty.

2. Israel will withdraw all its armed forces and civilians from the Sinai behind the international boundary between Egypt and mandated Palestine, as provided in the annexed protocol (Annex Ⅰ), and Egypt will resume the exercise of its full sovereignty over the Sinai.

3. Upon completion of the interim withdrawal provided for in Annex Ⅰ, the parties will establish normal and friendly relations, in accordance with Article Ⅲ (3).

Article Ⅱ

The permanent boundary between Egypt and Israel in the recognized international boundary between Egypt and the former mandated territory of Palestine, as shown on the map at Annex Ⅱ, without prejudice to the issue of the status of the Gaza Strip[2]. The Parties recognize this boundary as inviolable. Each will respect the territorial integrity of the other, including their territorial waters and airspace.

Article Ⅲ

1. The Parties will apply between them the provisions of the Charter of the United Nations and the principles of international law governing relations among states in times of peace. In particular:

a. They recognize and will respect each other's sovereignty, territorial integrity and political independence;

b. They recognize and will respect each other's right to live in peace within their secure and recognized boundaries;

c. They will refrain from the threat or use of force, directly or indirectly, against each other and will settle all disputes between them by peaceful means.

2. Each Party undertakes to ensure that acts or threats of belligerency, hostility, or violence do not originate from and are not committed from within its territory, or by any forces subject to its control or by any other forces stationed on its territory, against the population, citizens or property of the other Party.

Each Party also undertakes to refrain from organizing, instigating, inciting, assisting or participating in acts or threats of belligerency, hostility, subversion or violence against the other Party, anywhere, and undertakes to ensure that perpetrators of such acts are brought to justice.

3. The Parties agree that the normal relationship established between them will include full recognition, diplomatic, economic and cultural relations, termination of economic boycotts and discriminatory barriers to the free movement of people and goods, and will guarantee the mutual enjoyment by citizens of the due process of law. The process by which they undertake to achieve such a relationship parallel to the implementation of other provisions of this Treaty is set out in the annexed protocol (Annex Ⅲ).

Article Ⅳ

1. In order to provide maximum security for both Parties on the basis of reciprocity, agreed security arrangements will be established including limited force zones in Egyptian and Israeli territory, and United Nations forces and observers, described in detail as to nature and timing in Annex Ⅰ, and other security arrangements the Parties may agree upon.

2. The Parties agree to the stationing of United Nations personnel in areas described in Annex Ⅰ. The Parties agree not to request withdrawal of the United Nations personnel and that these personnel will not be removed unless such removal is approved by the Security Council of the United Nations, with the affirmative vote of the five Permanent Members, unless the Parties otherwise agree.

3. A Joint Commission will be established to facilitate the implementation of the Treaty, as provided for in Annex Ⅰ.

4. The security arrangements provided for in paragraphs 1 and 2 of this Article may at the request of either party be reviewed and amended by mutual agreement of the Parties.

Article Ⅴ

1. Ships of Israel, and cargoes destined for or coming from Israel, shall enjoy the right of free passage through the Suez Canal and its approaches through the Gulf of Suez and the Mediterranean Sea on the basis of the Constantinople Convention of 1888, applying to all nations, Israeli nationals, vessels and cargoes, as well as persons, vessels and cargoes destined for or coming from

Israel, shall be accorded non-discriminatory treatment in all matters connected with usage of the canal.

2. The Parties consider the Strait of Tiran[3] and the Gulf of Aqaba to be international waterways open to all nations for unimpeded and non-suspendable freedom of navigation and overflight. The parties will respect each other's right to navigation and overflight for access to either country through the Strait of Tiran and the Gulf of Aqaba.

Article Ⅵ

1. This Treaty does not affect and shall not be interpreted as affecting in any way the rights and obligations of the Parties under the Charter of the United Nations.

2. The Parties undertake to fulfill in good faith their obligations under this Treaty, without regard to action or inaction of any other party and independently of any instrument external to this Treaty.

3. They further undertake to take all the necessary measures for the application in their relations of the provisions of the multilateral conventions to which they are parties, including the submission of appropriate notification to the Secretary General of the United Nations and other depositaries of such conventions.

4. The Parties undertake not to enter into any obligation in conflict with this Treaty.

5. Subject to Article 103 of the United Nations Charter in the event of a conflict between the obligation of the Parties under the present Treaty and any of their other obligations, the obligations under this Treaty will be binding and implemented.

Article Ⅶ

1. Disputes arising out of the application or interpretation of this Treaty shall be resolved by negotiations.

2. Any such disputes which cannot be settled by negotiations shall be resolved by conciliation or submitted to arbitration.

Article Ⅷ

The Parties agree to establish a claims commission for the mutual settlement of all financial claims.

Article Ⅸ

1. This Treaty shall enter into force upon exchange of instruments of

ratification.

2. This Treaty supersedes the Agreement between Egypt and Israel of September, 1975.

3. All protocols, annexes, and maps attached to this Treaty shall be regarded as an integral part hereof.

4. The Treaty shall be communicated to the Secretary General of the United Nations for registration in accordance with the provisions of Article 102 of the Charter of the United Nations.

Annex Ⅰ

Protocol Concerning Israeli Withdrawal and Security Agreements

Article Ⅰ Concept of Withdrawal

1. Israel will complete withdrawal of all its armed forces and civilians from the Sinai[4] not later than three years from the date of exchange of instruments of ratification of this Treaty.

2. To ensure the mutual security of the Parties, the implementation of phased withdrawal will be accompanied by the military measures and establishment of zones set out in this Annex and in Map 1, hereinafter referred to as "the Zones."

3. The withdrawal from the Sinai will be accomplished in two phases:

a. The interim withdrawal behind the line from east of El-Arish to Ras Mohammed as delineated on Map 2 within nine months from the date of exchange of instruments of ratification of this Treaty.

b. The final withdrawal from the Sinai behind the international boundary not later than three years from the date of exchange of instruments of ratification of this Treaty.

4. A Joint Commission will be formed immediately after the exchange of instruments of ratification of this Treaty in order to supervise and coordinate movements and schedules during the withdrawal, and to adjust plans and timetables as necessary within the limits established by paragraph 3, above. Details relating to the Joint Commission are set out in Article Ⅳ of the attached Appendix. The Joint Commission will be dissolved upon completion of final Israeli withdrawal from the Sinai.

Article Ⅱ Determination of Final Lines and Zones

1. In order to provide maximum security for both Parties after the final withdrawal, the lines and the Zones delineated on Map 1 are to be established and organized as follows:

A. Zone A

(1) Zone A is bounded on the east by line A (red line) and on the west by the Suez Canal and the east coast of the Gulf of Suez, as shown on Map 1.

(2) An Egyptian armed force of one mechanized infantry division and its military installations, and field fortifications, will be in this Zone.

(3) The main elements of that Division will consist of:

a. Three mechanized infantry brigades.

b. One armed brigade.

c. Seven field artillery battalions including up to 126 artillery pieces.

d. Seven anti-aircraft artillery battalions including individual surface-to-air missiles and up to 126 anti-aircraft guns of 37 mm and above.

e. Up to 230 tanks.

f. Up to 480 armored personnel vehicles of all types.

g. Up to a total of twenty-two thousand personnel.

B. Zone B

(1) Zone B is bounded by line B (green line) on the east and by line A (red line) on the west, as shown on Map 1.

(2) Egyptian border units of four battalions equipped with light weapons and wheeled vehicles will provide security and supplement the civil police in maintaining order in Zone B. The main elements in the four Border Battalions will consist of up to a total of four thousand personnel.

(3) Land based, short range, low power, coastal warning points of the border patrol units may be established on the coast of this Zone.

(4) There will be in Zone B field fortifications and military installations for the four border battalions.

C. Zone C

(1) Zone C is bounded by line B (green line) on the west and the International Boundary and the Gulf of Aqaba[5] on the east, as shown on Map 1.

(2) Only United Nations forces and Egyptian civil police will be stationed in Zone C.

(3) The Egyptian civil police armed with light weapons will perform normal police functions within this Zone.

(4) The United Nations Force will be deployed within Zone C and perform its functions as defined in Article Ⅵ of this annex.

(5) The United Nations Force will be stationed mainly in camps located within the following stationing areas shown on Map 1, and will establish its precise locations after consultations with Egypt:

a. In that part of the area in the Sinai lying within about 20 Km. of the Mediterranean Sea and adjacent to the International Boundary.

b. In the Sharm el Sheikh area.

D. Zone D

(1) Zone D is bounded by line D (blue line) on the east and the international boundary on the west, as shown on Map 1.

(2) In this Zone there will be an Israeli limited force of four infantry battalions, their military installations, and field fortifications, and United Nations observers.

(3) The Israeli forces in Zone D will not include tanks, artillery and anti-aircraft missiles except individual surface-to-air missiles.

(4) The main elements of the four Israeli infantry battalions will consist of up to 180 armored personnel vehicles of all types and up to a total of four thousand personnel.

2. Access across the international boundary shall only be permitted through entry check points designated by each Party and under its control. Such access shall be in accordance with laws and regulations of each country.

3. Only those field fortifications, military installations, forces, and weapons specifically permitted by this Annex shall be in the Zones.

Article Ⅲ Aerial Military Regime

1. Flights of combat aircraft and reconnaissance flights of Egypt and Israel shall take place only over Zones A and D, respectively.

2. Only unarmed, non-combat aircraft of Egypt and Israel will be stationed in Zones A and D, respectively.

3. Only Egyptian unarmed transport aircraft will take off and land in Zone B and up to eight such aircraft may be maintained in Zone B. The Egyptian border unit., may be equipped with unarmed helicopters to perform their functions in

Zone B.

4. The Egyptian civil police may be equipped with unarmed police helicopters to perform normal police functions in Zone C.

5. Only civilian airfields maybe built in the Zones.

6. Without prejudice to the provisions of this Treaty, only those military aerial activities specifically permitted by this Annex shall be allowed in the Zones and the airspace above their territorial waters.

Article Ⅳ Naval Regime

1. Egypt and Israel may base and operate naval vessels along the coasts of Zones A and D, respectively.

2. Egyptian coast guard boats, lightly armed, may be stationed and operate in the territorial waters of Zone B to assist the border units in performing their functions in this Zone.

3. Egyptian civil police equipped with light boats, lightly armed, shall perform normal police functions within the territorial waters of Zone C.

4. Nothing in this Annex shall be considered as derogating from the right of innocent passage of the naval vessels of either party.

5. Only civilian maritime ports and installations may be built in the Zones.

6. Without prejudice to the provisions of this Treaty, only those naval activities specifically permitted by this Annex shall be allowed in the Zones and in their territorial waters.

Article Ⅴ Early Warning Systems

Egypt and Israel may establish and operate early warning systems only in Zones A and D respectively.

Article Ⅵ United Nations Operations

1. The Parties will request the United Nations to provide forces and observers to supervise the implementation of this Annex and employ their best efforts to prevent any violation of its terms.

2. With respect to these United Nations forces and observers, as appropriate, the Parties agree to request the following arrangements:

a. Operation of check points, reconnaissance patrols, and observation posts along the international boundary and line B, and within Zone C.

b. Periodic verification of the implementation of the provisions of this Annex will be carried out not less than twice a month unless otherwise agreed by the

Parties.

c. Additional verifications within 48 hours after the receipt of a request from either Party.

d. Ensuring the freedom of navigation through the Strait of Tiran in accordance with Article Ⅴ of the Treaty of Peace.

3. The arrangements described in this article for each zone will be implemented in ones A, B, and C by the United Nations Force and in Zone D by the United Nations Observers.

4. United Nations verification teams shall be accompanied by liaison officers of the respective Party.

5. The United Nations Force and observers will report their findings to both Parties.

6. The United Nations Force and Observers operating in the Zones will enjoy freedom of movement and other facilities necessary for the performance of their tasks.

7. The United Nations Force and Observers are not empowered to authorize the crossing of the international boundary.

8. The Parties shall agree on the nations from which the United Nations Force and Observers will be drawn. They will be drawn from nations other than those which are permanent members of the United Nations Security Council.

9. The Parties agree that the United Nations should make those command arrangements that will best assure the effective implementation of its responsibilities.

Article Ⅶ Liaison System

1. Upon dissolution of the Joint Commission, a liaison system between the Parties will be established. This liaison system is intended to provide an effective method to assess progress in the implementation of obligations under the present Annex and to resolve any problem that may arise in the course of implementation, and refer other unresolved matters to the higher military authorities of the two countries respectively for consideration. It is also intended to prevent situations resulting from errors or misinterpretation on the part of either Party.

2. An Egyptian liaison office will be established in the city of El-Arish and an Israeli liaison office will be established in the city of Beer-Sheba. Each office will

be headed by an officer of the respective country, and assisted by a number of officers.

3. A direct telephone link between the two offices will be set up and also direct telephone lines with the United Nations command will be maintained by both offices.

Article Ⅷ Respect for War Memorials

Each Party undertakes to preserve in good condition the War Memorials erected in the memory of soldiers of the other Party, namely those erected by Egypt in Israel, and shall permit access to such monuments.

Article Ⅸ Interim Arrangements

The withdrawal of Israeli armed forces and civilians behind the interim withdrawal line, and the conduct of the forces of the Parties and the United Nations prior to the final withdrawal, will be governed by the attached Appendix and Map 2.

一、导读

1948 年，以色列建国激起了阿拉伯国家强烈的民族主义情绪，使之结成了共同对抗以色列国的同盟。由于埃及的综合国力较强，因此，它实际上处于阿拉伯国家领导者地位。在数次中东战争中，它承担了大量的人力、物力和军费开支，损失极为严重。仅以 1967 年第三次中东战争为例，埃及在此次战争中大约有 1 万名士兵和 1500 名军官阵亡，3 万名官兵负伤，95%的飞机被炸毁，80%的陆军装备被破坏，具有重要战略地位和经济价值的西奈半岛被以色列人占据。1970 年，穆罕默德·安瓦尔·萨达特继任为埃及总统之后，针对国内军费开支庞大、经济萧条、人员伤亡惨重的局面，决意以埃及民族利益至上为原则，实行“疏苏亲美”“近以远阿”的国家战略，以期得到美国的支持，尽早结束与以色列的战争对峙状态，收回西奈半岛，集中力量发展国内经济，摆脱埃及当时的困境。但以色列方面因在第三次中东战争中大获全胜，民族自信心空前高涨，既不愿也不会归还所占领土。这迫使阿拉伯国家不得不再次寄希望通过战争打破中东地区的现状，以战求和，达到收复被占领土的目的。1972 年，埃及联合其他阿拉伯国家共同发动了第四次中东战争，迅速占领西奈半岛，希望通过军事手段迫使以色列与之和谈。在美国的积极斡旋和调和下，埃以和平谈判成为可能。1979 年，埃及总统萨达特与以色列总理梅纳赫姆·贝京在美国白宫签署了以《戴维营协议》为基础的《埃以和约》，规定以色列军队在 3 年内完全撤出西奈半岛，埃及承认以色列作为国家的合法性并与之建交等，从而结束了埃以之间长达 30 年的全面交战和对峙状态，实现了两国关系正常化。

《埃以和约》使埃及得以从阿以战争中抽离出来以恢复和发展国内经济。之后不久，埃及政府便采取接受美国经济援助、加速开放本国市场、加大石油出口等措施，仅一年时间，国内生产总值便增加了 10%左右，为 10 年来增长最快的一年。从短期效果来看，萨达特初步实现了既定目标，埃及经济危机得以缓解。然而，就长远而言，这反而将埃及进一步推向困境：

其一，萨达特的国家至上原则和利己主义行为，直接导致埃及与阿拉伯国家爆发了激烈的冲突，遭到了大部分阿拉伯国家的联合制裁，除了阿曼、苏丹、索马里继续与埃及保持外交关系外，其余阿拉伯国家先后与埃及断交。可以说，自签订《埃以和约》后，埃及便失去了以往在阿拉伯国家中的领导地位，陷入了空前的孤立。

其二，美国对埃及的经济援助（以贷款的方式）使得埃及背上了沉重的债务负担，加剧了国内的社会矛盾。1982 年，埃及需偿还的债务本息达 20 亿美元，外债总额已高达 211 亿美元，其中民用债务为 165 亿美元，军事债务为 46 亿美元。在外债高企的情况下，大部分经济援助资金反而为开罗和亚历山大的大公司瓜分，并未惠及普通民众，使得财富分配不均、贫富差距过大，大大激化了社会矛盾。

然而，《埃以和约》作为阿拉伯国家与以色列签订的第一个和平协议，具有划时代的里程碑意义。它不仅开创了埃以外交的新局面，亦提供了由武力冲突转向政治和解以解决中东问题的新思路，实质性地推动了中东和平进程。自此以后，中东地区的人民要求和平的呼声越来越高，与以色列的和平谈判也接连出现，如1993年巴勒斯坦解放组织主席阿拉法特与以色列总理拉宾签署了《奥斯陆协议》、1994年约旦国王侯赛因又与拉宾签订了《华盛顿宣言》等。可见，自《埃以和约》后，以和平方式解决国际争端越来越为广大阿拉伯国家的人民所接受。

二、注释

1. 本文节选自耶鲁法学院网页，http://avalon.law.yale.edu/20th_century/isregypt.asp。
2. the Gaza Strip，加沙地带。
3. the Strait of Tiran，蒂朗海峡。
4. the Sinai，西奈半岛。
5. the Gulf of Aqaba，亚喀巴湾。

三、问题探讨

1.《埃以合约》内容概述。
2. 试评价《埃以和约》。

四、参考文献

1. 孙振欧、钟实：《埃以和约签订一年来的中东形势》，《西亚非洲》1980年第2期。

2. ［埃］萨达特：《我的一生——对个性的探讨》，李占经等译，商务印书馆1980年版。

3. ［美］费希尔：《中东史》，姚梓良译，商务印书馆1980年版。

4. ［英］理查德·艾伦：《阿拉伯—以色列冲突的背景和前途》，艾玮生译，商务印书馆1982年版。

5. Gerald M. Steinberg & Ziv Rubinovitz，*Menachem Begin and the Israel-Egypt Peace Process: Between Ideology and Political Realism*，Indiana University Press，2019.

UNIT 24

A MULTI-CULTURAL SOCIETY FOR THE FUTURE[1]

ANY contemplation of the character which our urban society might assume by the year 2000 must naturally begin with a hard look at our present society and the potential forces of change already discernible. Any other approach to futurology would be day-dreaming.

Broad scope

Within the broad scope of this Symposium, areas such as education, the law, government, communication, religion, and the environment all figure prominently. Fundamental to every one of these topics is the question: What sort of people are going to provide the human factor in the year 2000 to flesh out our abstractions?

Societies, of course, are only composed of people. If a society is to claim any right to a long-term existence, it must also operate only for people, in the firm framework of justice and law.

My concept of a society able to sustain growth and change without disintegration is a society based on equal opportunity for all — a goal which no right-thinking person could dispute, but the striving for which has led traditionally to some of the deepest conflicts within society. This means full scope for all to develop their personal potential, no matter how diverse their origins, beliefs, wealth or ability. All too often in the past, equality of opportunity has been only reluctantly conceded to less privileged sectors of our community, or even withheld. I believe that by the year 2000 we will need to have perfected ways of inducing this equality for all, in fact as well as in law, by far-reaching legislative and ameliorative measures. The seer gazing into his crystal ball to discern the outlines of tomorrow's society needs a sound appreciation of the character, origins and history of his present society. I suppose an Australian Minister for Immigration occupies a strategic vantage-point from which to project his gaze into the future. He is heir to an extremely diverse society largely shaped by the policies of his predecessors of the past quarter century, during which the most dramatic changes in the composition, outlook and prospects of Australian society have taken place. Further, he is, within the framework of the parliamentary system, responsible for the formulation and implementation of policies which cannot fail to affect, in some measure, the continuing growth and rate of change within that society. Thus he must envisage some grand design or, at very least, long-term plans for that society as he exercises his options in policy-making.

National pride

I wish to record at the outset my conviction that the future of our society is essentially hopeful.

When we consider the achievements of the successors to that non-descript band of "assisted passage" migrants who landed at Sydney Cove[2] on the first Australia Day 1788[3], we must be pardoned for some small sense of national pride. This pride derives as much from the creation of a stable and relatively just society as from any material success. In this lie real grounds for hope for the future.

Again, I am hopeful because there has come about in our community in recent years a greater self-awareness and a new self-criticism which are indicative of our growing maturity. The "lucky country" syndrome is losing something of its cynical ring. The desire to do something with our heritage rather than simply live off it is becoming commoner, as is seen in the ecology movement. Today there seems to be more of a desire to see things re-ordered as they could be or should be, rather than simply retained as they have always been. These stirrings are triggered by, and in turn contribute to, the growth of a "new nationalism", as it is already being called. Who are we in Australia? What were our social origins? How should these origins influence us today? How can we build on them in shaping a better and more just future? Is the process to be one of steady evolution or noisy revolution? I see these questionings essentially as a hopeful sign, even if the whole range of prognostications can scarcely prove right.

National fabric

We may justly claim that to have woven our present national fabric from originally rather ill-assorted strands, but without suffering the major upheavals marking the history of other societies, is no small achievement. Again, to have built up hitherto a sort of national expertise in absorbing people from many different backgrounds lends us confidence as migration continues to strengthen and enrich the character of our society. In itself, however, this does not permit us to assume that solutions to yesterday's problems will provide answers to today's — or tomorrow's — challenges. For, as the very composition of our society changes, every problem takes on a new twist. The complexity of the issues now calls for a new flexibility of mind in approaching them and grappling with them. In this, demographic factors will increasingly come to our aid. It is a fact that 46 per cent of today's population is under 25 years of age. Thus, 46 per cent have no personal knowledge at all of an Australia without mass migration of great ethnic diversity, nor of the dynamic process of social and cultural change which it has brought about. Such change has always been a part of their lives and must be seen by them to be perfectly normal. In the face of such change and the increasing ethnic diversification which has provided the impetus for much of it, young Australians seem to exercise an admirable openness and tolerance.

Unfortunately, this cannot be said of all other groups in the community. Despite the diversity that has always been present in Australian society — and today is the very hallmark of it — many influential circles in the community show scant evidence of recognising its importance, or even its existence. A widespread ignorance seems to prevail about what is actually happening to the fabric of Australian society under the continuous impact of a migration which, in terms of proportionate numbers of newcomers to the base population, is virtually without parallel in modern times.

Conspiracy of silence

Something of a conspiracy of silence persists in many quarters about the social impact of other than Anglo-Saxon[4] influences on our national life. This was referred to a number of times in the reports recently submitted to me by the Task Forces set up by the Government in all States to examine problems experienced by newcomers settling in our midst. It deserves to be taken seriously.

To take a homely illustration, how often do our television screens reflect anything like the variety of migrant groups encountered in a real-life stroll through our city streets, or particularly our near-city suburbs?

The image we manage to convey of ourselves still seems to range from the bushwhacker to the sportsman to the slick city businessman. Where is the Maltese process worker, the Finnish carpenter, the Italian concrete layer, the Yugoslav miner or — dare I say it — the Indian scientist? Where do these people belong, in all honesty, if not in today's composite Australian image? Are they to be non-people — despite their indispensable economic contribution to our well-being — because they do not happen to fit the largely American-oriented stereotypes of our entertainment industry? It would seem a mark of national maturity to be able to identify firstly what is essential and distinctive about one's own land and its people, and then to portray it consistently with insight and sympathy.

Cosmopolitan

If it is a fact that Australia is now one of the most cosmopolitan societies on earth — and the evidence confirms that it is — it is time that all Australians were encouraged to develop a better understanding of what this implies.

Today there is a great deal of knowledge of the dynamics of majority/minority group relations available from generations of study and scholarship in — the United States, and increasingly also from Canada. In Australia, too, expertise in these fields is by no means lacking. Naturally, we cannot assume that North American experience will be directly relevant to the future interaction of the groups composing Australian society. But neither can we wait until the year 2000 to establish what patterns are likely to develop.

Back in 1966, Dr Charles Price, of the Australian National University[5], in a definitive essay on "The Study of Assimilation", in his Australian Immigration: a Bibliography and Digest, put forward three alternative social theories to describe the effects of large-scale migration on the character and structure of a society. Evaluating the American experience, he defines the three philosophies which have emerged from the voluminous literature on the subject, as follows:

1. The "Anglo-Conformist" view[6] which asserts that it is possible and necessary

for migrants to cast away at once their old language, customs and attitudes in favour of the basic Anglo-Saxon "core culture".

2. The "melting pot" view[7] — which in a more recent form has emerged as the "multiple melting pot" view — and which claims that it is possible and desirable for migrants and native-born alike to emerge from the crucible "melted, blended and reshaped" as a brand new species of man.

3 "Permanent ethnic pluralism" whereby each ethnic group desiring it, is permitted to create its own communal life and preserve its own cultural heritage indefinitely, while taking part in the general life of the nation.

"Family of the nation"

Personally, I must confess to something of an aversion to the technical jargon in the literature. To the average Australian, whether "old" or "new", terms like "assimilation", "integration", "homogeneous" or "pluralistic" society are probably meaningless. The concept I prefer, the "family of the nation", is one that ought to convey an immediate and concrete image to all. In a family the overall attachment to the common good need not impose a sameness on the outlook or activity of each member, nor need these members deny their individuality and distinctiveness in order to seek a superficial and unnatural conformity. The important thing is that all are committed to the good of all.

Of course, all labels have an unfortunate habit of becoming devalued with use, but a viable idea can nevertheless exist without a tag on it. Conversely it cannot be conjured up out of the air by hopefully coining a suitable slogan. It must evolve from real demand for it and ultimately come to stand on its own feet, if it is to prove viable with the passage of time. After all, history can only be written in retrospect. Today, irrespective therefore of what labels we use, the fact is that the increasing diversity of Australian society has gradually eroded and finally rendered untenable any prospects there might have been twenty years ago of fully assimilating newcomers to the "Australian way of life", to use a phrase common at that time.

Life styles

We might well ask ourselves: what is the Australian way of life today? The life style and values of the suburban housewife in Moonee Ponds, the Italian travel agent in Carlton, the Turkish car factory worker, the Slavic Orthodox priest, or the Aboriginal at Lake Tyers? It is all too easy to overlook the pre-existence in this land of the original Australians, millennia before the advent of us "white ethnics". In considering the applicability in Australia of the above American social philosophies, therefore, we must bear in mind that any theory that fails to accord these people an equal place in the family of our nation is out of the question today and in the future. Likewise, other ethnic groups introduced to this land by our migration programs may not be denied an equal place in our future society. It is obvious that on present trends, no one group in our society by the year 2000 will be able to exercise any inalienable claim to permanent dominance over all the others. This will not only be a matter of justice and human dignity, as it is today, but by then will be a simple matter of numbers and percentages in the population. The statistics tell their own tale.

Projections prepared by the Bureau of Census and Statistics indicate that, based on current trends and predicating a consistent annual net migration gain of a moderate 60,000, the population will grow to almost 21,000,000 by the year 2001, virtually the target date of this Symposium. By that time, the percentage of people born outside Australia and their children would probably be around 40 per cent on current trends. On these trends they are likely to be from more than 60 countries. In the face of such statistics, justice will never be done by blandly asserting that the cultural and social impact of such people shall be null and void, or that Australian society can pretend to a sameness. The situation today is already so advanced that such a hypothesis is simply unreal. The first of the American social theories is not a viable option for Australia, and it has never, in fact, been a viable option.

Dynamic interaction

My vision of our society in the year 2000 foreshadows a greatly increasing social complexity, in which the dynamic interaction between the diverse ethnic components will be producing new national initiatives, stimulating new artistic endeavours, and ensuring great strength in diversity. In foreshadowing the future character of this interaction, we do little service to our history to imagine that Australia could ever have become a pale reproduction of Britain, a pseudo-America, or a make-believe Asia. In this respect we have always diverged from the ethnically static societies of the Old World and share the potential dynamism of the developing societies of the New World. From the first days, there have been people here of at least several ethnic backgrounds. To start with, on the first Australia Day the vast majority of Australians were black. Moreover, anthropologists and linguists tell us that there were at least three different racial groups and more than 26 "families" of languages among these Aboriginal peoples, Australia-wide. How then could we ever have talked of homogeneity without gross offence to these oldest of Australians?

The newcomers, too, were an extraordinarily motley crew in backgrounds, manners, and morals. We may well suppose that no mistakes made by subsequent selection officers for our immigration program overseas could ever equal those perpetrated by the screening system of 1788! At the individual level, it is known that there were Negroes and Jews in the First Fleet; that the second language of the early goldfields was Chinese; that among the freedom fighters of Eureka were some from Italy, Britain, Germany, Ireland and Canada; that the highest peak in Australia was named by a Pole after his national hero; that Leichhardt was one of many German pioneers who challenged an alien environment; while another of his countrymen, Karl Linger, won the first national anthem competition in 1860 with his music for "The Song of Australia".

Individual pioneers

While history records the contribution of a Henry Lawson (or Larsen), a Ferdinand von Mueller, a Hans Heysen, or an Elioth Gruner, a nation's story is not only written in terms of its outstanding men of letters and sciences, its intrepid pathfinders, or its entrepreneurial geniuses. The multitudes of nameless individuals who cleared its land, built its ports and railways, fought in its wars, produced and consumed its products and created its riches, also deserve recognition, if only en masse. Among this anonymous cavalcade were many whose native tongue was not English, but whose contribution was no less significant for that factor.

Indeed, we must not overlook that there are also in our migration history numerous examples of "group settlement", some of which have been well documented along similar lines to those occurring at the same period in the Americas. Dr Price has described such examples of group settlement as that by

German Lutherans in South Australia in the 1830s, and by groups of Greeks, Dalmatians, Sicilians, Piedmontese, and Maltese in North Queensland earlier this century. A feature of this group settlement has been the movement to Australia by Italians, Greeks, Maltese, and Yugoslavs along more or less clearly defined "migration chains" that started off on a kinship basis and extended from individual clans, villages, and regions in the home country to certain country towns, rural settlements, and metropolitan suburbs in Australia. Thus the group settlement of Calabrians in Griffith, N. S. W., began in 1922 when three agricultural labourers settled there and began to bring out relatives and friends from Italy. By 1955 the total group settlement numbered more than 1,000. The same story can be told of Griffith and the Veneto.

Other group settlements of roughly the same period were founded by Dalmatians in the upper Swan Valley, W. A., and on the rural outskirts of Sydney; by Albanians at Shepparton, Victoria and at Mareeba, North Queensland; by Bulgarians on the outskirts of Adelaide; and by Macedonians near Canberra. More recent examples still are offered by the Italian settlement in the Ovens Valley, Victoria, where a thriving tobacco-growing community exists today; by the Estonian-Finnish settlement in the Picton-Thirlmere district of N. S. W.; by the Portuguese fishermen's settlement at Fremantle, W. A.; by the Sikhs established around Woolgoolga-Coffs Harbour, N. S. W.; and by the Russian Old Believers at Yarwun, Queensland.

Group settlement

A survey in the 1950s indicated that at that time the overwhelming majority of Mediterranean migrants had settled in Australia by village or district groups through this process of "chain migration". Indeed, it may seem surprising that even some British migrants have come to Australia on the basis of group settlement, under the Ex-Servicemen's Resettlement Scheme which operated in Western Australia in the mid-1920s.

The point I wish to make from this historical digression is that migration to Australia by no means takes place simply on the basis of individuals seeking economic or social advantages for themselves or their children, as superficially seen in the popular imagination, often encouraged by the 'economic growth at all costs' lobby. The guest-worker concept has never found favour in Australia among people concerned for human values and social justice. Even in North-Western Europe, where the concept developed, severe social strains are now appearing in the fields of industrial and communal relations.

Ethnic groups

The dynamism in an ethnically diverse society seems somehow related to the group life within that society. It is not simply the product of the individual differences between its citizens. These may indeed become blurred through interaction over a period of time, but the life of an ethnic group is more resilient and retains its integrity. Thus a social philosophy that presupposes the submergence of all ethnic diversity in a melting pot — at a time when current migration is continuing to infuse new members — also seems out of touch with the realities. Naturally, individuals are always free to move in society in whatever circles they prefer, but doctrinaire views should not inhibit that freedom. The corporate life of ethnic groups represents a great deal more than the simple totality of their individual members' lives and activity. To an extent, they have created their own national image. They have brought with them a common history and culture, an ideology different from the Anglo-Saxon. They perceive different goals and pursue them in their own traditional ways. In short, they lead a way of life which, while in living touch with its ancient forms and impulses, is imperceptibly coming to terms with — or at least learning to co-exist with — that of many other ethnic groups in our society and of course with the "old Australians". Such pluralism is not operating within a time scale, but looks ahead far into the future.

Ethnic links

While there seems to be no reliable way of establishing the degree to which individual migrants in Australia retain their link over the years with ethnic organisations, it is a fact that the strength of corporate ethnic group life is as strong today as at any point in our history. Indeed, I believe there is fair indication that it may be destined to become stronger as the overall percentage of recent migrant stock in our community increases, and as the threat of anonymity in our society impels people to assert their identity and distinctiveness. In any case, the incidence of ethnic group activity in Australia today is such that no impartial observer could possibly fail to assess its impact on Australian life as fundamental. Clearly, we must reject that chauvinistic view which conveniently devalues the presence and activity of ethnic groups as somehow un-Australian.

National narcissism

We may well ask why this narcissism in our national thinking? Are we such an alien outpost in an Asian world that we cannot venture far from the apron strings of our original "Nanny"? There is no doubt that in some periods of our history, and particularly earlier this century between the two World Wars, the official desire to promote an apparently — but never quite — homogeneous Anglo-Saxon population doubtless reflected most people's attitudes. That was a day of a rather closed, derivative, society dependent on the goodwill of Imperial Governments and haunted by fears of Asian "hordes". However, earlier there had been periods during which the promise of cultural diversity in Australia had made an appearance, only to be negated by restrictive legislation expressing an "intolerance of ambiguity". Admittedly, this was dressed-up in the guise of ensuring equality of opportunity for all. As Dr Barrie Pittock has said in another context, "newcomers were expected to see the self-evident proof that Anglo-Saxon ways were in every respect superior to their own. ...The established society came to fear the very existence of groups of free men who by choice lived according to different customs and traditions"?

An early flowering of cultural diversity was seen in the German communal life of the Barossa Valley. The earliest schools in this district were Lutheran private schools in which German was used as the medium of instruction for children whose mother tongue was German. Amid much bitterness in 1851 the South Australian Government withdrew its subsidy to the schools, refusing to allow any other language than English to be the medium of instruction. Matters came to a head in 1917 when all Lutheran schools were ordered to teach in English or be taken over by the State, a body blow against the transmission of group identity from generation to generation. In the absence of continuing German migration into that community, it became extremely difficult for it to resist cultural take-over by the majority. However, such is the underlying ethnic consciousness in this community that it has never quite been sapped even today by external pressures.

Social justice

However, in present-day Australia, the situation has changed quite dramatically in respect of the overall proportions of"old" and "new" Australians. In the name of social justice a society dare not, in the long term, devalue the presence of one in four of its members. Is one out of every four to be permanently denied the dignity of self-expression and self-determination-should he so desire — as taken for granted by the other three? We do not need to be gifted with a vivid imagination to picture the explosive pressures — or else naked repression — that would inevitably become the consequences of devaluing or ignoring ethnic communities till the year 2000.

Of course, it may be objected that the Australian talent for absorbing newcomers into its economy and its national life style will continue to operate to the extent of preventing the growth of "communities within the community". Unfortunately, this is wishful thinking, unsupported by the evidence available today. The real situation in the "migrant belts" of our great cities reflects the years of high migrant intake of the 1960s, when large numbers of settlers from many cultural origins came to Australia. The aspect which should have caused us most concern in this situation was the absence of any deep understanding of what happens when thousands of people from widely differing linguistic and cultural backgrounds crowd into small areas of Australian cities, without significant social or linguistic contacts with Australians or much chance of achieving them. Can they be expected to live in a cultural and social vacuum for years while learning to adapt to the life of Australians they seldom meet?

We might well ask ourselves whether Australians living overseas could be seriously expected to bring off such a prodigious feat. Or would they be more inclined to opt for the easier alternative of reconstructing a little corner of Australia in an alien land and peopling it with fellow Aussies likewise fleeing the social pressures to conform, haunted by memories of sun, surf, and gumleaves while indulging in a bit of harmless nostalgia? Even this analogy proves inadequate at two points: the Aussies overseas would most likely have little intention of staying for life, nor would they generally have children on whom to project their social and cultural sensibility as second generation migrant offspring.

The critics

There have been critics of the pluralist approach who have seen it as leading to a fragmented society, lacking in cohesion and threatening to produce a complete, permanent, and hostile segregation of one part of our population. I believe this is postulating an unreal threat — a sort of communal apartheid — which is not founded on fact. The situation in Australia today is that concentrations of multiple ethnic groups do exist in our major cities, and that these show signs of considerable durability. However, economically they are already integrated with our society by virtue of their involvement in the Australian work-force. Further, because of the co-existence in these localities of many different ethnic groups in close proximity, there can be no question of one part of the population permanently living in hostile segregation from the majority.

The various groups are constantly interacting and adjusting, slowly but steadily, to each other and to life in Australia, without losing — at least in the first generation — their essential ethnic character. In this situation, there is nothing threatening to Australia's future in the year 2000. We need to bear in mind that time is on our side. In terms of world history we are still a young country, and our achievements thus far lend promise for an even brighter future. It is only in recent years that our national resources have come to be realised as prodigious.

Human capital

But the most precious resource of our nation, like all others, is its people — its human capital. For the planners of the year 2000, the proper servicing of that capital must assume a higher priority than any merely physical developing program.

We are still very much a nation in the making, in terms of the destiny we hope to fulfill beyond the year 2000. A large proportion of our population has not been in this land long enough to have truly identified with it. Perhaps this is one reason why, after 27 years of our post-war migration program, more than a million residents of Australia have not yet adopted its citizenship. The flowering of a truly national spirit in Australia is not an optional extra, but a major objective to be sought in the next few decades. Individually, Australians do feel a pride in their country, I believe, but to newcomers this may be all too little apparent. We can hardly expect new migrants to feel a greater love for their adopted country than those born here appear disposed to show. Yet there is an encouraging measure of unity among our diverse population, perhaps more evident on subtle occasions than in the day-today routine of urban life. Our bid for inclusion among the final contenders for the World Cup soccer championship has set tingling a nerve of patriotism that has run right through our ethnic communities.

Listen to the conversation of any party of Australians overseas: some of the most forthright Australianism will be expressed in varieties of accented English. When the chips are down, and one's personal identity counts for something, most migrants will be at one with the older residents in feeling proud to belong to Australia. Migrant expressions of loyalty on those occasions represent by their awkward sincerity a more impressive token of national unity than the broader Australian vernacular.

Policy adjustments

There will, of course, be policy adjustments to be made and much scope for informed and enlightened judgment to be applied, if our society is ultimately to profit from the challenge of the present situation. The first prerequisite for this is an accurate perception of what is actually happening in our migrant communities in major Australian cities. In these centres, despite expectations that newcomers would blend in time into the local population, the fact is that today the local population is gradually moving out of many of the inner suburbs, to be replaced, to an extent, by incoming waves of newer ethnic groups — a quite classical phenomenon in American migration experience, where I understand it has been described in the literature as"ecological succession".

Further, there is evidence from recent surveys on poverty in Australia that ethnic groups are significantly over-represented among the poorer sections of society, tending to appear disproportionately in labouring, unskilled, and blue collar occupations.

Moreover, there is small evidence that the children in such migrant groups are broadly enjoying the benefits of real equality in education, rightly seen as the key to future social mobility. Yet, in many cases, this may have been a prime consideration in a migrant's decision to leave his homeland. Schools in migrant areas are also charged with failure to provide a curriculum that is culturally and linguistically relevant to the needs of migrant children. A recent critic characterised these schools as the "archetypal assimilationist agency".

This could be a serious criticism in a community which is moving away from such a goal towards greater freedom of self-determination.

Bilingual teaching

By contrast with the harsh treatment meted out to the German language schools in 1917, a current development in bilingual teaching in a State High School in Melbourne is a welcome sign. From the 1974 school year a totally new approach to First Form teaching at the Brunswick Girls High School will centre on language acquisition. All students will continue to learn in their mother tongue while likewise learning the standard forms of a second language. Sixteen periods covering language, natural and social sciences, each week, will be based on this bilingual approach using English, Turkish, Arabic, Greek and Italian, while the remaining fourteen periods will be drama, music and elective studies. This bold project seeks to minimise cultural and social conflict by encouraging the children of migrants to take a pride in their language, to become acquainted with its standard and literary forms, and thus engage the goodwill and co-operation of parents in the schooling of their children. It is hoped that this will reduce family tensions that can impose severe strains on migrant children and evoke a new respect by migrants for their adopted country's proclaimed belief in freedom and equality. I quote this interesting development in some detail because I would like to see it as a sign of a new day dawning.

Complex system

In a democratic system such as ours the only acceptable means by which disadvantaged groups may seek to reverse the forces militating against them is by participating in the processes by which the decisions that affect their lives are made. However, several recent studies of the participation of migrants in Australian political life reveal that migrant representation in local, State and Federal Government is negligible. One obvious reason for this is the ignorance and understandable apathy of new arrivals confronted by the complex and cumbersome Australian system of government.

As the reports of the Task Forces recently submitted to me indicate, the community itself must bear an increased responsibility for educating migrants in important citizenship matters. Justice demands that those who obey the rules should have some say in making them. Despite our belief in freedom and equality for all, we may have somehow managed to frustrate the hopes of too many members of our ethnic groups, particularly in the inner city concentrations. However, effective ameliorative measures will not be easy to conceive nor implement.

In the Meredith Memorial Lectures given at LaTrobe University in 1972, Professor Jean Martin argued that it is precisely the prevailing egalitarian ideology in Australia that withholds from ethnic groups any unique privileges or consideration of any kind. Yet such an ideology actually fosters inequality and in the long run is self-defeating. The response of many of the ethnic groups to this situation has been to develop alternative "micro-societies" which are becoming stronger as our migration program proceeds. They are thus intensifying relationships within their own communities, which in turn leads to a consistent increase in ethnic consciousness.

Social interaction

Our prime task at this point in our history must be to encourage practical forms of social interaction in our community. This implies the creation of a truly just society in which all components can enjoy freedom to make their own distinctive contribution to the family of the nation. In the interests of Australians of the year 2000, we need to appreciate, embrace and, preserve all those diverse elements which find a place in the nation today. This involves the most fundamental issues of human rights such as those enshrined in the United Nations International Covenant on Civil and Political Rights, which the Government has expressed its intention of ratifying. The Covenant guarantees freedom of social and cultural expression for all residents of countries ratifying it.

The social and cultural rights of migrant Australians are just as compelling as the rights of other Australians. The full realisation of these rights would lead to reduced conflicts and tensions between the groups which are weaving an ever more complex fabric for Australian society as we hurry towards the turn of the century.

My personal ambition is that Australians of all backgrounds will always be proud before the world to say in whatever accents, "I am an Australian", just as the proudest boast in the days of the Roman imperium was contained in the words, "Civis Romanus sum".

一、导读

多元文化主义政策，是澳大利亚基本国策，更是其经济、政治与社会赖以持续繁荣与稳定发展的基石。作为曾经有着100多年种族主义传统的西方发达国家，澳大利亚之所以会走上多元文化主义道路，实属历史发展之必然。

二战结束后直至20世纪60年代，澳大利亚民族国家建设的一个中心内容就是吸纳移民。这一时期澳大利亚引进移民的力度非常大，且在移民问题上举国一致，内部鲜有争议。当时，虽然在政府政策推动下，“1958年，有175名亚洲人获得澳大利亚公民身份，其中有129名中国人和39名日本人；1956—1962年，有2907名有色人种获得澳大利亚国籍；到1969年，该数字达到1.1万”。但是，由于欧洲人的语言、文化传统、生活习惯等与澳大利亚相近，容易融入澳大利亚主流生活，导致1947—1969年的20多年间，在澳大利亚总共吸纳的208.06万移民中，绝大多数还是来自欧洲地区的移民。换言之，澳大利亚移民政策虽然在理论上废除了种族歧视，但移民实践中仍然有种族选择之嫌疑。

20世纪六七十年代，一方面由于欧洲经济逐渐从二战破坏中迅速复苏，并取得了辉煌成就；另一方面则由于澳大利亚社会长期存在的、对非英裔族群的歧视，使得来自欧洲国家的移民人口数量逐年萎缩，且由澳大利亚又回流欧洲的人口数量则持续上升，导致欧洲移民占澳大利亚移民总数的比例不断下滑，澳大利亚经济与社会发展面临着前所未有的劳动力人口挑战。为解决这一问题，1973年工党惠特拉姆政府公开宣称，要采取一个无种族、肤色和国别背景歧视的移民政策。也就在此时，其移民部长阿尔·格拉斯比在一场高级别公开论坛上发表了这篇《塑造一个面向未来的多元文化社会》的演讲，宣布应将澳大利亚建成一个多元文化社会，并强调不同民族或种族文化应和平共处。随之，1975年上台执政的自由党弗雷泽政府也重申了澳大利亚的多元文化主义政策，指出这一政策“强调允许更鼓励人们维护自己的文化传统，我们都应当容忍相互间的差异”。多元文化主义逐渐成为澳大利亚政治与社会的共识。

1983年，工党霍克政府上台后，“立志为建设一个多元文化的新澳大利亚而奋斗”。事实上，也就是在霍克执政期间的1987年，联邦政府成立了隶属于总理和内阁的多元文化事务办公室（OMA），主管多元文化政策的相关工作，特别是于1989年又发布了受到国会两党一致支持的《一个多元文化的澳大利亚的国家议程》的政府文件。在这份文件中，霍克政府系统地制定了多元文化政策的范围、限制和目标原则，提出了一揽子实施多元文化政策的措施，使之成为澳大利亚多元文化社会发展的一块里程碑。从此，多元文化政策奠定了“澳大利亚基本国策”的政治地位，成为解决澳大利亚社会移民与民族关系问题的指导性纲领和基本原则。未来澳大利亚社会移民和民族关系的处理，亦主要依循多元文化主义的基本要求而展开。

二、注释

1. Selected from A. J. Grassby, *A Multi-cultural Society for the Future*, Australian Government Publishing Service, 1973.

2. Sydney Cove，悉尼湾。

3. the first Australia Day 1788，即 1788 年 1 月 26 日，为菲利普船长率领的第一舰队登陆澳大利亚杰克逊港的日子，后被定为澳大利亚国庆日。

4. Anglo-Saxon，盎格鲁—撒克逊。

5. the Australian National University，澳大利亚国立大学。

6. The "Anglo-Conformist" view，指"盎格鲁文化主导论"。

7. The "melting pot" view，即"熔炉论"。

三、问题探讨

1. 什么是多元文化主义？谈谈你的理解。

2. 根据文献内容，谈谈澳大利亚推行多元文化政策的必要性。

四、参考文献

1. 杨洪贵：《澳大利亚多元文化主义研究》，西南交通大学出版社 2007 年版。

2. 王鉴：《澳大利亚的多元文化主义政策》，《世界民族》2004 年第 4 期。

3. 王晓凌：《试论澳大利亚多元文化主义》，《安徽大学学报》（哲学社会科学版）2005 年第 4 期。

4. 王宇博：《20 世纪中期澳大利亚移民政策的变化》，《苏州大学学报》（哲学社会科学版）2009 年第 3 期。

5. 钱志中：《澳大利亚多元文化主义政策的历史选择与动态演化》，《世界经济与政治论坛》2014 年第 6 期。

UNIT 25

APEC ECONOMIC LEADERS' DECLARATION[1]

Meeting New Challenges in the New Century

1. We, the Economic Leaders of APEC, gathered today in Shanghai for the first time in the twenty-first century. We are here to explore ways to meet the new challenges confronting us. Convinced of the great potential of the Asia-Pacific region[2], we have resolved to achieve common prosperity through broader participation and closer cooperation.

2. Our meeting has taken place at a crucial juncture. The major world economies are experiencing a slowdown more severe than anticipated. Most economies in the Asia-Pacific region have experienced an economic downturn, with some emerging economies particularly affected by unfavorable external market conditions. In addition, the terrorist attack on the United States risks undermining some industries as well as consumer and investor confidence. In the long run, a major challenge for the Asia-Pacific community is to manage the profound changes brought forth by globalization and the New Economy and to benefit from the opportunities that abound.

3. As the premier forum for regional economic cooperation in the Asia Pacific, APEC is well suited to play a leading role in helping its member economies embrace these opportunities and challenges. We wish to send a clear and strong message on the collective resolve of the Asia-Pacific community to counter terrorism. We are determined to reverse the current economic downturn and maintain public confidence at a time of uncertainty by fighting protectionism and committing to the launch of the new WTO[3] round at the upcoming WTO

Ministerial Conference. These efforts are consonant with and contribute to the pursuit of the APEC vision of peace, harmony and common prosperity.

4. Inspired by such a vision, we are determined to work together for a more dynamic and prosperous Asia Pacific in the new century by promoting sustainable economic growth, sharing the benefits of globalization and the New Economy, and advancing Trade and Investment Liberalization and Facilitation (TILF). To this end, we reaffirm our commitment to achieving the Bogor Goals of free and open trade and investment in the Asia Pacific by 2010 for developed economies and 2020 for developing economies. We have also charted the course for the development of APEC in its second decade and beyond by adopting the Shanghai Accord.

Promoting Sustainable Growth

5. We affirm our unwavering confidence in the medium and long-term growth prospects for the Asia-Pacific region since the fundamentals of the region remain sound. As reforms and restructuring following the 1997 – 1998 financial crisis take effect, many emerging economies are now in a much stronger position to cushion themselves against the impact of the economic slowdown and unexpected shocks.

6. We undertake to adopt appropriate policies and measures to increase economic growth and resolve to enhance macroeconomic policy dialogue and cooperation not only to resume growth but also to build a stronger foundation for sustainable growth and broad-based development. It is important for all economies to take timely policy actions to strengthen markets and facilitate an early pick-up in global economic activity.

7. In this context, we pledge to accelerate our domestic efforts to build capacity and deepen structural reform so as to strengthen the market fundamentals across the region. To this end, we emphasize the importance of sound economic policies and corporate governance as well as the important role and responsibility of governments in shaping the legal and regulatory framework that encourages competition and innovation, with an increased emphasis on capacity building. Developing the social safety net is a high priority, as it can make an important contribution to reducing the harmful effects of economic

shocks on vulnerable groups. As noted in the 2001 Economic Outlook, enhancing financial efficiency is also essential to promoting growth. We thus welcome efforts made in these areas in APEC, including strengthening economic legal infrastructure, supervision of capital markets, corporate governance, and implementation of international financial standards, as exemplified by the work done through the Finance Ministers' process. We also welcome contributions by Pacific Economic Cooperation Council (PECC)[4] in these areas. We direct responsible Ministers and Officials to build on their work.

8. Recognizing the importance of promoting financial stability and crisis prevention, we stress the need to strengthen the international financial system. We urge continued efforts to enhance the effectiveness of mechanisms to prevent the recurrence of financial crisis. We welcome the important steps that have been taken to strengthen the international financial architecture including, for example, the review by the Financial Stability Forum of the effectiveness and the progress in implementing the recommendations from the Working Group on Offshore Financial Centers and Highly Leveraged Institutions. We emphasize the importance of ensuring that representation on the International Monetary Fund (IMF)[5] Board and IMF quota/share allocation appropriately reflects the current world economy. While the IMF and other international financial institutions play a pivotal role, regional cooperation can also be very useful in complementing efforts by these institutions to promote financial stability. In this connection, we welcome the substantial progress in implementing the Chiang Mai Initiative to strengthen cooperative financing arrangements among the Association of Southeast Asian Nations (ASEAN)[6] countries and China, Japan and the Republic of Korea. We also note the ongoing work in the Manila Framework Group. We support all these efforts and urge them to be strengthened.

9. The current economic slowdown underlines, above all, the importance of APEC's work towards more open and stronger economies. We reaffirm our unyielding commitment to free and open trade and investment and resolve to work together to fight against protectionism in all forms. We render the strongest support for an open, equitable and rules-based Multilateral Trading System, which is essential to sustain global economic growth. APEC must also stay on track with its own agenda on trade and investment and on capacity building.

Sharing the Benefits of Globalization and the New Economy

10. We are convinced that globalization is a powerful vehicle that stimulates economic growth, and holds great promises for delivering higher living standards to people and improving social well-being for our communities. We acknowledge that the New Economy has broad potential to raise productivity, stimulate innovation in economic organization and entrepreneurship, and create and disseminate knowledge and wealth. However, the opportunities arising from these processes are not sufficiently shared among and even within economies. Hence the need to enable all individuals in our communities to benefit from them. We emphasize the importance of capacity building, both human and institutional, as a key answer to the challenges and opportunities of globalization and the New Economy. Capacity building constitutes a key element of the balanced approach essential to the success of APEC along with market opening and full participation.

11. In this context, we reiterate that human capacity building (HCB) remains a central theme this year and the years ahead. We commend the success of the High-Level Meeting on Human Capacity Building, and welcome the Beijing Initiative as a comprehensive set of principles for human capacity building, which also provides opportunities for further work in the New Economy. We call on APEC fora and member economies to undertake follow-up activities in specific areas of their interest in the spirit of developed and developing economies complementing each other. We support the engagement of all key stakeholders in the region and, in particular, the establishment of the partnership of government, business, academic and training institutions for this purpose. We welcome the launch of the Consortium for APEC Cyber Education Cooperation initiated and sponsored by the APEC Education Foundation, the Human Capacity Building Promotion Program and the APEC Finance and Development Program. We also welcome the outcomes of the 4th Human Resources Development Ministerial meeting and support the Kumamoto Statement that makes a contribution to APEC Human Resources Development activities in the 21st Century as a basis for advancing social and economic development and the sharing of prosperity by our people.

12. Reaffirming the importance of Economic and Technical Cooperation (Ecotech) in achieving equitable growth and sustainable development, we welcome the progress that APEC has made in advancing Ecotech goals and underscore that Trade and Investment Liberalization and Facilitation and Ecotech should be mutually reinforcing. We call for efforts to this end to be further strengthened. We commend the formulation and submission of Ecotech Action Plans by individual member economies as a major step forward for promoting sound and balanced development of APEC and ask Ministers and Officials to develop the exercise as lessons are learned.

13. We also welcome the progress made in other areas of Ecotech. We endorse the APEC Strategy for Combating Infectious Disease and call on members and relevant fora to implement its recommendations.

14. Given the importance of Small and Medium-sized Enterprises (SMEs) and micro-enterprises, we instruct Ministers and Officials to build on APEC's Integrated Plan of Action for SMEs and place special emphasis on micro-enterprises. In this context, we welcome the High Level Meeting on Micro-enterprises to be hosted by Mexico next year.

15. Building on work done in Brunei last year, we have made further progress by formulating and delivering a long-term, forward-looking and more action-oriented e-APEC Strategy for the development of the New Economy through the promotion of information and communications technology (ICT) and its application in our region. The goal is to build APEC towards a digital society, with higher growth, increased learning and employment opportunities, improved public services and better qualities of life by taking advantage of advanced, reliable and secure ICT and networks and by promoting universal access. Such a society should bring equal opportunities and widely shared benefits for all member economies and individuals, including women, the disabled and others. We commend the crosscutting character of the e-APEC Strategy and urge APEC fora and member economies to implement the programs for collective and individual actions set out in the Strategy, as appropriate. Under the current circumstances, the early implementation of the Strategy will also support the revival of the ICT sector. We also welcome the progress in advancing e-commerce.

16. In September 2002 many of us will be meeting in Johannesburg for the

World Summit on Sustainable Development, to reinvigorate our commitment to sustainable development in pursuit of enhancing economic growth, promoting human and social development and protecting the environment as interdependent objectives. We will consider how APEC, which has undertaken a broad range of activities in this area, can contribute to the success of the World Summit and take forward the outcomes in its work program.

17. We realize that there is an ongoing public debate on the benefits and costs of globalization. Such debates are healthy when they are informed by rigorous and comprehensive analysis of the impact of globalization. The time has come for APEC to come forward and lead the public debate in a constructive manner. We instruct Officials to convene an APEC Dialogue on Globalization and Shared Prosperity, focusing on, among other issues, structural adjustment and its impact. At the same time, APEC should reach out to business and other stakeholders to communicate APEC's objectives, activities and benefits to ensure that they participate in and benefit from the APEC process and globalization at large. In particular, we thank APEC Business Advisory Council (ABAC) for its report and value the interaction with the Council and other business representatives. We also direct our Ministers and Officials to develop and implement programs to give effect to the APEC Communications and Outreach Strategy as well as the conclusions of the Ad Hoc Group on APEC Interaction.

18. Noting that sustainable growth in the APEC region also requires the ability to feed a growing and increasingly prosperous population, Leaders call for accelerated implementation of the APEC Food System initiative. Recognizing the benefits of biotechnology in improving productivity, increasing nutrition, and reducing the environmental impact of agricultural production, we reaffirm the importance of safe introduction and use of biotechnology products based on sound science. We also welcome the initiative to hold a policy-level dialogue on agricultural biotechnology and call for more related capacity building activities.

19. We take satisfaction at the significant progress made, through the leadership of the Ad Hoc Group on Gender Integration, in the capacity of APEC to address gender equity in its work. Our commitment to a wide distribution of the economic opportunities of our era requires the application of gender perspectives in APEC's work, we welcome the decision to hold a Second Ministerial Meeting on Women in Mexico in 2002, as an opportunity to make

further progress.

Supporting the Multilateral Trading System

20. Trade and investment liberalization and facilitation hold another key to realizing our vision for reduced disparities and common prosperity. They have taken on increased importance at a time when rapid changes are reshaping the global marketplace. Hence, we commit to further efforts in advancing trade and investment liberalization and facilitation both within our region and globally.

21. In November, a major decision will be taken at the Fourth WTO Ministerial Conference. Its outcome will have long-term implications for our future. Our choice is unmistakably for a stronger Multilateral Trading System with greater opportunities for all. We strongly support the launch of the WTO new round at the conference, recognizing that the current slowdown in the world economy has added to its urgency. We agree that, once launched, the new round should be concluded expeditiously.

22. We emphasize the need for a balanced, sufficiently broad-based agenda, which is achievable. This is essential to the successful launch and conclusion of the New Round. We agree that the agenda for the New Round should include further trade liberalization, the strengthening of WTO rules, implementation issues, and reflect the interests and concerns of all members, especially those of the developing and least developed ones. We also agree that such an agenda should address the challenges in the 21st century and support the goal of sustainable development. This will help ensure that the prosperity flows from growing trade and investment is accessible and equitably distributed to all. In this context, we also emphasize the importance that the New Round be supported by all WTO members, and hence the need for effective implementation of special and differential treatment and for enhancing WTO's internal transparency.

23. We reconfirm the commitment to the APEC-wide moratorium on the imposition of custom duties on electronic transmissions, and agree on its extension until the Fifth WTO Ministerial Conference, recognizing the importance of relevant WTO agreements for electronic commerce.

24. We reaffirm the importance of APEC WTO-related capacity building activities which realize the objectives of the Strategic APEC Plan as a unique,

substantial contribution to strengthening the Multilateral Trading System, and call for the accelerated implementation of the Plan to assist developing economies in implementing the WTO agreements.

25. We applaud the conclusion of all negotiations on the terms for China's membership in the WTO as a historic development that not only helps make WTO a truly world organization but also reinforces the underpinnings for global economic cooperation. We urge that the decision on final approval of China's accession be taken at the upcoming Ministerial Conference. We also reiterate strong support for the final approval of the accession by Chinese Taipei at the Conference and the advancement of WTO accession by the Russian Federation and Viet Nam.

26. We reaffirm that regional and bilateral trade agreements should serve as building blocks for multilateral liberalization in the WTO. We affirm that the existing and emerging regional trading agreements should therefore be consistent with WTO rules and disciplines. We also believe that these arrangements should be in line with APEC architecture and supportive of APEC's goals and principles. We note the initiatives on exchange of information in this regard.

Sharpening the Vision for the Future

27. APEC has come a long way since its inception in 1989. So has the world around it. These changes have not in any way lessened the need for a vehicle of cooperation like APEC in our region. On the contrary, they have made it more compelling for us to remain fully committed to the APEC process, to the vision of a peaceful and prosperous Asia-Pacific community of diverse yet interdependent economies that has evolved from Seattle to Brunei, and above all, to the Bogor Goals. We also reaffirm our belief in the unique APEC Approach based on the fundamental principles of voluntarism, consensus-building, combination of individual and collective actions, flexibility, comprehensiveness and open regionalism, which has inspired and underpinned our successes.

28. At the same time, we recognize that APEC must demonstrate its dynamism in advancing with the times by responding and adapting to changes in the global and regional economy. As it enters the second decade, it is important for APEC to enrich, update and sharpen its vision for the future. In this respect,

we envision that APEC's objectives in the second decade are to make continuous progress in achieving the Bogor Goals; deepen the spirit of community by sharing the benefits of growth more widely and equitably; and build APEC into a closer, stronger partnership for regional economic cooperation.

29. To this end, we announce today the Shanghai Accord as a strategic, forward agenda for the development of APEC in the coming years. The Accord not only gives voice to our common resolve to fulfill our commitments, it also stands as a template laying out some key steps to be taken to achieve our Goals and Objectives. Reflecting the diversity of APEC's membership, it incorporates trade and investment as well as economic and technical cooperation as two mutually supportive and reinforcing elements.

30. In the Shanghai Accord, we commit to:

— Broadening APEC's vision for the future by identifying a conceptual and policy framework to guide APEC in the new century. Such a framework recognizes the changes entailed by globalization and the New Economy and reflects the need to extend the APEC agenda to cover reforms and capacity building at both domestic and international levels;

— Clarifying APEC's roadmap for achieving the Bogor Goals on schedule with a mid-term stocktake of the overall progress in 2005, including by broadening and updating the Osaka Action Agenda, adopting a pathfinder approach in advancing selected APEC initiatives towards achieving the Bogor Goals, promoting the adoption of appropriate trade policies for the New Economy, following up on the APEC Trade Facilitation Principles, pursuing greater transparency in economic governance; and

— Strengthening APEC's implementation mechanism by strengthening the Individual Action Plan Peer Review process, reinforcing Ecotech and capacity building efforts.

31. We direct our Ministers and Officials to follow up actively on the Accord. We have no doubt that with our concerted efforts the vision we set here will over time come to full fruition, culminating in a stable, secure and prosperous Asia-Pacific community.

一、导读

亚太经合组织（Asia-Pacific Economic Cooperation，APEC）是亚太地区级别最高、涉及领域最广、影响力最大的经济合作机制。1989年11月5日—7日，澳大利亚、美国、日本、韩国、新西兰、加拿大及当时的东盟六国在澳大利亚首都堪培拉举行APEC首届部长级会议，标志着APEC正式成立。该组织现拥有21个成员，分别是澳大利亚、文莱、加拿大、智利、中国、印度尼西亚、日本、韩国、墨西哥、马来西亚、新西兰、巴布亚新几内亚、秘鲁、菲律宾、俄罗斯、新加坡、泰国、美国、越南，以及中国香港、中国台北。此外，APEC还有3个观察员单位，分别是东盟秘书处、太平洋经济合作理事会、太平洋岛国论坛秘书处。该组织成员所辖总人口达27亿，约占世界总人口的40.5%。根据国际货币基金组织公布的数据，APEC成员经济总量约占世界经济总量的53%，贸易总量约占世界贸易总量的43%。该组织主要宗旨是为本地区人民的共同利益推动经济增长和发展；促进成员间经济相互依存；加强开放的多边贸易体制；减少区域贸易和投资壁垒等。

APEC共有5个层次的运作机制：

（一）领导人非正式会议。1993年11月，首次APEC领导人非正式会议在美国西雅图召开，之后每年召开一次，每次会议结束时，与会领导人会一起发表《领导人宣言》。

（二）部长级会议。包括双部长会议以及专业部长会议。双部长会议每年在领导人会议前举行一次，专业部长会议定期或不定期举行。

（三）高官会。每年举行4～5次会议，由各成员指定的高官（一般为副部级或司局级官员）出席。

（四）委员会和工作组。高官会下设4个委员会，即贸易和投资委员会（CTI）、经济委员会（EC）、经济技术合作高官指导委员会（SCE）及预算和管理委员会（BMC）。各委员会下设多个工作组、专家小组和分委会等机制，从事专业活动与合作。

（五）秘书处。1993年1月在新加坡设立，为APEC各层次的活动提供支持与服务。秘书处负责人为执行主任，2010年起设固定任期，任期3年。

自1989年诞生以来，APEC主要关注贸易投资自由化、贸易投资便利化和经济技术合作等三大经济领域，即所谓“三个支柱”。在这三大领域中，贸易投资自由化的目的是减少关税和消除非关税壁垒，并取得了一些成果，使得亚太地区的平均关税从APEC成立之时的16.9%，降到了2011年的5.7%，低于10.3%的世界平均水平；贸易投资便利化则主要是方便亚太地区的商业人员从事商业活动，以促进亚太地区经济繁荣，这包括简便海关程序、推动商务人员通行便利化等多个领域，这是 APEC 取得成就最为显著，也最惠及各成员利益的经济领域。然而，与其在贸易投资自由化、便利化领域取得的成绩相比，APEC 在经济技术合作领域却少有建树和实效，甚至受人诟病。

此处选录的《APEC 经济领导人宣言》发表于 2001 年在上海举办的第 13 届亚太经合组织领导人非正式会议。该宣言及其附件《上海共识》《数字亚太经合组织战略》和《反恐声明》，共同推动了亚太经合组织成员在多边贸易体制建设、人力资源能力建设、电子 APEC、新经济及反恐合作等多个领域的进一步合作。

二、注释

1. 本文节选自美国政府出版办公室网页，https：//www. gpo. gov/fdsys/pkg/WCPD—2001—10—29/pdf/WCPD—2001—10—29-Pg1525. pdf。

2. the Asia-Pacific region，指“亚太地区”。

3. WTO，世界贸易组织。

4. Pacific Economic Cooperation Council (PECC)，太平洋经济合作委员会。

5. the International Monetary Fund (IMF)，国际货币基金组织。

6. the Association of Southeast Asian Nations (ASEAN)，东南亚国家联盟(东盟)。

三、问题探讨

1. 谈谈你对亚太经合组织的认识。

2. 评析 2001 年亚太经合组织《领导人宣言》的价值和意义。

四、参考文献

1. 蔡鹏鸿、王泠一：《中国与 APEC》，文汇出版社 2001 年版。

2. 宫占奎：《APEC 运作机制研究》，南开大学出版社 2005 年版。

3. 刘重力等：《APEC 贸易便利化问题研究》，南开大学出版社 2012 年版。

4. 张伯伟：《APEC 贸易自由化及其影响：兼析开发的区域经济组织》，经济科学出版社 2001 年版。

5. 朱彤等：《“后危机”时代的 APEC 及其新增长战略研究》，南开大学出版社 2013 年版。

后　　记

《世界历史文献选读》即将付梓之际，我们有如释重负之感。与其说这是江苏师范大学“十三五”本科教育教学教材和2018年江苏省高等学校重点教材项目成果，不如说这是编者同仁在长期教学过程中慢慢积累、不断鞭策、砥砺前行的结果。

为适应学校人才培养创新改革的需要，根据学校新编2014版历史学专业人才培养方案，世界史教学团队开始给2014级历史学专业本科生正式开设“世界历史文献选读”课程。苦于当时没有合适的教材，我们决定根据各自研究领域，自己精选文献，然后印刷编订成册供学生使用。每次使用之后，任课教师都会根据教学效果和学生意见反馈进行适当调整、完善与补充。总体而言，自编教材在教学适用过程中效果很好，学生普遍反映在拓宽知识、感受历史、解读史料和学习语言等方面获益良多，考研同学的感受尤为深刻。这次《世界历史文献选读》有幸列入江苏师范大学“十三五”本科教育教学教材和2018江苏省高等学校重点教材。为了更好地完成教材编写任务，我们先后多次召开教材编写会议，对文献选择、内容编排、格式体例等反复商讨，交流意见，希望把教材编得更好。经过大家的共同努力，这部教材最终得以如期顺利完成。

江苏师范大学教务处处长赵鹏教授、副处长汪颖教授，历史文化与旅游学院院长张文德教授、副院长朱锦程博士、副院长刘德州博士等对教材立项和编写给予了大力支持。国内世界史同仁对教材的编写也给出了许多有益的意见和建议。对此，我们深表感谢！合肥工业大学出版社对本教材的出版提供了很多的帮助，我们在此也深切致谢。

本书是集体智慧的结晶，具体分工如下：

第1—4单元：蒋保教授编写；

第5—8单元：鞠长猛副教授编写；

第9—13单元：张荣苏博士编写；

第14—17单元：宋严萍教授编写；

第18—21单元：赵辉兵教授编写；

第22—25单元：颜廷副教授编写。

全书最后由蒋保教授负责统筹和统稿。

为了配合世界通史教学，在文献编写的过程中，我们尽可能选取具有代表性的资料，尽可能做到较为客观的评介。但是由于研究领域和研究水平所限，教材会存在这样那样的问题或者不足。我们真诚地希望世界史同仁以及广大读者能够提出宝贵意见，以便在以后的修订工作中进一步修改完善。

2019年4月